Traditional Archery

Sam Fadala

STACKPOLE BOOKS

0 11557 02943 7

Published by
STACKPOLE BOOKS
5067 Ritter Road
Mechanicsburg, PA 17055
www.stackpolebooks.com

Printed in the United States

10 9 8 7 6 5 4 3 2

First edition

Cover design by Caroline Stover

About the Cover
The unique Black Widow recurve bow was introduced in 1957, with continuous manufacture to this day. Each one is personally customized for the individual archer, including draw length and weight, special order handle shape, bow length, elevated arrow rest or off-the-shelf shooting. Many other options are available, such as multiple limb sets that can be ordered without sending the riser back to the shop for fitting. Constructed for high performance and long life, the reverse handle, with limbs behind the riser, promotes smooth drawing.

Library of Congress Cataloging-in-Publication Data

Fadala, Sam, 1939-
   Traditional archery/Sam Fadala. — 1st ed.
      p. cm.
   ISBN 0-8117-2943-5
      1. Archery 2. Archery—History. I. Title
   GV1185.F33 1999   98-43191
   799.3'2—dc21   CIP

For my Nancy

Contents

Acknowledgment

Special gratitude goes to Herb Meland of Pronghorn Custom Bows, Casper, Wyoming, a man born to make traditional longbows and recurves. Thanks, Herb, for making great bows and for sharing your knowledge of archery.

Preface

So long as the new moon returns in the heavens a bent, beautiful bow, so long will the fascination of archery keep hold of the hearts of men.

James Maurice Thompson,
The Witchery of Archery, 1877

In 1991, a part of the ancient world was lifted from the ice by the hands of fate, a far-off desert storm raining sand down on the peaks of the Italian Alps, caused a warming trend that melted the frigid tomb of a lone figure who met his fate 5300 years earlier. Two German hikers spotted the body as they paced along a cloud-high trail on the mountain. Their discovery was reported as another victim of mountain climbing in the Alps, until someone realized that here was not an unfortunate modern-day hiker, but a man from a distant past. Scientists pulled threads of information together with needles of modern technology until they wove a fabric that told a fascinating story about the ancient "Ice Man."

The man himself was immensely important, but it was his tools that brought marvel to the eyes of those who saw them. His ax was made of copper, changing the previously accepted historic dating of that era. His knife was constructed of flint, a material used to this day for delicate surgery, for it can be rendered far sharper than the finest scalpel known to modern man. Most wondrous of all to some of us, the Ice Man carried a longbow. It was approximately seventy-two inches long and made of yew, a wood still considered useful in bowmaking. Made from shoots of the wayfaring tree (*Viburnum lantana*), his arrows were round and straight, three-fletched, with grooves cut into their shafts for mounting the feathers straight, true, and long-lasting. Two arrows had flint arrowheads cemented with birch tar into deep notches. His basic archery equipment, all in all, resembled what thousands of devotees of the sport have turned to once again—traditional equipment.

In contrast to a background of high technology, traditional archery has returned to delight bowshooters the world over. While longbows and recurves never died out entirely, they were eclipsed by the shadow of the compound bow in all but the most remote Third World countries, where tribes of the Amazon and other cultures never put aside the ten thousand-year-old tool, still using it as part of their daily living. No one can say what prompted archers in a world of computers, satellites, and radio telescopes to look once more upon bows of the past. Some think it was the advancement of the compound bow itself. "I quit shooting bows," one archer reveals, "because I wasn't having fun anymore. It wasn't archery. It was cold, hard, high-tech gear made of synthetic stuff."

I, too, set the bow aside for a while. My compound was a heavy, bulky, wheel-and-pulley bow that shot a wonderfully fast arrow, and once sighted in—which was no big trick—could be counted on to whack a beverage can at twenty yards every shot, as long as the exact distance was known. In time, a six-inch target at fifty yards was no challenge. Man is never content leaving well enough alone; that's why he has physics, medicine, and electronics. So the continued mechanical improvement of the compound bow is as natural as looking for a better cold medicine. Likewise, we will see trends to improve on longbows and recurves, now that they represent a large market share of the archery industry. However, the turn-back to the traditional bow tells us that not everyone wants high-tech in everything.

Thousands of archers who love cell phones and e-mail decided that when it came to bows, they preferred doing it as the archer Howard Hill said, "the hard way." The rush was on. In a few years there was a bowyer on every street corner, it seemed. "Anyone who can glue two pieces of wood together is making a bow," one old-time craftsman complained. He was right, but he failed to consider that the new traditional bow fully encompassed handling and other features of the originals. These bows were the genuine article. But two things were quite different: Dedicated bowyers were using fine, up-to-date materials not available in the heyday of the traditional "stick," and they knew more about bow geometry than their predecessors.

The result led to a minor paradox. Modern longbows and recurves were shooting faster arrows than most early compounds, and they weren't that far behind many of the more ordinary "round wheel" mechanical bows of the day. Naturally, none of these "stickbows" whipped the fastest mechanical models; however, neither were they slowpokes. More importantly, enlightened design made a more efficient bow that delivered a higher percentage of stored energy to the nock of the arrow. None of this, however, trampled on the nature of the stickbow. Happily, it remained the same tool enjoyed in the past in all respects—except with better shooting qualities and ballistics. There was good reason to be excited.

Today's longbows and recurves have not risen from graves of obsolescence, mere zombies of the past masquerading as something new. They are new, and yet absolutely true to yesteryear. As this is written, there is no end in sight to their popularity, as hundreds of bowbenders enter the ranks of traditional archery every day. Several magazines dedicated solely to the simpler bow now thrive, and traditional archery organizations abound. At one large 1997 bowshooter's jamboree, of the few thousand participants on the grounds, close to half carried a longbow or recurve. Where traditional supplies were once difficult to find, there are now dozens of companies dedicated to providing the archer with everything from the bow and its arrows to every conceivable piece of tackle. A few tiny sparks sprinkled down by the spirit of the archers of yore have set a blaze in the field of modern archery. Its light can now be seen from border to border and across the globe.

In the midst of this happy rebirth comes this book, dedicated to both the veteran and novice stickbow fan. It is about the longbow and recurve, as each exists today—AND NOTHING ELSE—only the bows, their arrows and tackle, plus how to gain the most enjoyment and fulfillment from traditional archery.

What Is Traditional Archery?

Although it's impossible to divide the world of the bow into perfect niches, three major camps can be recognized: primitive, traditional, and high-tech.

Following the history of archery is like navigating a wild river with its rapids, shining pools, waterfalls, placid waters, and myriad sidestreams. No one knows when the gleaming light of invention cast its rays on the mind of ancient man to create a bow, but we are certain that the strung stick changed the world of man for millennia. The course of history would have flowed on an entirely different current without the invention of the bow. Unfortunately, it was employed in hate, anger, and possessive greed as well as for procurement of food, and, as with so many of man's tools, also honored the art and culture. The twang of its string was music to the ear; the smoothness of the stick was a pleasure to the touch. Special designs were commonly placed on the bow as art, with many a bow rising from the ranks of an impersonal implement to a friend with a special name. The bow was then, and is now, far more than an instrument used to cast an arrow.

The archery world was swept up in a whirlwind of longbows and recurves in the past decade. Longtime companies like Bob's Archery Sales were there to meet the increased demand for traditional bows, arrows, and tackle.

A small segment of modern archery remains dedicated to the primitive bow. These bows are mainly modeled on original designs, if not entirely, then at least in spirit. Many are cast in the image of the bow of the American Plains Indian, a true bow warrior. His bow procured food, figured in religion and mythology, and was a symbol of power and of course a weapon of war. Other bows follow the line of the English longbow, with its rich history and legend.

There are two major styles of primitive bow construction: self-bows and composites. A bow made of yew and yew only, for example, is a self-bow. Although it may use a hemp string and leather handle, the bow itself is constructed of one product. Composite bows are primitive bows made of more

Seasoned bowyers like Keith Chastain of Wapiti Archery provided not only longbows and recurves, but traditional equipment and supplies as well. Wapiti, for example, sells cedar shafts for arrowmakers.

Large companies, such as Bear Archery, brought stickbows back to meet the new traditional tackle demand. Here, author Sam Fadala, right, along with Bear Vice President, Bill Krenz, look at a recurve and longbow from a well-known company.

than one material. Their ancestry also reaches back into the past.

Every student of anthropology should study the history of archery, for he will find in it the true nature of man. Never again will he think of the prehistoric person as a lump-jawed anthropoid dragging his knuckles on the ground in search of an acorn. Ancient man possessed design knowledge and building skill, both clearly exhibited in his bows. Materials varied by culture and geography, of course. Whereas, the Ice Man's bow was made of yew, others were built of many other woods, as well as horn, animal sinew, and even met-

Newcomers to the sport were greeted by companies such as G & G Traditional Archery, who not only sold new bows, but used models as well—a good way to get started with modest cash outlay.

al. An example of the latter is an ancient Persian bow. Made entirely of metal, this short bow was calculated to have a draw weight of 90 pounds. Animal sinew and other products were sometimes attached to bows as "backing" to increase strength and life. The glues used may have been crude, but we still have intact examples of such composite bows from the distant past.

The first composite bows are credited to the Asians. Adding horn or animal sinew to a wooden core escalated the power of his bow, giving him the

This ancient Persian bow was undoubtedly one of the earliest takedowns and shows the beautiful decoration common to many bowshooting nations.

This Persian bow used a threaded stud for takedown.

capability of launching an arrow to great distances. The mounted Asian archer became one of the most formidable soldiers the world has ever known. The oriental bow was not only made of joined materials for improved ballistics, it also carried a unique design, with curved limbs constructed of layered materials that stored and released great energy. Anyone who doubts the traditionalism of the recurve bow need look only to the remarkable models of the distant past to realize the antiquity of the concept. Combining the recurve effect with composite construction rendered these bows startling in their ability to fire an arrow with great force. The composite recurve had no trouble driving an arrow through metal armor, for example, although it must be admitted that the self-bow of the English archer could do likewise.

A composite primitive bow might have horn, which is a compressible material, layered upon its belly (that part of the limb the archer looks at when shooting his bow). On the back of the bow (the limb surface away from the shooter) there might be animal sinew, an elastic product. These were both permanently attached to the wooden core of the bow, then sealed with a moisture-proof lacquer. When the bow was drawn, the horn belly compressed as the sinew backing stretched. Upon release, the compressed horn flew back to its original station like a recoiling spring, while the sinew relaxed upon release of the limbs.

This book is not the forum to detail the wonderful properties of bows from around the world. That subject would require a book of its own. The amazing little Eskimo bow, the bushman's small poison-arrow

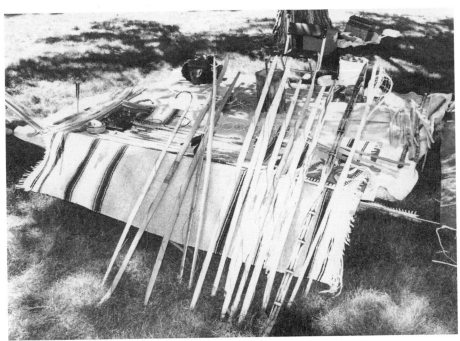

A step back from the traditional bow is the primitive model. These were built by Bob Aragon of Colorado, who specializes in pretraditional tackle.

These handsome David Carrick self-bows are true to original Indian designs. Note the interesting arrangement of the string grooves on the left-hand bow. By offsetting the string, the bow became somewhat center-shot.

thrower, the ancient Japanese bow with which the soldier of the sixteenth century outshot the musket of the time with greater accuracy—all demand attention. The unusual Andaman Islander bow had uniquely shaped limbs widening beyond the rounded handle, then slimming rapidly down to extremely narrow bow nocks, making it look like a thin, two-bladed paddle with sharp ends. The North Andaman bow had one limb bent outward, almost as if

Examples of the atlatl, or spear-thrower, have been located all over the world.

attempting a recurve design, whereas the South Andaman bow had even limbs. Both were significantly taller than their users, in absolute contrast to so many of the North American Indian models.

Before leaving the trail of the primitive bow, mention of the atlatl, which preceded it, is warranted. The atlatl was essentially a spear-thrower, also known as a throwing stick, spear sling, dart thrower, and Woomera (Australian), to mention some of its other names. The naturalist Nuttall gave the tool its popular name in 1891, translating two Aztec words, one for "throwing" and the other for "on the water." The atlatl seems to have roots in Peru, North America, Australia, Europe, and many other geographic locales.

Ken Wee, who makes atlatls as well as primitive-style self-bows, prepares to launch a dart at the target.

Using a swinging forward motion of the arm, the atlatl propels a long spear-type arrow toward the target.

Whereas the bow and arrow provided a greater chance of hitting the target, the atlatl was far more effective than a hand-thrown spear.

As a spear-thrower, the atlatl added much greater thrust potential. Rather than simply throwing the spear by hand, it could be propelled by a sort of sling. Atlatl handles were made of ash, hickory, cedar, oak, maple, mountain mahogany, and Florida ironwood. Some were possibly constructed entirely of bone or antler. Handles were normally around fifteen to twenty-four inches long. Some had wrist loops; others did not. Some had dart rests; others apparently had no gripping attachment. Are we surprised to find that atlatl handles were often decorated with paint, inscribed or fixed with leather, stone, porcupine quill, and other fetishes?

By attaching the butt of the spear to the handle, lifting the combination above the head, drawing way back, then thrusting forward, the spear took off from the handle like a jet from the deck of an aircraft carrier. The dart thrown by the atlatl is much like a very long arrow with a rounded shaft, a point, and feathers on the rear to guide it. But rather than a true nock, the butt is flat-based with a beveled cup. These "spears" were called darts or ar-rows, as well as harpoons, lances, veras, rods, and javelins. Speeds of eighty to one hundred miles per hour were, and still are, achieved with the atlatl's arrow, measuring three-eighths to one-half inch in diameter. According to one study, this represents an advantage of two hundred times the thrust available by hand alone.

The atlatl, like the primitive bow, is far from dead. Each summer in Casper, Wyoming, a national contest is held for atlatl throwing, with participants from many states and foreign countries showing up to compete; this truly ancient tool has survived to the space age. Atlatls have been located in the La Brea Tar Pits in California, as well as in many other parts of the world. Putting a date on its inception is risky at best. Some place it close to the advent of the bow. Nobody, of course, knows the truth. We do know that Eskimos used it to procure waterfowl or throw harpoons. Its one-handed nature was perfect for steering a boat while simultaneously launching a

This dart, made of cane, is certainly no match for a fine arrow; however it will fly with sufficient accuracy to hit a target downrange.

harpoon. There is no easy jump from the atlatl to the bow, however. The two couldn't be more different. The atlatl offers an extension of the arm for much improved leverage, but the bow stores energy within itself. Even in its simplest form, it is a tool that holds power to be released on demand.

That's a glance at the primitive bow and the atlatl that came before it, but before going into traditional sticks, let's consider the compound. As with so many other inventions, there is nothing terribly new about the compound bow, either in concept or design. A professor in the state of Washington put a compound bow on the drawing board as an experiment at least fifty years ago, and the patent of the idea came from an ingenious fellow in the 1960s. The first compounds were ugly and test fired arrows that were no faster than arrows fired from many stickbows of the day. I had a chance to chronograph an early model. It propelled a 500-grain arrow 180 feet per second. The 1957 Black Widow recurve bow was faster than that, as was the Groves recurve.

But the compound did have one marvelous property going for it—the relaxation factor. Even the earliest models offered a "break-over" that really gave the archer a break. Once drawn about halfway back, the draw weight of, say, a 70-pound bow was reduced to 50 pounds. That was a bargain. The

The flying dart is just visible as it flies downrange. Note the high trajectory that will drop it into the target.

bowbender had to hold back only 50 pounds while gaining 70 pounds pull. Things got even better. A relaxation factor—also known as letoff—in the 50 percent range was soon a reality. Before long, the wheels, pulleys, and cables intended for mechanical advantage came to the fore with new designs, and the compound bow realized its potential. Jenning's four-wheel Arrowstar had variable letoff, was easy to tune, stayed that way, and shot a fast arrow. I have chronographed many compounds since, and not one has truly put the old Arrowstar under the table.

Nowadays, compounds have even greater letoff—80 percent for some models. They are short and handy and they shoot extremely fast arrows with a flat trajectory, especially when those darts are light in weight. Highly practiced compound shooters can hit a beverage can at seventy paces. These bows are highly accurate, especially when good sights are used with a mechanical release to turn the arrow loose. Overdraws are also commonly used.

An ancient idea, the overdraw was found on Turkish bows centuries ago. The *siper*, as it was known, fit on the archer's arm to provide a platform for the arrow so a very short shaft could be used. Today's overdraws, which fit on the riser of the bow, serve the same function—the use of a very short arrow. The short arrow is stiffer for its length and also lighter than a longer shaft of the same construction. The overdraw principle was not left out of the stickbow. The Black Widow company at one time had a bow with a unique forward handle design that put the arrow rest much closer to the archer.

The compound bow today remains number one in popularity. Because it has sights and high letoff capability, it's easier to master than either the primitive or traditional bow. Why, then, have thousands of archers turned to the traditional bow? Perhaps the answer was given in the preface: The compound bow has become too mechanized for these people. They want something simpler with a bit more romance, a little more beauty. Few will disagree that a longbow or recurve enjoys more graceful lines than a compound, and also carries much lighter in the hand. One may argue that each one is a machine that does work, and that's true, but a stickbow is to a compound what a violin is to a jukebox; they both make music, but entirely differently.

Now we come to the traditional bow. Recall that many primitive models were self-bows. Traditionals can also be built of one material, but most are composites joining wood and fiberglass with fine adhesives. While flatbows, which have limbs that are wide and flat, are not unheard of,

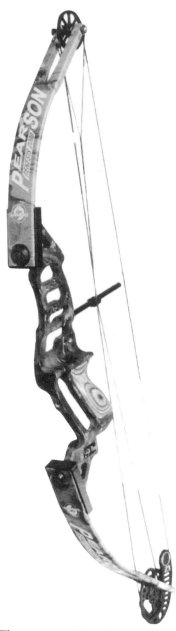

The compound bow is more machinelike than the longbow or recurve. It's a fine-shooting instrument on the cutting edge of high technology, but a different nature and personality compared with the stickbow.

A Few Good Reasons to Shoot Traditional Bows

1. Recurves and longbows are fun, even a joy, to use. They're simple—once set up—uncomplicated, and user friendly.

2. Traditional bowshooting can become a way of life, much more than a passing fad or temporary interest in a hobby.

3. There is a beauty in longbows and recurves, not only in the bows themselves, but in the arrows as well, in flight as well as appearance.

4. There is a challenge in shooting longbows and recurves in the instinctive style. You want to master them, to draw, hold, and release without conscious aim—accurately.

5. Traditional bows lend themselves to more shooting than mechanicals, the archer firing arrows smoothly and naturally.

6. The simpler bow has a long and amazing history that in many ways embodies the story of man himself. It has cultural value.

7. It's exciting to shoot longbows and recurves, in part because the arrow can be seen in flight, even though it is by no means slow.

8. Traditional archery is a visit to a simpler world, relaxing and recreational.

9. Roving with a traditional bow is healthy exercise.

two designs reign upon the traditional throne: longbow and recurve. Longbows have thick-cored, narrow limbs, and recurves have thinner cored, wider limbs that turn back on the ends. The popularity of the traditional bow peaked in the 1940s, 1950s, and 1960s, with Frank Eicholtz earning the title "father of the laminated bow," due to his experiments in the middle forties. He tried a plastic material first—Lamicoid. He finally got a bow to hold together, but was dissatisfied with it. In 1944 he talked a chemist into making him a bit of fiberglass, using this to build two improved experimental bows.

Lowell Drake fired a shaft an official five hundred sixty-seven yards with a 65-pound Eicholtz bow. Frank continued using Lamicoid along with fiberglass. Glass backed the tension side, Lamicoid the compression side, with a yew core between the two. In 1948 Eicholtz began working with George Gordon to develop a unidirectional fiberglass to replace the woven glass of the day. The breakthrough allowed mass production of viable composite laminated bows at affordable prices. Frank built a 52-pound bow using the new glass, strung it, and hung it on the wall. For two years he tested the draw weight of the strung bow. It always measured 52 pounds. Strings wore out

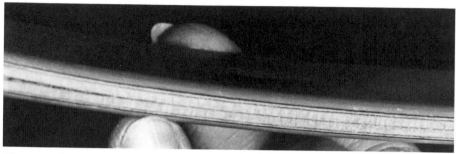

The arrival of a workable fiberglass created a new world of bowcrafting. Here, an early Bear bow shows a lamination process that allowed good traditional-style bows to be made in large numbers.

and had to be replaced, but the new laminated bow remained good as new, unstrung only to change strings.

The bows of those decades, in spirit if not exact style and materials, live again today. Bear, Shakespeare, Pearson, Herter's, Colt, Howatt, Hoyt, Black Widow, Wing, York, American, Smithwick, Howard, Perry, Drake, Groves, Fleetwood, Saunders, Martin, Staghorn, Hill, Blackhawk, White, and Jaguar were only some of the names appearing on longbows and recurves during this time period, the majority by far composites of wood and glass, just like our current traditional models. The state of the art was quite elevated at the time. For example, on July 5, 1958, Norman Richards set a new flight record with a Perry Flight Bow. The 72-pound bow with overdraw launched a 16½-inch, 103-grain arrow a distance of 842 yards, 1 foot, and 6 inches. A Howard Hill recurve bow from Howard Hill Productions in Sunland, California, won first place in the 1959 barebow (no sights used) competition in the hands of Jim Darling, whose high scores could never have been accomplished with a poor-shooting bow.

Most of the names above no longer appear on bows, but many of the companies active during that time are back. Howard Hill bows are still available, for example, although the recurve that won the above competition is not among the lineup, only the famous English-style longbows. Black Widow has been in business from the company's inception in 1957 to the present. The company continues its tradition of making one of the finest recurve bows in the world. Bear has reintroduced an entire lineup of recurves, as well as a longbow. Jack Howard has returned with his famous recurve. Groves bows are back; so are Martin recurves and longbows. The Hoyt and Howatt names, and many others, are found on stickbows. Now add to these nationally known brands the hundreds of names of custom bowyers (see appendix B) and the impact of traditional archery registers 6.0 on the Richter scale.

Archers today shoot traditional bows as a way of life, not merely as a sport. They realize that more practice and dedication are required to stay on top of the simpler bow, and they also shoot off the shelf with an instinctive, barebow style. The handsome high-performing bows, most of them made with wood handles, some with well-grained exotics, represent personal pride in manufacture and ownership. Shooting traditional bows has become part of the total body workout for many, also stimulating mental improvement through concentration and relaxation. There is no doubt that the traditional bow will see the dawning of the twenty-first century. Moreover, it will have captured more of the archery market by that time, even if the present trend slows down by half, which it shows no signs of doing.

Relegated to the attic by the compound bow in the 1970s, the stickbow has returned, and it looks like it's back to stay.

Today's traditional bow, like this Black Widow recurve, is the best ever, due not only to advanced design knowledge, but also to space age components.

Today's Traditional Longbows and Recurves

The function of a bow is storage and release of energy. The nonmechanical stickbow is basically a spring. It's bent to store energy, then snapped back to original configuration to release that energy. If a bow were 100 percent efficient, which is impossible, all of its energy would go into propelling the arrow. In reality, part of the bow's "power" is absorbed by the rebounding limbs (heavier limbs soak up more energy than lighter ones) and even the vibrating string itself. However, the arrow does receive considerable force at the nock.

Drawing a bow is like pulling a spring to store power. When the bowstring is released, a portion of that stored energy goes into propelling the arrow.

This generated power causes it to fly downrange. It seems pretty simple on the surface. However, a full understanding of a bow's action requires knowledge of geometry and physics. We're not interested in that kind of knowledge here. All we care about is how longbows and recurves work for us.

Ancient bowyers must have learned quickly that certain woods were right for bowmaking, and others useless, which is absolutely correct to this day. Even when two woods are both worthy, they can give different performance results. For example, a bowyer made two identical recurves—same length, same draw weight—using impregnated (with epoxy under force) hickory risers but two different woods for their limbs. Even though these bows were very similar, they did not "feel" the same, nor shoot the same. The difference was in the two woods used in the limbs. It had to be; everything else was the same. The smoothest-drawing bow I ever shot had Tonkin bamboo limbs. I tested another like it and it, too, was unbelievably smooth drawing. Of course, it's easy to be fooled. One bow, made with glass in its limbs, was slower shooting than its twin without the glass. So it wasn't a wood difference in this case.

When recurves and longbows again rose to prominence in the early 1990s, bowyers came out of the woods like the men of Sherwood Forest, only in far greater numbers. These men had many good books to read, as well as a group of old-timers to consult who never stopped making stickbows when the compound boom broke the sound barrier in the early seventies. Competition ran high.

This self-bow, handmade by Ken Wee, is an example of the many different woods used in today's bows, including yew, Osage orange, and other woods popular through the ages.

Parts of an Arrow

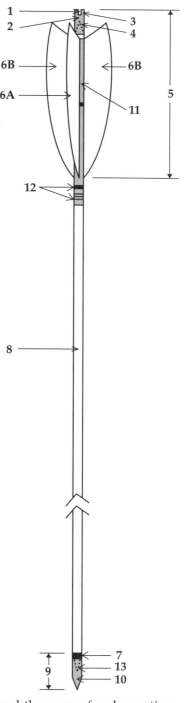

1. The *nock throat* is the slotted section of the nock into which the string fits.

2. The *nock* is the small, usually plastic, fitting glued onto the nock taper to contain the string.

3. The *nock lip* is either side of the nock.

4. The *nock taper*, also known as the butt of the shaft, is the pointed back end of the arrow onto which the nock is glued in place.

5. The *heel* of the arrow is the section that runs from the forepart of the fletching to the back of the nock.

6. *Fletching* for traditional bows consists of the guidance feathers attached to the back portion of the arrow. (A) The *cock feather* projects away from the strike plate when the arrow is nocked on the bow. (B) The *hen feathers* are the other two on an arrow fletched with three feathers. These project inward toward the strike plate.

7. The *breast* is that part of the arrow that touches the shelf of the bow.

8. The *shaft*, which was called the stele at one time, is the full body of the arrow, the dowel or cylindrical part that takes the nock, fletching, and point.

9. The *foreshaft* is the part of the arrow that lies anterior to (forward of) the breast.

10. The *point*, or pile, is the hard attached piece that protects the end of the shaft from shattering when it strikes a hard object. In older archery literature, the pile was a target point that could be blunt or pointed.

11. The *cap dip* is a contrastingly colored (painted) section of the arrow from the nock forward, under the fletching, covering about nine or ten inches of the shaft (length can vary). Normally of one color, but it can be of different colors. Useful in identifying an individual's arrow in group shooting.

12. *Cresting* is the colored bands that go around the arrow for decoration, also serving to personalize an arrow.

13. The *point taper*, also called the tongue or tang, is the angled forepart of the shaft that accepts the point.

To make a living with his trade, or even part of one, each bowyer had to create his best product. The rush was on to experiment with all types of materials and designs, which resulted in the superbows we enjoy today. Osage orange and yew, two wonderful woods, have long been considered ideal for making self-bows. Many other woods have come to the attention of the modern craftsman, including a list of exotics for risers with names like cocobolo, bloodwood, bocote, and zebrawood.

Few modern archers really know wood, but bowyers do. It's part of their trade. Ask one and he'll recite the properties of a specific wood. For example, as I became more knowledgeable about custom recurves and longbows and felt comfortable asking for increased input on construction, I asked one bowyer, "What about lignumvitae?" No good for bows, he said. And he went on to explain that lignum vitae is one of the hardest woods known, that it is even harder than some metals, with a specific gravity of 1.10 to 1.34, and that it will not float. He told me that because it is resinous and oily, it resists rot and has been employed for years for the bearings lining the stern tubes of steamship propeller shafts, where it's known to outlast brass and babbitt bearings under water by several times. Such are the properties of lignum vitae,

The return of the traditional bow includes self-bows like this one, which was built by its owner.

which means "wood of life." While lignum vitae is strong, it is overly heavy for bowmaking. But wood is only one product used in the making of the modern recurve or longbow.

Parts of a Bow

A recurve bow is featured, but parts are essentially the same on a longbow.

1. The *working limb* is the "live" or moving portion of the limb from fade-out to bow tip that stores and releases energy to the arrow.

2. The *recurve* is that portion of the limb that turns away from the bow. It serves to store and release energy. On a recurve limb, the string runs upon a section of the recurve itself, whereas on the longbow, the string does not lay on the limb.

3. The *upper limb* is topmost when the bow is held in the normal shooting position.

4. The *lower limb* is the bottommost when the bow is held in the normal shooting position.

5. The *tiller* is actually a point from limb to string that is a measurement for tillering the bow. With the usual two fingers under the nock, and one over, the upper limb is generally made a little weaker than the lower limb in order to compensate for the added drawing power applied to the lower limb.

6. The *bowstring* has loops on either end that slip onto the ends of the bow, as well as a built-up area in the middle (about).

7. The *serving* is the built-up portion of the string that accepts the nock of the arrow. It aids string life, and also promotes good nock fit.

8. The *fadeout* is the area on the limb between the rigid riser and flexible limb.

9. The *back of the bow* is the part facing away from the archer when he holds the bow in the normal shooting position.

10. The *face of the bow* is the part facing toward the archer when he holds the bow in the normal shooting position.

11. The *riser* is the entire rigid center section of the bow.

12. The *handle* of the bow is also known as the *grip*. It's that part of the riser that the archer's bowhand grasps during shooting.

13. The *throat* is the deepest section of the grip.

14. The *shelf* of the riser contains the arrow rest.

15. The *arrow rest* is the horizontal pad on which the arrow glides during the shooting of the bow.

16. The *strike plate* is the pad on which the side of the arrow glides during the shooting of the bow.

17. The *sight window* is the entire cutout portion of the riser that contains the shelf of the bow and also provides the center-shooting aspect of a bow.

18. The *brace height* is the measurement from the serving of the string to the throat of the grip.

19. The *nocking point* is the precise location where the nock of the arrow fits into the string.

20. The *limb bolt* retains the limb or the riser of the bow.

21. The *riser platform* is the flat spot on which the limb is attached via the limb bolt.

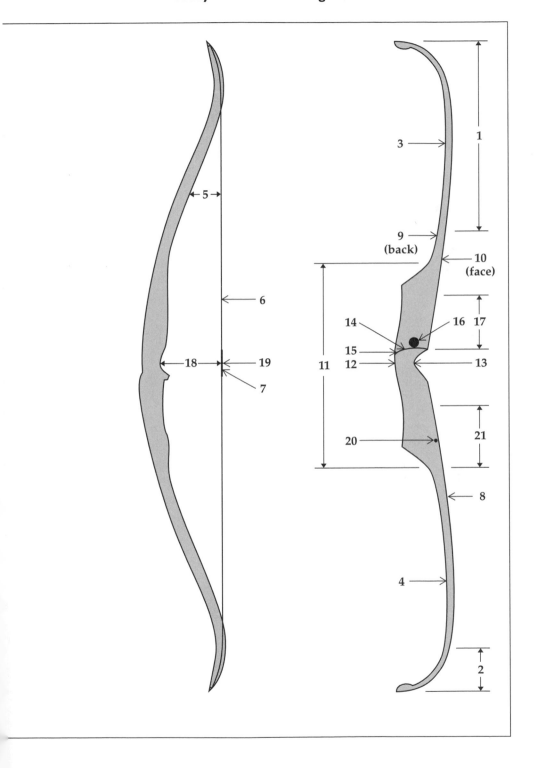

There are also many synthetics that go into the modern stickbow. Is this really traditional? By definition, yes—traditional, but not primitive. Ideally, the true replica of the primitive bow would use animal sinew, ancient adhesives, basic woods, horn, and so forth, properly made by hand with the most simple of tools, but don't be surprised to hear the hum of modern electric tools from a primitive bowyer's den. The letter of the law may not always be followed, but the spirit is. The traditional bow, on the other hand, is a product of modern mind and knowledge, even computer-generated modeling, along with E-bias fiberglass, carbon (sometimes), high-class epoxies, Gordon glass, space age strings, and more. So what criteria should an archer look for in a traditional bow? I'll discuss ten, but first forget all old ideas about longbow and recurve characteristics. The rules have changed.

Although many modern traditional bows, such as this Bear Kodiak Magnum, follow the exact lines of the original, the newest examples are often better performers due to improved materials.

Longbows have always been considered slower shooting than recurves. They may still be, but the gap is narrower. Longbows firing medium-weight arrows in the 200-feet-per-second domain are now common. Old-style longbows generated hand shock and "recoil," but the better reflex-deflex designs no longer do. Longbows have always been much lighter and trimmer than recurves. That generally remains true, with exceptions like the Ghost, a superlight recurve with extremely trim lines.

Today's recurve bow may have a deflexed riser, the bow's limbs pointing back toward the archer after the fadeout section, with the recurve portion beginning a few inches from the tip of the limb. Ancient bowyers learned that curving the limbs out and away from the back of the bow (the surface of the limb facing away from the archer) stored more energy than straight limbs. That's a law of physics, but the differences today in the shooting abilities of the two bows are less than they once were.

Many different materials go into today's traditional-style bows. This Sky Archer Target Supreme TD (Takedown) has a die-cast magnesium riser.

You can, however, spot the difference in looks in a second. The longbow's limbs are straight. When strung, the string does not lie on any portion of the limb, as it does with the recurve. And it's still safe to say that the two bows feel different in the hand, do not carry alike, and have, all in all, different natures.

At the close of this chapter, selection features such as bow length, mass weight, draw weight, draw length, riser size, and handle shape will be discussed. For now, let's look at ten general characteristics—positive and negative—of modern longbows and recurves.

Imparting a reasonable *arrow speed* is an important job for any bow, mainly because the faster arrow creates a flatter trajectory, making shots beyond twenty or thirty yards more reasonable. The traditional recurve of the past was a worthy bow, but across the board it rarely fired a 500-grain arrow much beyond about 180 feet per second. There were exceptions, the Black Widow being one mentioned earlier. Recently, I chronographed a handsome old bow I carried in the late fifties and early sixties. A 410-grain arrow broke away from the riser at a mere 162 feet per second. I recall replacing that under-50-pound-draw recurve with a 75-pound composite Ben Pearson longbow that the archery shop owner couldn't give away. I bought it for twenty bucks. It threw a heavy arrow at least as fast as my pretty recurve shot its light arrow.

In the 1980s, Dan Bertalan took on an interesting project, traveling across the country to meet with bowyers. Along with conducting interviews, Dan chronographed many custom bows, the work ending up in a book, *Traditional Bowyers of America*. No two bows will provide absolutely identical

Bear Archery Company's Montana Longbow was designed to meet the roving interest in the older-style traditional bow.

arrow speeds due to minor variations in materials, right down to specific individual woods used. However, Dan did provide an excellent across-the-board data base of modern traditional bow speeds. For example, a Fedora 60-inch one-piece 68-pound recurve launched a 28½-inch 2117 aluminum 530-grain arrow wearing three five-inch feathers 213 feet per second. A Rocky longbow with similar statistics drove a 460-grain arrow 205 feet per second.

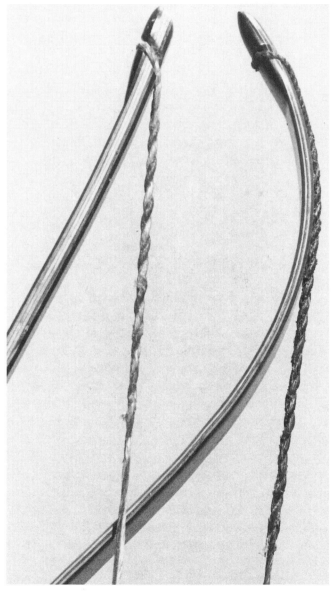

These two examples show their origins immediately. The longbow's string, left, does not ride on the limb, whereas the recurve's does.

I, too, have chronographed a number of bows. One 67-pound Black Widow fired a 540-grain arrow 217 feet per second. My own 63-pound Black Widow drove the same arrow 209 feet per second. A Pronghorn longbow kicked a similar arrow just over 200 feet per second.

Hand shock and recoil in a bow may be a problem. Hand shock is felt as a vibration. It can be annoying to some, even painful to others. Archers with a touch of arthritis may go so far as giving up traditional archery because of hand shock in a bow. On the other hand, some of the greatest archers living today shoot bows that have plenty of hand shock; they simply ignore it. I have personally watched two bow experts hit tiny targets out of the air with bows that had hand shock.

Recoil is the feeling that the bow would like to follow the arrow downrange. Once again, it's a bothersome trait to some and absolutely no problem for other bowshooters. As long as a bow "handles well" for its owner, hand shock and recoil are meaningless.

Forgiveness is a positive trait in a bow, albeit a little difficult to define. This trait can, however, be discovered in a bow. I've shot bows that demanded a near-perfect arrow release, spot-on anchor point, and a dead steady bowarm. These factors are necessary for all good shooting, but a forgiving bow seems to put that arrow near the mark even when the archer does not do his part expertly. The opposite of a forgiving bow is a sensitive bow, where any detour from near-perfect form dooms the arrow's flight from the start. Forgiveness in a bow reveals itself through hands-on experience—shooting lots of arrows.

An undesirable trait, *stacking* means that the bow does not progress evenly in draw weight. Pounds of force per inch varies, especially toward the end of the draw. There isn't an experienced stickbow shooter who hasn't shot a bow that stacks. Stacking is usually related negatively with smoothness of draw: A bow that stacks is not a smooth-pulling bow. My bowpartner, the late Ted Walter, had an all-fiberglass 55-pound recurve bow that stacked like a deck of cards. Yet, Ted could hit small targets close, and medium-sized targets far with that bow—consistently. Stacking is not a desirable trait, but once again, it can be lived with, at least by some archers.

The less *noise* a bow makes the better. There are two sources of sound when a bow is fired: the arrow and the bow itself. Noisy arrows often have loose screw-in points of overly large feathers. Noise from bows is normally a string sound, either from vibration or slap against a limb. Even though the string itself is the problem, some bows are very hard to quiet down, no matter what kind of silencer is used on the string, and a bow that cannot be quieted with silencers is a nuisance. Twang! Twang! Twang! Naturally, all bows make noise when an arrow is turned loose. But with string silencers, this should be more a hum or buzz than a twang. The quietest bows I've ever shot were longbows, perhaps because of their reduced string contact with the limbs. However, today's better-designed recurves are also extremely quiet. For ideas on cutting down on bow noise, see chapter 8. Before leaving this topic, I must admit that some archers love bow noise. The last thing they want is a hum when they can have a big healthy twang and hiss. It's part of archery for them, something they picked up from Robin Hood movies, perhaps. These shooters have even been known to use large feathers on purpose, even flu-flu styles, just to enhance arrow flight noise.

Accuracy is obviously important for any shooting instrument. The modern stickbow is no exception. What is interesting here is that all tests I have been associated with reveal equal *potential* for bow accuracy among the different types. The compound bow is often considered more accurate than longbow or recurve because of its appointments and characteristics, including top-grade sights, even scopes, string peeps, bubble levels, stabilizers, mechanical releases, and high letoff, which make physical mastery easier. Put a longbow, recurve, or compound in a shooting machine, use only matched high-grade arrows, and all will shoot accurately. In short, longbows and recurves also have fine accuracy potential. It's up to the archer to realize that potential.

Seemingly, *longevity* should have nothing to do with recurve or longbow performance, since an otherwise fine-shooting bow could be prone to an early demise. But the inherent lifespan of a bow does matter. We're talking about relatively expensive toys here, well worth every farthing, since one or two can serve an archer for years with great pleasure and value. But it's safer to say that "good bows" are well made, and well-made bows don't break easily or wear out through normal shooting over a short span of time. Part of this criterion is reliability. A breakage-prone bow simply cannot be called reliable, and reliability is a handmaid to performance.

Bow quiver and other add-on options should be available for the recurve. The modern longbow can sidestep this one, I feel, because it stands alone so well. In fact, I prefer a longbow bereft of add-ons. But I think a recurve should be capable of bow quiver attachment without a hitch, sights, and if the owner so desires, a stabilizer as well, even though I personally feel that cushion plungers, stabilizers, and other attachments finally nudge the recurve out of its traditional ranking. Actually, archers of the past were more likely to add sights to a recurve bow than today's stickbow set, who prefer shooting instinctively, barebow style.

Relatively easy *mastery* of the high-grade traditional bow is possible if it is correctly designed and manufactured. In level of difficulty the longbow seems slower to fully control than the recurve, but this is not always true. There are bowshooters who quickly take to the longbow. Mainly, it's the

Included in the exciting traditional revolution is a renewed interest in old bows, such as this venerable model from Bear Archery displayed by Claris Butler.

smooth-pulling, forgiving bow that is easiest to master, regardless of its type, in contrast to a misbehaving bow that is difficult to control. And any stick is tough to master if its draw is too heavy for the archer.

Ease of tuning and staying tuned are valuable bow traits. Although most sticks require very little "messing with," and once set up tend to stay that way, there are some bows that are finicky. It takes a lot of fooling around to get these models to throw an arrow hot, straight, and true. Some of these bows are so fussy that if the string stretches a little or a strike plate becomes worn, arrows that once flew well go haywire. The good stickbow tunes easily and stays that way.

Most of the above ten points influence the performance of the traditional bow. When all are positive, the result is a fine-shooting, reliable instrument that handles at least a minor array of arrow types without porpoising or fishtailing, the dart gliding from the bow cleanly, flying point-on to the target. The bow is also a pleasure to shoot and highly reliable in all regards, including longevity. The above points deal with the bow itself, but what are the deciding factors in choosing a specific stick? That's really another matter, and so here are nine more points to consider.

One bowyer may insist that longer limbs are faster than shorter ones and are also responsible for a smoother-pulling bow. Another holds that short limbs are faster and not at all exclusive of draw smoothness. Both are right—or wrong. Unique design is actually more important than overall *limb or bow length*. However, this does not mean that a person with a long draw should insist on a short bow. There are limits. Extremely short bows can exhibit many problems, not the least of which is a slow arrow. There are no formulas to set down because bow designs differ. The buyer must listen to his bowyer. If, for example, the bowyer feels that his design requires a 60-inch bow or longer for a 28-inch draw, take his advice; he knows the idiosyncracies of his product.

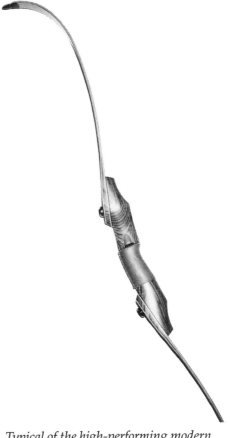

After deciding on bow length, it's time to look at *draw weight*. Perhaps the single most common mistake in going from compound to longbow or recurve is "overbowing," which means buying a model with an unwieldy draw weight. Compounds enjoy letoff; sticks don't. You pull and hold the whole enchilada. With a little personal conditioning, it's no problem for most of us. However, going from a 70-pound compound to a 70-pound traditional bow can totally discourage the archer. There is also efficiency to consider, a factor that is often overlooked when bow shopping. Given two traditional bows, one with a 55-pound draw, the other with a 70-pound draw, which is more "powerful"? The latter? Not always. It takes a chronograph to tell.

If the 55-pound model gets 200 feet per second with a 500-grain arrow, and the 70-pound model gets 200 feet per

Typical of the high-performing modern traditional bow, this Ferret from Pronghorn Custom Bows shoots well over 200 feet per second with a 500-grain arrow.

second with the same arrow, the bows are obviously equal in power. The archer is just tugging more pounds for nothing with the heavier model. This does not mean that heavy bows aren't powerful. They certainly are. In many cases, the heavier bow will shoot a heavier arrow at a similar speed to the lighter bow and arrow, which means more kinetic energy. Ideally, the bow carries sufficient force to drive an arrow at good velocity for that flat trajectory mentioned earlier. With a bow like that, a shot across a little gully at a pine cone becomes a lot easier than with a slowpoke that loops its arrow toward the clouds to span the ravine. Going to the superlight trend of the late '50s, however, is probably heading too far in the light-draw direction. But muscle-wrenching weights are even worse.

If the archer cannot fully control his bow, then no matter how strong that bow is, its inherent energy is a waste, for it cannot be realized. Better to draw a 50-pound bow to full anchor point than to short draw a 65-pound bow. Finally, there's a law of diminishing returns with increasing draw weight. In most of my tests, I've found that above 60-pounds of pull, increases in arrow speed become less dramatic. Were I given a choice between a 55-pound bow that launched a 500-grain arrow 195 feet per second and a 65-pound bow that sent the same arrow 200 feet per second, I'd take the 55-pounder every time.

Another important factor in selecting a personal traditional bow is *bow weight*. Many of us got away from compounds because they did not satisfy our archery psyche, but also because they weighed a ton. Admittedly, the same fellows, including me, often admire a heavy rifle for its stability on a target bench. However, rifles are rifles and bows are bows. I want my longbows on the light side and my recurves about medium weight. For example, my one-piece 60-inch quiverless Pronghorn longbow weighs 18 ounces. My Black Widow recurve goes about 3 pounds. I'm content with those weights. Others may prefer a little heavier longbow and perhaps a little lighter recurve. That's personal preference. Distribution of the weight is important too. My Widow, for example, feels stable because it is heavy through the handle. The Pronghorn longbow is much lighter in weight than the Widow, but it too has mass in the riser for excellent weight distribution.

Draw length is another important item to look at. Archers going from a compound to a traditional bow often want to stay with their compound bow draw length. That's a mistake. Because the compound is shot "straight up," it's easy for a person with average "arm spread" to draw 29 or 30 inches with a compound. My compound draw length was 31½ inches. But I shoot my sticks at 28-inch draw. Why? Because the shooting style is entirely different with the longbow or recurve—much more compressed. Also, most of us shoot stickbows canted, not straight up and down, although there is nothing wrong with that style if an archer likes it (see chapter 6 on shooting styles).

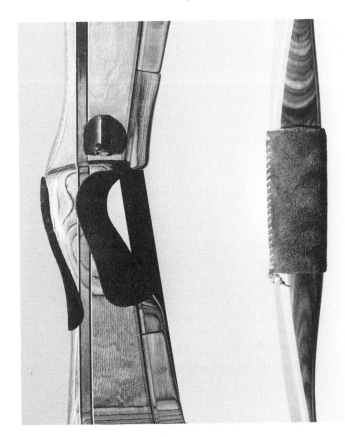

Here is a perfect example of the wide range of styles available in today's traditional bows. On the left is a Black Widow recurve. On the right is a recurve from Great Northern company. Note medium-wrist grip on the Widow, "broom handle" low-wrist grip on the Great Northern Ghost.

The archer exchanging compound for stickbow should borrow a bow first, and learn to shoot it in the traditional style before deciding on his true draw length. (See chapter 11 for using the "try arrow" to determine draw length.)

The *size of the bow* is another factor to consider. Once again, it's a matter of personal preference. I don't like bulky bows, but others love them. A huge riser, for example, does nothing for my shooting or my eyes. Others find big bows appealing. They like the feel of a huge handle; they enjoy the extra wood, which lends itself to sculpturing or other decorative features. Some may prefer these bows because they hark back to the "good old days" when big risers were popular. I'm really not sure. All I know is that I want my bows to be large enough to fill my hands, and not much bigger.

Grip shape is another important factor. As the grip goes, so goes the hand. I want my bowhand (the one holding the bow) to form a fist on which the arrow seems to rest. This means a grip where the riser shelf is located just above the hand. Deeply cut grip throats tend to drop the bowhand downward. That produces the bent-wrist or high-wrist hold. Even on recurves, I prefer a much straighter wrist posture. To that end, all my recurves have

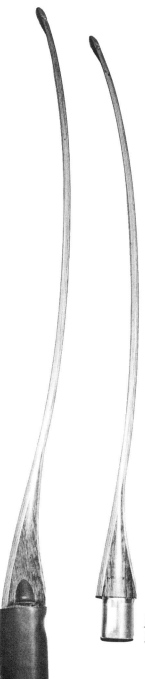

what is called a longbow grip, including my Black Widow. For an extra fee, that company offers a custom grip, which for me meant a low-wrist design that looks more like a broom handle than anything else. Of course, personal preference is key to these choices because longbows and recurves are not only mechanical things, but extensions of the mind and body of the archer. Many bowbenders love the high-wrist hold, for it tends to accommodate a thumb-finger circle of pressure, while the palm of the hand simply rests in the grip. And there's nothing wrong with that plan at all.

Takedown versus one-piece is another choice that has to be made. Although both are excellent, the takedown has certain merits that make it hard to turn away from. Whereas the one-piece, with its unbroken lines, is arguably more handsome, the takedown offers greater practicality. Broken down, a takedown bow fits into a modest-sized case, handy not only on an airplane, but also in a motor vehicle, a boat, or on a backpacking trip. One takedown bow with two sets of limbs of different draw weight makes two long bows. Or with two sets of nearly identical limbs, the takedown is a bow with a backup. If a limb gets caught in a car door, for example, there's another set ready to go into action.

Just one of many different takedown designs, this Pronghorn longbow comes apart at the riser.

Glaringly different are these two bows. The recurve, below, has wide, narrow limbs, whereas the longbow's limbs are much narrower with a thicker core.

How the bow looks is a matter of personal taste. I admire nice wood, for example, and find my bocote riser recurve stunning, especially with its matching bocote lams. However, I also like bows that are made of nothing more than Actionwood, which is essentially a pile of hard maple strips laminated together. All the same, beauty is important in a longbow or recurve because these are bows that become part of the archer. He should find them beautiful, therefore, if only in his own eyes.

Finally comes perhaps the most important decision: Should you go with a *longbow or a recurve*? Generally speaking, the longbow is a more lithe and lively creature, smallish in the hand, large in performance, and lightly carried over long trails. In contrast, the recurve has a look of power with its shapely curves, and some feel that its wider limb makes it more stable in the hand and easier to master. Since both of these bows are shot as part of the archer's own body, the obvious path to a choice is studying each to see which one "fits" best. I own both. Wouldn't have it any other way.

3

The Custom Bow

Many companies have come back "on line," once more offering longbows and recurves, including Martin Archery, Bear Archery, Browning Archery Company, and other manufacturers that once turned out numbers of traditional bows annually. Companies associated with compounds are also offering factory-made stickbows in response to archer demand, such as PSE, long known as a compound-only concern. Semicustom bows, such as the Black Widow, are also available. Each bow is made by hand, but with a team doing the job, not one bowyer, and production is quite high. Finally, the true custom bow may be had. Although these bows also follow general specifications (there is no confusing a Black Swan custom longbow with a Roger Rothhaar recurve), each one is built from the ground up by one, two, or a few bowyers.

The big difference between the factory, semicustom, and custom bow is degree of personalizing possible. Factory bows usually come in many models, but the archer does not have a choice in exact draw weights or lengths, or the materials blended to manufacture the bow. The semicustom bow offers more options, but it's highly unlikely that a bowbender will talk the company into a wood that is not normally used, or a specific bow length not ordinarily offered. The custom bow cannot be ordered to the exact specifications of the buyer either, because there are limits that the bowyer must insist on. In fact, archers often tend to get carried away with personalizing their custom bows.

A real conversation I overhead between a prospective customer and a custom bowyer startled me. It went something like this:

"I'm looking for a longbow and I hear you make a good one. Do you do all the work yourself?"

"Yes, I do. I'm a one-man shop. I grind my own laminations and make every bow by hand."

"Okay. What lengths do your longbows come in?"

"I offer 56-, 58-, 60-, 62-, and 64-inch longbows."

Arvid Danielson of Black Swan working on one of his custom bows. Today, there are several hundred traditional bowmakers at work in the country.

"Oh, I really wanted a 57-inch longbow."

"Well, I guess I can do that."

"All right, but I have a long draw length."

"How long?"

"I draw a 30½-inch arrow."

"You mean with your compound, don't you?"

The conversation went on and on. When the bowyer said he could not build a short longbow for a long draw, and that he wouldn't make it over 65 pounds pull because he didn't believe in going beyond that draw weight, the sale was off. In fact, the bowyer knew what he was talking about. He agreed to make a 57-inch bow, which was not in his normal lineup, when he knew

Herb Meland of Pronghorn Custom Bows discusses traditional archery with interested bowshooters. If a prospective customer can see the work of a bowyer firsthand, all the better.

perfectly well that the archer would never be able to tell the difference between that and a 58-inch model, and he even agreed to use a riser wood that he did not like working with. But when the customer insisted on a product that would be no darn good, the bowyer drew the line because his reputation was at stake.

Custom bowyers are building many different types of bows these days, including English-style longbows, reflex-deflex longbows, shorter and longer longbows, recurves of all types, bows with longer risers, others with shorter risers, flat bows, slim bows, thick bows, and so forth. By flipping through the pages of any archery magazine, you can pull out the names of custom bowyers by the handfuls, especially if the periodical deals with traditional equipment only, as does *Instinctive Archer* magazine. It's impossible, and it would be wrong if it were possible, for anyone to dictate to another what bow he should shoot. In the previous chapter a few features worthy of consideration were laid out. Now, let's see what goes into making a custom bow so the reader can evaluate the cost of one of these handmade models.

The March 1960 issue of *Archery Magazine*, a major bowshooting periodical of the day, contained a number of advertisements for bows, most of them from manufacturers, not custom bowyers. The semicustom Joe Fries bow, from the company of the same name, sold for $75.00. The Staghorn, a semicustom, sold for $85.00. Howard Hill offered a recurve bow with pistol grip for $85.00, plain grip $75.00. Dick Green's bow sold for $69.50, the Steiner Fury went for $72.50, and Herter's had a lineup of recurves that ran between $30.00 and $50.00. The Damon Howatt Diablo sold for $59.50, and the Indian Archery Company's Seneca fetched $45.00. One of the more expensive bows advertised was a Wing Presentation recurve at $100.00. The Black Widow, then made by the Wilson brothers, ran $75.00.

Custom bows these days cost more—a lot more. Part of the increase lies in normal inflation, of course. A good car in 1960 didn't cost a bushel basket of greenbacks, and gasoline ran around 30¢ to 35¢ a gallon where I lived. Today, $600 for a handmade longbow or recurve is not unheard of, although the buyer does have to beware. Prices can be inflated. A perfectly excellent stick can still be found for under $500 with a little shopping. In fact, I recently

The primitive bow has not been left out of the custom picture. Ken Wee creates fine custom primitive longbows.

tested a highly expensive bow against one that sold for $450 and the less expensive bow performed better. So the reader must be prepared to spend up to $750 or so for the custom bow of his dreams. What goes into the making of a fine custom bow that shoots a fast arrow with good handling characteristics? Let's find out.

Bowyer Herb Meland of Pronghorn Custom Bows places a set of limbs in the form for a three-piece takedown bow.

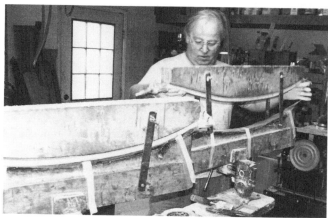

The top of the form is put in place and bolted to hold the limbs as the adhesive cures under properly heated conditions.

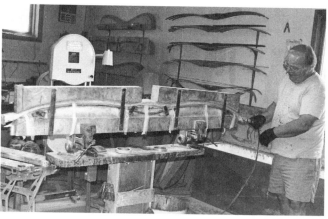

With the limbs set in place in the form, the bowyer connects an air bag (air hose) to the form. When the hose is inflated, proper pressure is applied to the laminated limbs in the form, causing them to set up correctly as the bonding cures.

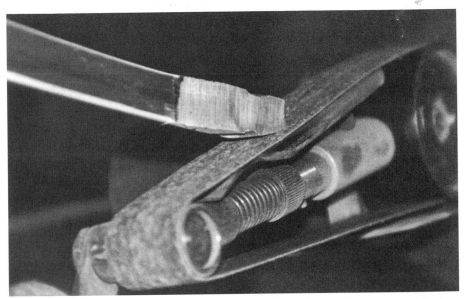

Rough-shaping a bow tip with a belt sander. Although custom bows are handmade, many tools are used in the process.

Design precedes everything else. A bowyer has to have, in his mind, a plan of merit that results in good looks and top performance. Some bowyers don't possess the knowledge or imagination to design a truly great bow. Either they make one that doesn't look good or shoot well, or they pirate a competitor's model. One fine little longbow I know of has been copied by several bowyers around the country, including a few who originally didn't care for the bow they now imitate because it didn't have the English longbow look.

A person I know claims there are no true customs—only "individually made bows." I say custom means "made for an individual on special order," and although the customer cannot expect a bowyer to change his whole design to meet one archer's demands, there are quite a number of appointments that can be personalized. Most bowyers build more than one model, for example, so that's a starting point. Which model does the customer want? Longbow, recurve, one-piece, takedown? What overall length? What draw weight? Right-handed, left-handed, special grip (low wrist or high)? What limb material? What handle material? Which overlays? How about riser lamination options? Exotic wood? Plain wood? How about enhancing options, such as bow quiver inserts? Some bowyers offer bamboo, yew, red elm, or other limb wood options not simply for the sake of appearance, but also because different woods respond differently to compression, energy storage, and energy release.

It's beginning to look a little more complicated than whittling on a chunk of wood until it turns into a bow, isn't it? Compatible materials for the riser and limbs are selected, and laminations are ground with extremely close tolerance, in thousandths of an inch in most cases, to create the core density necessary for the specific draw weight the customer ordered. In making limbs, fine quality adhesives must be used with accurate pressure, heat, and timing for proper bonding. The limbs have to cure for a specific period as well, cooling, usually overnight, while still under pressure.

Many details must be attended to, such as laying the bow out accurately, roughing it out, gluing tip overlays properly, cutting string grooves precisely, aligning tips, and tillering the bow so that the limbs draw evenly without one limb fighting the other. The limbs must be worked during the tillering process to ensure the right draw weight, the one ordered by the customer. On this dimension, there must be some slack allowed. If I ordered a 60-pound bow and got a 58- or 62-pound pull, I'd not complain. The bowyer does need a couple pounds leeway so he can work on tillering the limbs. Other details

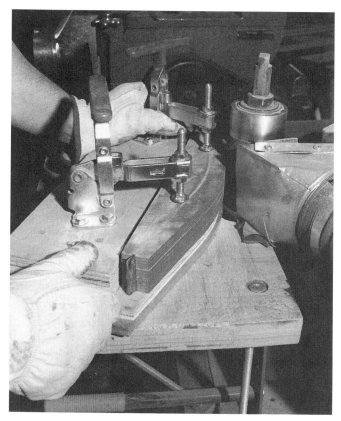

The back of the riser is shaped using a specific jig to guarantee perfect dimensions.

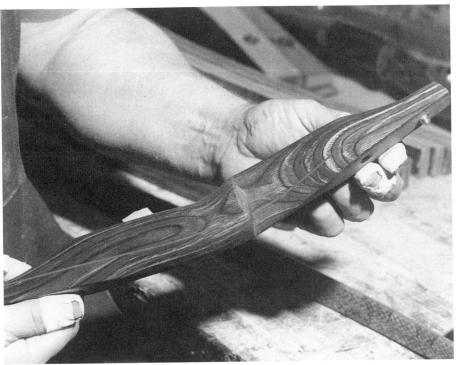

Checking sanding for scratches. A well-crafted custom bow never shows scratches left in the wood from tools.

include final shaping, careful wood filler application, lots of sanding for a smooth finish, and a final lacquer coating to seal the bow against the elements. The bowyer might add a leather handle, snakeskin on the limbs, inlays, or any number of other minute features. I had two of my bows built with locators—small cutouts that my pinky finger sank into—indicating by feel that I was gripping the riser the same way every time for uniformity in shooting.

Obviously, the custom bow is a product of its maker's imagination and planning, as well as hard work and skill in craftsmanship. The good ones merit their price tag. They'll last a long time, giving a great deal of pleasure. Unfortunately, there are some badly overpriced bows available too. For the reader's convenience, here are some tips to buying a custom or semicustom bow.

If you are a newcomer to traditional archery, you should consider starting out with a used custom bow at a moderate price that fits your general needs, or a standard "factory" bow, with a custom to follow later. It may take a while to decide what you really want or need, and requirements and desires change with time. After you know just what you want in a longbow or

Herb Meland checks the decorative copperhead snakeskin backing on one of his Pronghorn one-piece longbows.

recurve, then you can place an order for that truly special custom bow. I learned this the hard way when returning to the ranks of traditional archery after a long layoff. In a magazine I saw a bow in the hands of a well-known archer and decided he must surely know a good product, so I followed suit.

The recurve I got was bulky, overly long, and on the heavy side. It wasn't terribly expensive, but for its performance it cost too much. I ended up getting rid of it. After shooting a few stickbows at a local archery shop, I learned something, and my next bow was a good purchase. I still own and shoot it. Appendix A has a list of used bow shops for the reader's convenience.

The custom bow is not a panacea. It will never make up for lack of practice or make a good archer out of a poor one. The good custom bow should do what it was created for, but it's not magic. If you can handle 50 pounds pull, for example, and the bow you order is 65, no amount of fine workmanship in that stick will improve your shooting ability. When looking for a custom bow, you must carefully consider what you really want, and what you can shoot well, before plunging in. It's also wise to shop around. There are literally hundreds of bowyers plying their trade these days and making a multitude of different-style sticks.

Some stickbows are experimental in nature—buyer beware! One bowyer built an extremely short recurve with solid carbon limbs. It had hand shock and fired a slow arrow. Being a man of high reputation he remedied the problem by throwing the bow away and not making another like it. Ask the

---

Ordering a Custom Bow

1. Seek out a bowyer of high reputation.

2. Try to find a bow like the one you intend to buy, shooting it to see if it matches your style, your likes, and dislikes.

3. Don't buy a bow too heavy for your ability. Being overbowed takes the fun out of shooting. Remember that it's efficiency that really counts. An efficient 55-pound bow may outshoot a "doggy" 65-pound bow.

4. If you're coming from the compound, your draw length will be reduced when shooting traditional style. Most archers do well with a 28-inch draw.

5. No matter how fast a bow shoots, it won't be enjoyable if it handles poorly. A smooth-drawing, no-hands-shock bow firing a slightly slower arrow beats a fast, bad-mannered bow every time.

6. Ensure that the grip of the riser fits your hand. Most custom bows, even from multiworker shops, offer personal grip fits.

7. Consider a takedown bow if you plan to travel with it.

8. Choose a bow that pleases your eye, but never buy on looks alone.

9. Expect a waiting period while your bow is being built. I consider a year long enough; however, after taking receipt of a particular takedown longbow, I admit I would have waited three years for that beautiful stick.

10. Expect to pay half down, the rest on delivery.

11. Expect to receive some sort of warranty; however, I've witnessed some customer abuse. Recently, a bowyer was asked to repair—free of charge—a broken longbow. The bow was guaranteed for one year. It was now three years old. When I bought my new Chevy truck, it was warranted for three years or 36,000 miles, whichever came first. Had I asked for free repairs four years or 40,000 miles later, Chevy would have said no. Likewise a bow warranty. When it runs out, it's finished.

bowyer if the models he's selling are tried and tested, or hot off the drawing board. Ideally, you should go to the bowyer's shop and try a few different models before plunking your money down, but this is not always practical. Long-distance buying is necessary because there are so many fine bowmakers scattered over the country. An archer in New York, for example, may be thrilled with a custom bow from Montana, and he should have it.

The archer must consider the custom bow "individually made," rather than built solely for one customer. It's impractical to think that a bowyer could afford to set up all new implements just to make a one-of-a-kind bow. On the other hand, you should know what options you have. Certainly, you'll have a choice of a right-handed or left-handed model. You will also have a range of draw weights to choose from. You must select a draw length as well. The custom bow will often come in different overall lengths, and sometimes their dimension is limited by draw length. For example, if you are thinking about ordering a Black Widow MAII Takedown Recurve, the company will provide you with a draw length per bow length reference chart. For draw lengths of 24 to 28 inches, 58-inch limbs are suggested; for draw lengths of 26 to 30 inches, 60-inch limbs are listed; for draw lengths of 28 to 32 inches, 62-inch limbs are in the lineup; and for 30 to 40 inch lengths, Black Widow offers 64-inch limbs for its MAII bow.

Some custom shops cut your choices way down. One, for example, offers a particular recurve model only with 58-inch limbs for drawing lengths ranging from 24 to 29 inches. This bowyer does not feel that even a seven-foot-tall archer needs to draw beyond 29 inches, and he has found that his particular recurve functions ideally at a 58-inch overall length. I've tried his bows and agree with him. The bowyer knows more than the customer concerning a

Riser blocks: the lower block shows decorative spacer, and the upper block reveals the double-threaded insert epoxied in place.

particular bow that he, the bowyer, makes. As for the above-mentioned MAII Black Widow, the company knows that there is a *range* of practical application when it comes to bow and draw lengths with that particular model.

Now you must decide on draw weight. Today's better customs and semi-customs are efficient bows, and they don't require superheavy draw weights to launch an arrow a reasonable distance with a flat trajectory. There are bow-benders who can pull 100-pound longbows and recurves, shooting them with accuracy. My own brother had a 107-pound model he enjoyed for a few years, but later abandoned it for an efficient 63-pound bow. For those who enjoy tugging the weight, and who are built to do it, fine. The rest of us should look at the 50- to 60-pound range in a man's bow and perhaps 35 to 50 pounds in a woman's bow, with target models running lighter than utility bows.

There often are wood choices to be made with custom bows. Bowyer Mike Steliga prefers various hardwoods for the risers of his custom Bruin bows. He says his favorite is bubinga, "because of the variation of its striking grain contrasts that combine with the warmth of its reddish tones." Mike goes on to note that bubinga is "very dense and strong." Herb Meland of Pronghorn Custom Bows offers a variety of wood choices for the riser,

Herb Meland checks the riser on one of his Pronghorn Three-Piece Takedown Longbows with leather handle.

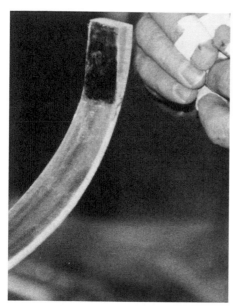

A micarta tip overlay, glued in place, awaits further shaping and finishing.

including zebrawood, bubinga, cocobolo, bocote, birdseye maple, curly maple, shedua, East India rosewood, bloodwood, moradillo, and others. Along with riser wood choices, there may also be limb laminations to select from, such as red elm, bamboo, yew, or Osage orange.

Takedown or one-piece? That's another choice to be made. The attributes of the takedown were noted earlier. A custom or semicustom bow may also offer a choice of handle shape, sometimes cut from a tracing of the buyer's hand. A shiny or dull finish is another possible choice. Three fingers under the nock is another option. (Some shooters prefer this style of drawing the bow, and the bowmaker must know that ahead of time so he can do the necessary tillering adjustment for this type of draw.) There may be insert options as well, for bow quiver, sights, stabilizer, or cushion plunger. Or the bow may be left without any inserts. Inlays and special touches are possible, including messages or names written on the bow, even line drawings. Pronghorn Custom Bows has a special model with professionally woodburned limbs depicting Indian arrows and other designs. The customer better ask about options, for there can certainly be a lot of them.

When looking for a custom or semicustom bow, buy from a bowyer who is known for a specific model. Clones may be as good as originals, but the original comes with its own earned reputation. Although clever bowmakers have successfully cloned a number of good bows over the past several years, this does not mean that the workmanship is on par with the original. Dedicated bowyers who have cut their own trails through the woods of the trade learned a lot on the way. Not all of their tricks have been revealed. Some are quite subtle, right down to the perfect alignment of a bow quiver insert.

Asking for customer references is all right, but you shouldn't rely on it in choosing a custom or semicustom bow. The reason is simple: Traditional archery is so personal that one man's meat is another's poison. I was slightly disappointed in a particular custom bow I happened to test. I tried two samples from the bowmaker and they were beautiful in workmanship, but definitely had some hand shock. Maybe I was too critical, but at the price of these bows, I expected better shooting manners. A fellow archer came along as I was chronographing and working with the bows. He asked to shoot them, and so he did. The first comment he made was, "They shoot so smoothly, and not a bit of hand shock!" I thought maybe it was just me, so I had another bow-bender friend, who happens to know a good deal about archery, try the bows. He handed them back with the comment that they were beautiful, but both had hand shock. That's why I'm skeptical about customer references when it comes to traditional bows.

It's a big mistake to let others dictate when it comes to the long-bow or recurve, too. Some of the finest archers in the world today—men who shoot aspirins out of the air—are doing it with bows that may not be right for the "average" bow-shooter at all, and probably aren't.

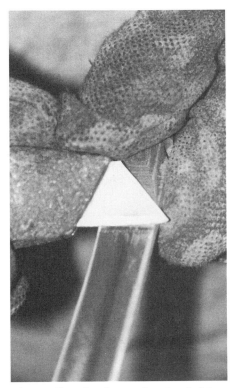

The smallest detail must be attended to in making a true custom traditional bow. Here, the bowyer removes all traces of excess adhesive using a razor knife.

But in the hands of these people, the bows are absolutely great.

Ask the bowyer about his stick's vital statistics, too, which include brace height, strings, and arrows. Not that a buying decision should be made on the basis of these matters, but it's important to find out what the maker of the bow uses in his own creations. Are Fast Flight strings recommended? The bow tips may not be made to withstand these strong strings, although I believe most custom and semicustom shops have gone to the newer materials now. If a recommended brace height seems extremely high, that's worth asking about, too. Does the bow handle a variety of arrows? It really should. Most sticks do, and although you may feel that only wood arrows are right for traditional bows, you'll come to find that aluminum, carbon, fiberglass, and other materials have been used for ages in longbows and recurves, and you, too, may wish to try them. Today's carbon arrow, for example, is only yesterday's fiberglass taken to another level.

When you find a bow you like, stop searching and buy it. Otherwise, the process of shopping can get out of hand. There are archers who are in and out of bows like socks because they continue to look for the perfect bow. Well, it doesn't exist. We have to remember that we are obligated to adapt to the bow a little, rather than expecting a bow to perfectly match us. Any bow is right if its owner has it mastered, enjoys shooting it, and can hit the target with regularity. Likewise, any bow is wrong if its owner cannot do these things, even if the strung stick is a masterpiece of design and beauty. It's impossible to list all of the traits that a bow *must* have because a bowshooter will come along with a model that exhibits opposite characteristics and he'll shoot it perfectly. The way to find out if a bow and an archer are compatible is simple. Shoot the bow; give it a good chance with an array of arrows, and make certain that it's tuned correctly to give it a fair chance. Also, although some archers and their bows are as compatible as rattlers and mice at first, "getting used to" these "bad" bows through lots of practice can override the mismatch.

When you excitedly remove that new bow from its package, you owe it to the bowyer to follow the rules. Set up the bow as prescribed by its maker with the correct string (which comes with the bow) and the right brace height as well as nocking point. Naturally, the bow must be tuned to your style of shooting, but these starting points are imperative. Also, shooting a batch of mismatched arrows is no way to test how well a bow does, and it's downright unfair to expect the bow to perform with them. Remember, too, that spine charts are only a starting point. Individual bows handle arrows individually. For example, one 55-pound bow may shoot an arrow of 70-pound spine (stiffness) well, whereas another bow of the same draw weight may shoot 55-pounds of spine best.

The custom or semicustom bow marks the apex of the modern traditional archer's equipment. Except for the few who can truly build a good bow of their own, and there are people who can do that, the custom and semicustom longbow or recurve is a shop and buy proposition.

4

Testing Traditional Bows and Arrows

Testing traditional bows and arrows can be done in two ways: one technical, the other hands-on. The first uses a chronograph to determine how fast a bow can drive arrows of various weights; in feet per second, along with a precision scale to determine not only the weight (in grains) of arrows, but also their variance. The second method of testing is "by feel and eye." The archer determines how a specific model works for him by shooting it. He can tell, with experience, whether a bow handles smoothly or with recoil, and if it suffers from stacking, hand shock, or other less desirable traits. While the hands-on approach is unscientific, it can be more important than the technical method, the reason being that shooting longbows and recurves is subjective and definitely varies for different people. That's why we see certain archers shooting dimes out of the air with a bow that has hand shock, whereas others can't hit a straw bale with the same bow at twenty paces.

"Traditional" in archery means the best of the past blended with the best of the present. Our longbows and recurves are imbued with the

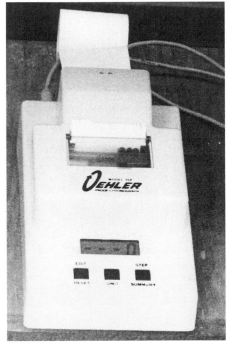

Although "shooting for cast," or distance, is worthwhile, a chronograph like this Oehler 35P Proof provides more accurate and reliable data in bow testing.

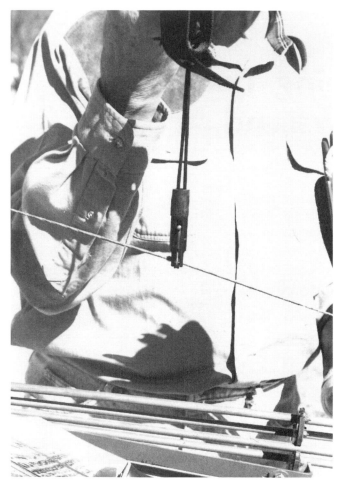

A modern mechanical release can be used when testing longbows and recurves to eliminate the human element in drawing, holding, and releasing.

best of the past, but they are twentieth-century products constructed of space-age materials and modern know-how. Because they blend the old and the new, we test them both ways—technically and by hand. The chronograph is now in widespread use over North America because superb machines have risen in quality and features while falling dramatically in price. My major machine is an Oehler 35P Proof model with both digital and tape readouts. It registers blunt-tipped arrows best.

When an arrow passes through the three skyscreens of the Oehler chronograph, two velocity readings are taken automatically. That's why the machine is called a Proof model. If the two figures are not close to identical, this indicates a problem and retesting is called for. Several arrows can be fired with accumulated results. I shoot twenty across the screens if I am hand-holding the bow, only five if the bow is in a shooting machine, which holds the bow "cocked" at a specific draw length until the trigger is tripped and the arrow is sent through the chronograph screens. The chronograph provides five pieces of information for accumulated shots: the highest velocity recorded, the lowest velocity recorded, the average, or mean, of the shots, the greatest spread between the highest and lowest figures, and the standard deviation of the group.

Because a person is not able to pull a bow perfectly every time to an absolutely consistent draw length, arrows receive slightly different energy levels delivered to the nock, resulting in variations in velocity. In practical terms, this is no problem. Reverend Stacy Groscup can shoot an aspirin out of the air with his stickbow, making it obvious that slight variations in draw length do not destroy the effectiveness of the bow. But determining speed with a chronograph is an exacting program, and high and low figures for handheld bows should be dropped from the group before averaging, thereby giving a weighted average.

Below is a list of twenty shots from a 60-pound longbow firing a 485-grain arrow. Four of the figures are a bit too low, indicating that the archer had a short draw that failed to deliver the full thrust of the bow to the arrow. One figure is on the high side, showing that one shot was overdrawn past the normal anchor point for the archer. Since the bow was rated for 60 pounds at 28 inches, it should be tested with the arrow drawn to exactly 28 inches.

Twenty shots with the test bow ran (in feet per second) as follows: 204, 202, 191, 204, 199, 203, 199, 189, 202, 190, 186, 204, 211, 199, 202, 204, 200, 204, and 201. The straight average for the twenty shots, including the one high and four low figures, is 199.75 feet per second, which rounds to 200 feet per second. By removing both the one high shot (211) and four low ones (191, 189, 190, and 186), the average comes to 202 feet per second, which is slightly more accurate for the bow than 200 feet per second.

Is this nitpicking? In this case, yes. However, sometimes weighted averages really pay off. I chronographed one recurve bow that proved amazingly fast. In fact, I did not trust the high figures. I finally had another archer, a powerful person capable of holding full draw with a clean release, zip twenty shots across the screens. He did a remarkable job—except for one shot. Somehow, he short-drew that one. A bow spitting its arrow out at over 215 feet per second, suddenly fell to 166 feet per second. That's when, by removing that one obviously low reading, the weighted average stepped forward to set the record straight. The shooting machine, however, shows us how remarkably close arrow velocities can be one to another. I have seen variations of only 3 feet per second from all types of bows, sticks as well as mechanical. We know that the 60-pound longbow in the above example shoots a 485-grain arrow at, let's call it, 200 feet per second, just to round it off. So what?

Since arrow speed is important in archery—high-tech or traditional—it's nice to know the facts about a given bow's velocity potential. Arrow speed is less important than handling characteristics, but a fast arrow does produce that flatter trajectory for easier hitting downrange. Also, there's nothing wrong with verifying an advertised velocity. Bowyers don't lie about how fast their bows shoot. It would be a foolish thing to do; too many of us have chronographs. However, figures for a given bow may be honest for that specific test product, but a little optimistic for the average bow coming from that shop. Because the very wood that goes into a bow can alter performance, we cannot expect two bows, even the same model and draw weight from the same shop, to produce the exact same velocities. But neither should the bows we buy fall way short of advertised arrow speed. The chronograph will reveal the truth.

Arrow energy can be figured once we know how fast a specific shaft flies. In the above case of the 60-pound longbow spitting out a 485-grain arrow at 200 feet per second, kinetic energy is derived by first squaring arrow speed, which comes out to 40,000. That figure is divided by 7000 to convert grains to pounds, because we want foot-pounds, not "foot-grains," of energy. This leaves 5.7142857. That figure is divided by 64.32, a constant for gravity.

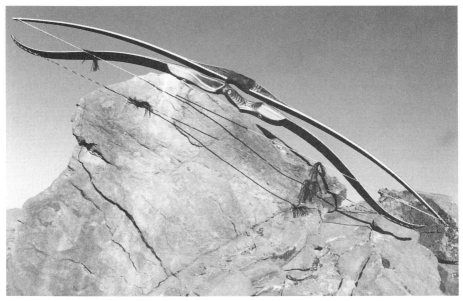

Bows must be set up properly before any testing is attempted. The differences between longbow and recurve setup can be great. For example, the reverse handle longbow, top, built by John Schulz, has much lower fistmele than the Brackenbury recurve shown with it.

Now we're left with only .0888415, which is the number of foot-pounds for 1 grain of arrow. Because our arrow weighs 485 grains, we multiply the figure by 485 to get 42.821603, which we round off to 43 foot-pounds. Although it's interesting to know that a 485-grain arrow shot at 200 feet per second *starts out* with 43 foot-pounds of energy, it doesn't prove much, except that arrows don't carry high kinetic energy, compared to, say, a bullet. A 22 Long Rifle cartridge shooting a 40-grain bullet at 1200 feet per second produces 128 foot-pounds at the muzzle, while the little 22 Short rimfire with a 29-grain bullet at 1100 feet per second earns 78 foot-pounds.

A bow reveals much of its nature through field-shooting. Positive and negative handling characteristics show up after only a few shots.

I pointed out that my particular chronograph yields five pieces of information. When using a shooting machine, I run a string of only five shots, since variation in velocity is so low. The machine automatically reveals the highest and lowest velocity in the string, the average velocity, as well as the greatest spread between the high and low shots. And it also provides a standard deviation from the mean, or average. Standard deviation, a measure of variance, shows how reliable the results are. In arrow shooting, standard deviations can be very low (excellent). The reasons are clear. First, bows can reliably produce the same arrow velocity shot after shot. Second, arrows can be made to very close tolerances, as indicated below. Add good "ammo" to an instrument that throws this ammo (arrows) at a consistent velocity, and standard deviations will be low. Out of a shooting machine, figures as low as 3 or 4 feet per second are common.

Scientific bow tests include force versus draw curves, which show how a bow builds and holds its power. But the resulting figures are not that useful to the grassroots archer, which most of us are. A simple bowscale can be useful, however, in determining the exact draw weight of a bow at a given length of pull, while also revealing if the bow stacks. The bow is set on the scale and drawn to specific lengths while noting what draw weights the scale shows. The tale is told toward the end of the draw, say around 25 inches for a 28-inch draw bow. For example, one longbow drew 3.0 pounds per inch at 25, 26, 27, and 28 inches, indicating no stacking, whereas another gained 3.0 pounds per inch at 25 and 26 inches, then the last couple inches saw the bow gaining 4.5 pounds per inch. That's stacking, which some bowshooters handle well, and others don't.

A scale like this fine RCBS Partner was originally intended for weighing reloading components; however, it works magnificently for weighing arrows and arrow parts for testing. The electronic Partner weighs within one-tenth of one grain. There are 7,000 grains in one pound.

The scale I used for my work is an RCBS electronic model with high capacity to handle arrows that weigh well over 500 grains. (A grain is a very small unit of weight, there are 7,000 in a pound and 437.5 in an ounce.) The simple scale can reveal important information about the quality of arrow shafts and arrows. I ran a set of one dozen barreled cedar arrows through my RCBS scale, which weighs to the tenth of one grain. Here are the twelve 60/65 spine arrow shaft weights (in grains):

353.4	350.9
356.7	354.6
358.4	353.7
354.2	354.8
354.7	353.4
355.3	354.5

These arrows have a spread of only 7.5 grains. Considering what a grain of weight represents ($\frac{1}{437.5}$ of an ounce), the tolerance of this fine set of shafts is obviously extremely close, showing what can be done with wood that is carefully worked. But how about the nocks, feathers, and points that go with them?

Here is what a set of twelve 125-grain field points weighed (in grains):

125.1	124.9
125.3	125.0
125.4	124.7
125.8	126.1
124.6	124.2
125.1	125.6

The spread of this set of field points is only 1.9 grains. Now how about feathers? Will they upset the apple cart? Here are thirty-six feathers weighed out (in grains):

3.8	4.1	3.9
3.9	3.6	4.0
4.0	3.9	4.3
4.0	3.9	3.7
4.1	4.1	3.5
3.7	3.7	3.9
3.6	3.6	4.1
3.5	4.0	3.7
3.7	4.3	3.5
3.8	3.7	4.0
4.0	3.6	3.4
3.9	3.7	3.5

The spread of these thirty-six feathers fell at 0.9 grains. Once again, the variation proves quite low, leaving only nocks to consider (irrespective of finishing the arrows with stain and gasket lacquer). Twelve nocks weighed as follows (in grains):

12.1	12.2
12.1	12.2
12.0	12.0
12.2	12.0
12.1	12.0
12.2	12.3

That's a spread of only 0.3 grains. This means that no component, from shaft to nock, varies enough to cause a problem with this particular set of arrows. Of course, the shafts were top grade. I've seen others that varied 100 grains in a set of twelve samples. But the point is clear: Arrows can be prepared to extremely close tolerances.

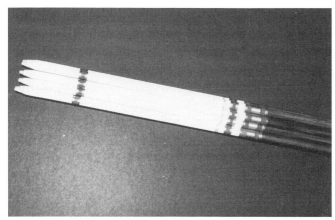

Arrow weight is vital in testing any bow, affecting not only velocity, but also handling characteristics. Shafts like these tapered cedars from Raven come with a notation of weight range, such as 360 to 370 grains spread.

What does finishing an arrow do to its weight? I stained twelve barreled cedar shafts with Tandy red leather dye, then gave them eight coats of clear gasket lacquer. Here are the results:

	Weight Before Dipping	**After Dipping**	**Difference**
1.	352.4 grains	373.6 grains	21.2 grains
2.	348.7 grains	370.7 grains	22.0 grains
3.	351.2 grains	374.5 grains	23.3 grains
4.	353.0 grains	374.8 grains	21.8 grains
5.	352.7 grains	376.4 grains	23.7 grains
6.	352.0 grains	374.0 grains	22.0 grains
7.	356.2 grains	379.9 grains	23.7 grains
8.	352.8 grains	375.8 grains	23.0 grains
9.	354.6 grains	377.3 grains	22.7 grains
10.	352.2 grains	375.6 grains	23.4 grains
11.	348.5 grains	372.7 grains	24.2 grains
12.	356.0 grains	379.5 grains	23.5 grains

These figures show that finishing an arrow with eight coats of gasket lacquer added 20+ grains of weight to each shaft.

Using test machinery wipes out such nonsense as "Boy, she sure looks fast!" Maybe she does, but let's find out for sure with a chronograph. The slowest bow I've tested to date "looked fast" because we were only shooting it at twenty paces. The little recurve, belonging to a friend, was praised as a

real ripper. "There's no flies on this bow," my buddy proudly assured me as he launched an arrow. He wanted to see just how fast that little ray gun truly was, so we turned from guessing to testing. The first string of arrows cut the atmosphere at a startling average velocity of 125 feet per second. My buddy stared, perplexed, at the information tape. We tested again, and again, finally using a second chronograph. Suddenly, my buddy fell on the ground laughing. "I bought that thing because it was supposed to be the fastest bow in the state," he roared.

Comparing today's traditional bows with yesterday's has been enlightening. The bows of the '40s, '50s, and '60s were darn good, but today's are better, across the board. As noted before, the reason is advanced design and materials. "When I made my first bow in the sixties," one bowyer said, "the adhesive I used hardened in thirty minutes, so I had a half hour to get the job done. When I got to that last lamination, I might put my stick in the jar and, thunk! The glue was set. Now what?" Today's adhesives are far stronger than those of the past, as well as slower drying to allow more work time.

Along with modern adhesives, other materials have improved, including fiberglass, to create stronger bows with improved performance. Phenolic resins are now used for bonding. Wood can be treated to epoxy impregnation under pressure, making stronger risers. Because of the chronograph, end results are no longer guessed at. Instead of "Boy, she sure looks fast!" the little beady-eyed machine tells us exactly how fast she is. That's how we learned, for example, that different woods used in limbs made an actual difference in arrow velocity. The chronograph said so. New bow chemistry and new materials can also be tested.

In spite of chronograph and scale testing, however, the hands-on shooting of a bow continues to be highly important. Hand shock and recoil may not be testable with machinery most of us have nearby, but our hands can detect these things. Shooting arrows for distance is also a reasonable measure of a bow, provided there's a safe area in which to do that. All things being equal, the faster arrow flies farther than the slower one. So if we are testing Bow A and Bow B with an identical arrow, and Bow A shoots that same arrow farther

The Black Shaft from The Game Tracker company is carbon, and as such uses a special nock and converta-point system. In testing, the weight of the arrow is essential, of course. So when this carbon is entirely set up with point, it will be weighed before doing any chronograph work.

than Bow B, it's safe to say that Bow A is faster than Bow B without turning to a chronograph for definitive results.

These are a few tests that archers can run with today's stickbows. Although hands-on shooting remains the most certain way for a bowbender to decide on the right longbow or recurve, it's also nice to have machinery available that augments the human element.

There is much to be learned from shooting experiments. For example, a long-believed theory concerning left-wing versus right-wing feathers was disproved using a shooting machine, as explained later in this chapter. Left-wing/right-wing refers to the wing of the bird. Determining which is which is simple: Hold both hands up in front of your face. Cup them. Each hand represents the normal curl or bend of the right-wing/left-wing feather. When mounting feathers on arrows, the proper jig clamp must be used: left-wing clamp for left-wing feather, right-wing clamp for right-wing feather (see chapter 11). However, left-wing feathers are perfectly all right for right-handed archers, and vice versa.

Fletching makes a difference in testing. Low-profile feathers, like these copied from an original Plains Indian arrow, have less drag than larger feathers; however, higher profiles may be necessary for arrow stabilization in some bows.

Ten Old Wives' Tales about Traditional Bows and Arrows

Bamboo is the best limb lamination material. Such was the belief not that long ago among quite a number of archers and bowmakers. There are hundreds of different bamboos, and some are superb for limb laminations. Perhaps the smoothest-shooting bow I've ever drawn had Tonkin bamboo limbs. Tonkin is fast and also downright beautiful. However, while bamboo is a fine lamination wood for bow limbs, it's difficult to call it the best. Bowyers usually end up with a wood they prefer for the style bow they build. It's wise to listen to them.

A bow can have high velocity, but poor cast. This notion was around when Robin Hood was still in short pants. The idea was that some bows shoot fast arrows, but don't cast an arrow very far, whereas others shoot slower arrows but cast them farther. As noted above, if you shoot identical arrows at different speeds, the fastest one flies the farthest. Period.

Heavier-drawing bows always shoot faster arrows than lighter-drawing bows. Bow efficiency, which we've touched on, answers this one. It's possible to have an 80-pound traditional bow that won't shoot an arrow any faster than a 60-pound bow. Also recall the point of diminishing returns. Above about 60 pounds pull in modern stickbows, arrow speeds climb slowly, even when bows are almost identical. This is not a black mark against heavy bows. They're great. But they don't always outshoot lighter-draw models.

Right-handed archers should use right-wing feathers and vice versa. Testing with a shooting machine proves that flight with left-wing or right-wing feathers does not vary. The same results show up when right-handed or left-handed archers hand shoot arrows with opposite wing fletching.

Only large feathers are correct to use in stabilizing arrows from longbows. Large feathers do overcome the archer's paradox (see chapter 11) more quickly than smaller feathers; however, there are other factors at play. Varying archer form alone may alter arrow fletching size.

Traditional bows should be well over 60 inches long. This notion stems from the idea that finger pinch and poor shooting qualities exist in shorter longbows and recurves. The worst snail I ever owned, albeit not as slow-shooting as some, was a short recurve that got 150 feet per second. But properly designed bows today can be *relatively*

Certain characteristics of fletching, especially from arrows of the past may be for performance, and others are cosmetic. The gap shown here provides an extra tie-on location to secure the feather, while the little "wings" coming from the front of the fletching are ceremonial in nature.

short while retaining good shooting properties. It depends on the design of the bow. However, there is no doubt that two factors concerning bow length remain true. Long limbs do promote a smooth draw. They may also add to recoil, since they are heavier than shorter limbs.

Leaving a bow strung causes it to lose power. For self-bows, yes, but after the invention of unidirectional fiberglass (mentioned in chapter 1), this was no longer true. Recall that its inventor left a bow strung for two years without the bow losing draw poundage. Nonetheless, if a bow is stored for a while, it should be unstrung, not only as a good maintenance policy, but also for safety.

Shooting through the gap produces better arrow flight. This method is explained fully in chapter 8, but it's worth touching on briefly here. As a test, the archer is invited to turn a feather-fletched arrow "wrong way round" with cock feather against the strike plate. Because feathers are forgiving, this arrow will fall into the same group with those shot through the gap. Plastic vanes, however, won't shoot off the shelf at all.

Recurves are trickier to shoot than longbows. Certain recurves of the past may have been tricky to shoot, but well-designed models of today are not. In fact, some archers feel they can master recurves more easily than longbows.

Traditional bows are limited in accuracy by their design. Not true. Longbows and recurves have high accuracy potential.

$$\boxed{5}$$

A 5,300-Year-Old Archer

What does a fifty-three-hundred-year-old archer have to do with modern-day traditional bowshooters? Quite a lot. A fascination with nonmechanical bows winds around the story of the Ice Man, as he was called, like friendly smoke curling above a midnight campfire. After all, Otzi, the name ascribed to this ancient bowman, carried the same equipment traditionalists admire today—in function and spirit, if not in exact dimensions, materials, or design. Modern archers who choose bows and arrows that predate traditionals are even more closely allied with this mountaineer who died more than three thousand years before Christ was born, before the pyramids were built, and long before Caesar met Cleopatra. This man and his equipment bear witness to the degree of sophistication reached by people of prehistoric times.

The story begins with dust from a Saharan desert storm appearing over the Italian Alps in March 1991. The glacial winter had been comparatively mild, without the usual snowfall, warmer than normal for the area. The

This is Otzi, the 5,300-year old Ice Man, as he was found in the ice of the Italian Alps by a mountain climbing couple from Germany.

warmish southerly air current carried the dust from faraway North Africa, which settled upon the rugged mountains, turning the ordinarily white ice fields a yellowish brown. In mid-July, a second covering of desert dust appeared. The darker landscape absorbed radiated heat and an amazingly rapid melting began. And thus the body of the Ice Man was slowly uncovered from its frigid grave. Normally a body would have been destroyed over the millennia by glacial movement, but Otzi had died in a depression that guarded his remains for over five thousand years.

Now enter Erika and Helmut Simon of Nuremberg, Germany, expert mountain hikers who vacationed in the Alps every year. The couple trekked the South Tyrol in September 1991, taking shelter in a hut on the eighteenth. Early the next day, they made one of the most startling discoveries in modern history. Helmut reported that "from a distance of 8 or 10 metres we suddenly saw something brown sticking out of the ice." They thought it was rubbish or a large doll, until Erika realized it was a man. They had found Otzi. Helmut snapped a photograph with the last frame of film in his camera. Austrian officials were contacted, as it appeared that the body was on the Austrian side of the Alps. A recovery team went to work. Unfortunately, the body was treated as an ordinary corpse and much damage was done.

Officials can hardly be blamed for initially thinking this was another ordinary casualty, perhaps a hiker lost many years ago and just now emerging from a glacier. After all, more than two hundred people die annually climbing the Alps. One man picked up a scrap of wood and used it to hack away at the ice. He did not realize that he was using a piece of the Ice Man's pack frame. An ax was found that was made of copper, but patina discoloration gave the impression of iron or steel, and it was thought to be a modern mountain-climbing tool. A birchbark container was trampled underfoot with its contents. Leather leggings were found, along with a "stick" stuck in the ice. This turned out to be Otzi's bow, which was snapped in the recovery efforts. A strange piece of wood with regularly spaced holes resembled a flute. Later, it was identified as part of the archer's back quiver. Some members of the team began to think they had found a soldier from World War I, as they sensed a lag in time. There was a hole in Otzi's head, which scientists later determined was the result of a medical procedure known as trepanning, in which a piece of bone was surgically removed from the skull, presumably to reduce pressure—possibly a cure for headaches.

Though the body is an amazing study in itself, the Ice Man's equipment is fascinating to the modern archer. The ancient man's bow, which was about 72 inches long, is shrouded in mystery. It appears to be unfinished, because there are no nocks on its ends to hold a string. But *The Traditional Bowyer's Bible*, Vol. 2, shows how to tie a bowstring on the ends of a bow that has no

Otzi's longbow remains a fascinating subject of study. It's made of yew wood, a material used for centuries after the age of the Ice Man. With the bow are pictured some arrows found at the scene.

grooves. When viewed under a microscope, however, the ends of this bow show no sign of string wear, indicating that it had not been used. The bow is yew (*Taxus baccata*), which to this day is used by archers to make self-bows and is often included by bowyers in composite bow limbs. As late as the sixteenth and seventeenth centuries, yew was exported from the Tyrol to England. In an issue of *Alaska Bowman* (vol. 2, no. 1), Doug Elmy explained: "One reason why yew was chosen as a bow wood was that it provided its own backing. Two things can be seen in any yew log: the dark red hardwood and the pale green sapwood surrounding it. The hardwood is brittle by itself, but naturally bonded to the sapwood, it performs extremely well."

The Ice Man's back quiver is rectangular with a narrowed bottom. The flutelike stick served as a stiffening strut. The middle piece was missing when Otzi laid his quiver down over five thousand years ago, showing that the quiver had been damaged. The Ice Man had the same problem we do with rain and feathers, and so his quiver wore a cover or cap. The quiver held four bound stag antler fragments, an antler point, string-bound sinew, and a finished bowstring. Investigating scientists concluded that it was from a previous bow and was too precious to throw away when the old bow broke.

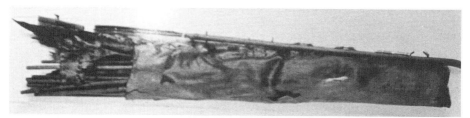

The quiver once had a covering that would have been used to protect the three-feather fletching of the arrows. Note that it is narrow and compact in design.

There were twelve shafts but only two finished arrows. The unfinished wooden shafts, made of long, straight shoots of the wayfaring tree (*Viburnum lantana*), are extremely straight, smooth, round, and tough. Flint arrowheads were attached to the two finished arrows via deep notching and were thickly cemented with birch tar. Three radially mounted feathers were cemented into grooves. Researchers are still trying to determine the source of the feathers. Some likely possibilities are the black woodpecker, alpine rook, alpine crow, common raven, or golden eagle. The two finished arrows differ markedly from each other. One is longer than the other and may be a composite.

Two-part arrows were sometimes used in ancient times. The forward portion could be replaced if broken, rather than building a whole new arrow. Otzi's two-part arrow was joined together with birch tar, the front made of wood from the Cornell tree, the back portion from the wayfaring tree. Today we have footed shafts, returned from the golden age of archery, when the traditional bow was king. These shafts are also made of two different types of wood, generally a cedar main part with a front section of carefully spliced purpleheart, wenge, or other extremely strong hardwood. Since the forepart of the shaft takes a greater beating, footing makes for a long-lasting arrow of medium weight.

Otzi was, without doubt, an experienced man of the Alps. It was his home. His equipment proves that he knew what he was doing. His wooden pack frame, with well-made string support cords and a fur pack sack, served the same function as today's models. He carried a copper ax with a head less than four inches wide, possibly used in bowmaking. The handle is the only known shaft made of yew wood. Carefully worked with a high degree of skill, the handle was designed for strength. Birch tar cement was applied between the wood and the metal, and a binding was made of narrow leather or hide strips. The ax head was made of 99.7 percent copper, 0.22 percent arsenic, and 0.09 percent silver. It was probably cast in an upright position in a ceramic pot used to melt the copper at temperatures reaching eleven hundred degrees Celsius. The copper ax upsets prehistoric dating, for it precedes the so-called Copper Age, altering previous scientific deductions.

Otzi also had a birchbark coal carrier to keep embers hot for the next fire, and cords and fragments of a second birchbark container that was built like a flattened tube. Its use has not been determined, but we know from prerescue photos that it was intact until a member of the recovery team stepped on it. Perhaps it was another carrying device, something like a pack sack. A smartly crafted retoucheur was used to flake flint. It resembles a short, thick carpenter's pencil, but instead of lead, a tiny piece of antler protrudes from its center. Marks show that Otzi shaved the wood back to reveal more antler

Otzi's ax set the world of paleontology on its ear. It was made of copper, thereby altering previous dates of the Copper Age.

spike when necessary, like sharpening a lead pencil. No similar retoucheur has ever been found.

There were many other well-designed, workable tools, including a bone awl designed to punch tiny holes for sewing and a knife classified as a dagger because it had two cutting edges, the blade so small that it resembled an arrowhead. Made of flint, it would have been extremely sharp, as flint can be made sharper than the finest surgical scalpel. The ash handle of the dagger, though damaged by an ice pick during recovery, is quite rigid. Thread made of animal sinew, about as strong as nylon, holds the blade to the handle. A scabbard, also damaged, was cleverly crafted of plaited lime tree bast, the fibrous inner bark of trees used in making cordage, a serviceable material from the distant past.

A small belt pouch made of calf leather held the bone sewing awl, three flint tools, and a piece of tinder. One flint tool was a blade scraper for cutting, carving, planing, and smoothing. The second was a flint drill, and the third was a small thin flint blade, possibly used to cut feather grooves, arrow nocks, or notches for arrowheads. The pouch still contained samples of pyrites, spark makers probably used to ignite fungus tinder. The Ice Man also carried two birch fungi; a tassel with a stone bead; a sloe, the fruit of the

Otzi's knife and scabbard are extremely interesting in both design and materials. The short blade is flint, which we know now can be sharpened to a super keen edge. The sheath was fully protective of the blade and the handle.

blackthorn (*Prunus spinosa*), extremely sour but with a high vitamin and mineral content; a net, possibly used for fishing; and six small tools made of stag horn, each of which served a different function.

All these items were preserved because they were frozen with Otzi's body in the glacial ice. The Ice Man's gear was certainly top-rate for so early a time, yet why the bow and all but two arrows were unfinished remains a puzzle. Adding to the puzzle, the two finished arrows were both broken—up front, as if from shooting.

What befell our long-ago archer? Was he adequately prepared when he began his journey into the high and rugged Italian Alps? No real food supply was found near the body, but Otzi seems to have been appropriately dressed. He wore leggings made of fur, although they now appear to be smooth leather because the fur has fallen off. His loincloth was leather, not fur. His shoes were also leather, with cowhide soles. They were still stuffed with knotted grass for insulation. He also wore a grass cloak long enough to cover the knees and a large, domelike hat shaped like a blunt cone with a chin strap.

Otzi's body bore tattoos, but their meaning is unknown. His teeth were basically intact. He had no superfluous body fat. Apparently, his diet was such that he burned up whatever food he ate. His body showed no signs of battering from a fall or other catastrophe. Did he simply lose his way in the mountains and perish in a sudden deadly storm? That is rather unlikely, considering his equipment and the fact that he was an outdoorsman who

Otzi's shoes were stuffed with grass for insulation. They must have been at least marginally effective against the high mountain cold.

lived year-round in the elements. It seems that Otzi started out from home well prepared for the trail.

Maybe he carried two bows, one ready to shoot, the other in a state of manufacture. He may have had several shootable arrows as well, all lost in some kind of battle with man or beast. How did his quiver get broken? Did he fall with it? He shows no broken bones other than those fractured during his rescue from the ice. Did he meet with a human adversary? Researchers are still trying to determine the whole scenario. Some of them believe that the Ice Man suffered a violent confrontation with an enemy preceding his death. Evidence shows that he may have been forced to make a somewhat hasty retreat, leaving behind certain items, possibly including a shootable bow. Much of his equipment is intact at the site of his death, but at the same time, certain things, such as the belt that would have held his accessory pouch, are definitely missing.

We do not have all the answers to the mystery of Otzi, but we do know that several thousand years ago, archers roamed the countryside carrying bows and arrows. They were good bows and arrows—not as fine as our traditional tackle today, because they were, after all, primitive by our standards, but they certainly cast an accurate arrow.

Traditional archers, one and all, share a kinship with the Ice Man of so long ago. Though his bow and arrows were far more than recreational for him, it's a good bet that from time to time he shot at a twig here, a leaf there, simply because he loved to watch an arrow fly to the mark, to hear the song of the string, and to feel the power of his body flow into his bow. I would have enjoyed shooting arrows with the Ice Man. I don't know a traditional or primitive archery fan who wouldn't have.

6

Instinctive Shooting

Arguably, there is no such thing as instinctive shooting. Instinct is an inborn, specific response, like an English pointer puppy lifting its forepaw to hold steady on a feather. "Reflexive" may be a better term for the hand-eye coordination naturally allowing archers to guide an arrow to the target without the use of sights. But since "instinctive" shooting is the term that has caught on, we'll stick with it.

Few are those who haven't tossed stones at a tree stump, a baseball to home plate from the outfield, or a football with just enough lead to intercept a running player downfield. Rock, baseball, football—none has sights. They're thrown through the air instinctively toward their mark. It's a matter of coordination, matching the computer (the brain) with the machine (the body) to accomplish the job perfectly. Physical condition and strength play a role. An archer incapable of controlling his bow could never be a good instinctive shooter. Struggling to get full draw, for example, takes away from the natural flow between mind and muscle, causing a different anchor point, or none at all, for every shot.

Wouldn't it be easier to fix up a set of pins and literally sight the bow in like a firearm? Perhaps, and if that's the individual's desire, fine. Target shooters attach sights to their Olympic-type recurves. But the rest of us will be missing out on something very special if we ignore instinctive shooting and go with sights on our longbows or recurves. All primitive archers, as far as I know, shot instinctively. Native bowmen of most countries still do. It's an effective, accurate process, with excellent arrow grouping possible. Good form and style are demanded, and once achieved, the joy of natural shooting is complete, making archery a great sport, even a way of life for many.

I recall roving with a gentleman one day. He used a compound; I carried a recurve bow. "Go ahead and shoot away," he finally said. "You don't have to wait for me." Since he didn't mind, I relaxed and fired arrows at will, aiming at bits of wood and similar targets out to forty paces or so. I shot at least

*Handling the bow
with ease and
fluidness is what
instinctive shooting is
all about.*

a half-dozen arrows to every one of his. I also think I had more fun than he
did. I wasn't hurrying to get arrows away. It was simply natural for me to fix
an arrow on the string, draw, anchor, and release, while my friend had to
judge range, line his bow up, choose the right sight pin, get his mechanical release in place, and then aim for several seconds before turning an arrow loose.

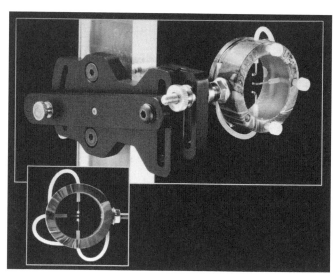

*In contrast to how the
instinctive archer
"aims," here is a
modern TRUGLO
"Range Rover" sight,
which makes a bold
comparison with "off-
the-shelf aiming."*

A slight bending of the head helps put the instinctive bow-shooter "into" his stance. This archer also tilts his bow almost to the horizontal.

Furthermore, I was able to hit some targets he couldn't even try for. When he knew the range, he shot better than I did, holding his bow at the perpendicular and putting arrows on target like bullets. (Compound bows won't take a bashing in this book. They're fine-shooting machines.) But my stickbow was king when it came to crouching, kneeling, bending, or holding the bow at the horizontal while sending a dart under a bush thirty paces away. All postures felt natural with my unencumbered recurve. I like that word—unencumbered. It explains what traditional tackle is: clean, pure, light in the hand, workable from standing, sitting, kneeling, crouched, or even prone positions.

It wasn't stance alone that allowed me to send several well-directed arrows out of my bow faster than the compound shooter; I didn't consciously aim. Notice the word consciously, which was carefully chosen—I didn't say

A perfect example of bent-knee shooting form—slightly crouched, but loose. Also note the excellent follow-through. The arrow is gone, but the archer remains in his preshooting posture.

Instead of bent knees, this bowman bends at the waist. His bow is dramatically angled, almost to the horizontal. Note, too, his solid anchor point.

Not quite "straight up," Bill Fadala steps into his shot, leaning forward, but with very little bow cant.

I wasn't aiming. The beauty of instinctive shooting is in its naturalness. The compound shooter always has to figure or gauge the range. But using the barebow method, the archer practices until shooting is second nature.

Throughout this book, many ways to accomplish a given task with traditional tackle are suggested. Shooting styles are no exception. I know what I have to do in order to hit the target, and there may not be another archer in my state who follows the same routine. First, I cock my head almost imperceptibly to the right. If I don't, there's a tendency to shoot "straight up," like a compound archer does. But if I bend my head slightly to the right, keeping my knees loose and slightly bent, my bow naturally cants (angles) so that the bottom tip swings left, the upper tip right. This canting maneuver creates a V-shaped trough from the usually horizontal arrow rest and vertical strike plate. Canting the bow also centers the eye over the arrow.

I recommend that all traditional archers try this style of holding the bow, quickly adding that it's not for everyone. My own brother shoots his recurve bow straight up, like a compound, unless he is forced to cant it in brush or trees. He also uses an elevated arrow rest rather than shooting off the shelf. But I suggest canting the bow, and if it doesn't work, then the archer can resort to the straight-up approach.

The second step in my style of shooting is bringing the bow to full draw with a push-pull technique. Some archers prefer holding the bow out at arm's length, then drawing the string back. This is also a good method, and it may aid some shooters in reaching full draw.

A smooth, continuous draw is recommended, but some archers use "double-clutching," which means drawing the bow almost to full, stopping a couple inches before reaching the nocking point, then finishing the draw. A friend of mine, an expert marksman with his longbow, once used this method, but for some reason trained himself out of it. Another friend still double-clutches his draw, pulling back until the string is a couple inches in front of his face, stopping, quickly drawing farther, touch-anchoring, then letting fly. If there's something wrong with how he draws his bow, he should keep right on doing it, because his arrows zip where he wants them to go.

The third step in my shooting style is gaining the anchor point. I've always told myself that my anchor point is the second fingertip of my right hand at the corner of my mouth. But I suspect that I naturally gravitate to feeling the first knuckle of my right index finger against the point of my cheekbone. Others anchor entirely differently. Howard Hill had a specific lower jaw tooth that he touched with the middle finger of his string hand every time. Some of our nineteenth-century predecessors, especially serious target shooters, anchored with the string hand under the chin. An expert group of Montana bowshooters uses the high-anchoring method; all of the archers in the club hold three fingers under the nock and locate the nock of the arrow just below the right eye, since all are right-handed. They're superior shooters, every one. Fred Bear called himself a snapshooter because he used a touch-and-release method of anchoring. An arrow went on the string, his 65-pound recurve came to full draw, and zip! The dart was gone—with

Fred Bear's anchor point is clearly shown here.

superior accuracy. (I met the late Fred Bear on two occasions. His personality seemed to be as rapid and precise as his shooting style.)

The use of a variable anchor point, also known as the floating anchor, on the face of it, seems to constitute a violation of good form. But some archers do it successfully. It can't be too difficult, because I manage it with good results, raising my anchor point nearer to my eye for extremely close shooting only. The floating anchor point is normally unwarranted, but it's an example of the flexibility of traditional archery.

In step three I reached anchor point. Now it's time to aim. "Aiming" for me means boring a hole into the target with my eyes, both open. The better I concentrate on this, the better I shoot.

To understand instinctive shooting better, let's look at other methods of aiming. Sights vary from a simple large-headed pin taped to the riser all the way to telescopes. Using sights requires conscious, deliberate aiming. Secondary vision (split-vision, or "gap-shooting") was Howard Hill's way of aiming, where he visually judged the distance (gap) between his arrow point and the target, thereby knowing how to direct his shot. (I never knew anyone, personally, who mastered this technique.) The point of the arrow has also been used to judge hold on a target. I did know someone who used this system of aiming a bow. He did not consider the gap between arrow point and target, as Hill did. He sighted the point of his arrow somewhere in relationship to the target, using a varying nocking point to change the trajectory of the dart. I tried shooting in this "points-on" style and didn't even get to first base with it.

The release comes next. There are at least two basic ways to release an arrow: popping the fingers open like the petals of a flower, instantly releasing the arrow, or the pull-through method. I suspect the first is best, but I can't seem to master it, so I use the pull-through technique. I like the pop-open method because it doesn't disturb the anchor point. In letting an arrow go the pull-through way, the hand has to move at least a little off of anchor. My hand slides back. Whereas at the anchor point my first knuckle rested against my right cheekbone, when the arrow is gone, that knuckle ends up closer to my ear.

In the pop-open method, with fingers popping out, the string may creep out an inch or two before the arrow gets away, shortening the draw. There is less tendency for string creep with the pull-through release. The real pros get it right either way. They put it all together in a single smooth operation, coordinated without conscious thought.

The arrow is away. Now comes follow-through. Ideally, the archer should remain in the same stance he held before the arrow was launched.

That's good follow-through. If he holds his bow somewhat tightly, it may tip forward only a little when he shoots. If he grips more loosely, the top bow tip may bend forward like a knight bowing to his king. Dropping the bowarm is one of the worst follow-through mistakes. The arm that holds the bow should remain as close to its prelaunch position as possible after the arrow is heading downrange, regardless of how much the bow tips forward.

Now let's consider how the body meets the bow. There are various finger positions for the string hand. Most common today, the Mediterranean draw uses the first three fingers, the nock of the arrow resting between the index and second finger. Sometimes called the English or split-finger hold, it transfers a lot of pulling power to the string. Three-fingers-under is another good way to draw the bow. The first three fingers of the bow hand all go beneath

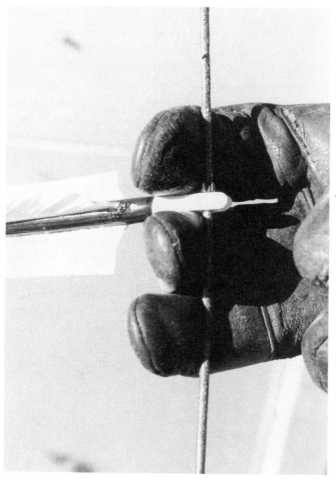

The Mediterranean hold uses one finger above the nock, two under, as shown here using a full glove (not a shooting glove). Also, this is a deep hook grasp, with the string well placed into the first joint of the fingers.

the nock. Along with good power transfer to the string, this method promotes a clean release of the arrow, because the nock is not pinched between fingers. Michelle Boss, daughter of Colorado bowmaker Dick Boss, is a prize-winning barebow shooter who improved her marksmanship considerably after going to the three-fingers-under string hold.

There are so many other string holds that the rest of this chapter could be filled with them. When I was a kid, I naturally pulled the bow with what's known as the primary release, the string more or less pinched between thumb and forefinger for a clean let-go; few people can pull stronger bows this way. The secondary, or Cheyenne, string hold, also uses the thumb, but two fingers attach to the string below the nock. The tertiary, or Sioux, string hold, brings all the fingers and the thumb into contact with the string, unlike the Mediterranean style, where thumb and pinky do not touch the string at all. Ishi, the last Yahi Indian, who taught Dr. Saxton Pope so much about archery, mainly employed his thumb to power the string back.

In the Mediterranean and three-fingers-under holds, the archer can place the string on the pads (balls) of his fingers in between the tips and first joints, or into the first joints of the fingers, called the "deep hook" method. The goal is to pull the string without torque, releasing without plucking, while keeping the hand straight. Once again, styles vary with the individual. The deep hook allows a more relaxed hand, which can lead to a better release, whereas using the pads of the fingertips lets the string get away with very little drag.

How the hand controls the grip of the bow is also vital to good traditional bowshooting. Very generally speaking, the broom handled longbow calls for a little more hand pressure than the deep-throated recurve. The heel of the hand takes the most pressure with the

The broom handle grip has gained in popularity in the new age of traditional archery. This bow has a gentle locator, which is the slight indentation just below the shelf into which the web of the hand fits.

straighter grip. Also, it appears that alteration in hand grip causes less disturbance to arrow flight with the longbow than with the recurve—or so it seems to me. The center of the bow is generally the throat of the handle grip, which is more pronounced on the deep-throated recurve than on the broom handle-style longbow. Hand placement is important because it contributes to the hand-eye coordination that is vital to instinctive shooting. The hand rests so closely below the shelf of the bow that it appears that the arrow is shooting off the fist instead of the shelf, with the arrow resting between the eye and the hand. It's almost like pointing the fist itself to direct the arrow to the target.

General stance normally puts the archer's feet angling somewhat to the right of the target for a right-handed shooter, the angle varying with different archers, with forty-five degrees considered a lot of angle. This stance directs the left shoulder toward the target, which promotes drawing strength. The position of the shoulder can change the pointing direction of the hand. Wrist position alters the shoulder, too. It's easy to demonstrate this by holding the left arm out with fist perpendicular to the floor, then rotating the fist to the right, clockwise. The shoulder angles a little upward. Shoulder and elbow are mildly locked as the bow is drawn. This, along with a fairly stiff bowarm, creates consistency with both push-pull or straight-arm drawing styles.

Target panic is a frequent affliction of archers. It has been defined as "premature arrow release with a short draw and no anchor point." There are several reasons for target panic. Anxiety can promote target panic. Some of us shoot fairly well when we're alone, but with others watching, we get nervous and shaky and lose concentration. We may be overbowed, which precludes full draw, denies an anchor point, and makes us let go of the arrow as soon as possible because we can't hold the string back very long. Or we refuse to let go of the arrow until after full draw is reached, which impairs hitting the target because concentration is directed on drawing the bow, not shooting it.

Target panic is such a widespread problem that there are books, videos, and magazine articles on the subject. Fortunately, target panic can be cured. A first step is going to a more manageable bow weight, at least for a while. I have a beautiful Ferret recurve takedown bow with two sets of limbs. I had bowyer Herb Meland of Pronghorn Custom Bows build a "regular" set of limbs, along with a matching set drawing only 45 pounds. When target panic tries to get ahold of me, I slip the lighter limbs in place, shooting at close range—only five yards or so—with concentration on a very small target. I shoot a lot with the lighter limbs in place until my form is back. When my draw, anchor, and release are all where they should be, only then are the heavier limbs replaced on the bow.

Working out can also help stem target panic, because physical strength has a lot to do with the ability to fully draw the bow. I use a little device offered by Saunders Archery Company. It looks like a slingshot with weights at the bottom. Two flexible tubes project out of the frame. These can be pulled one at a time, or together. One tube draws 24 pounds at 28 inches, the other 28 pounds at the same draw, or both can be pulled for 52 pounds. This exerciser tones muscles. It's also great for practicing shooting style, especially anchor point. Another good way to fight target panic is with a clicker. I use the Crick-It. This is a simple, but effective, device that adheres to the face of the bow on the upper limb seven to nine inches from the tip. A short chain projects from the body of the Crick-It, with a thin "drawcheck cord" leading from the chain attached to the bowstring just below the serving. The chain portion of the device is used to perfectly adjust the length of the cord. When full draw is reached, the Crick-It sounds off, letting the archer know he has achieved his goal. No click means a short draw.

The human brain is the computer center that directs the aiming of the bow in the instinctive style of shooting. It can also play mind games with the archer. One Sunday morning a breeze playing at the corners of the house woke me. Wind in Wyoming is like rain in Southeastern Alaska; you expect it. Blowing a bit, yes, but the sky was clear and the sun was warm, so I grabbed a bow and quiver full of arrows. The first thing I saw on my archery range was a defunct cedar arrow shaft punched into the ground. An arrow neatly sliced its top off with fractured pieces flying in the air. I nocked another dart. The second arrow sideswiped the shaft, pushing it askew. A third popped it out of the ground. "How did I do that?" I muttered softly to myself.

About forty yards away a cardboard oatmeal box lay against a bank of soft earth. An arrow punctured it. "How did I do that?" I asked myself out loud. Off to the side at about 30 yards rested a straw bale, several hundred times larger than the cedar arrow I just hit, and dozens of times bigger than the oatmeal box. My first arrow went over the bale. "Pick a spot," I scolded myself. The second arrow hit the bale, but not dead center. The next half dozen wouldn't cluster in a watermelon. I had "psyched myself out," my own mind becoming an enemy.

Then there's focus, fixing the eye on just one thing, along with concentration, closing the mind to everything but the target. Failure to focus and concentrate destroys bowshooting accuracy, which in turn undermines confidence. I lose focus and concentration occasionally. Instead, I question myself, which destroys the naturalness of my shooting. There is a story about a millipede that was strolling down the avenue. A spider stopped him. "How do you keep all those legs moving without tripping?" the spider asked.

A Brief Troubleshooting Primer
for Instinctive Shooting

"I've been trying to learn instinctive shooting for two months now, but I still can't hit the target."
Start with the bow. Does it have hand shock and recoil? Is it pleasant to draw? Be honest—is it difficult to draw and anchor? If the bow is manageable, and all tackle is matched (see chapter 11), try again, starting at only five yards aiming at very small targets, such as a one-inch paper circle pinned on a target bale. Keep at it. If things don't go better, get a coach to watch you shoot. Also, try a high anchor point, near the eye, for a while, with the intent of lowering it later on. This can help by putting the eye more in line with the arrow.

"I can pull my bow to full draw, but it's not easy. How can I make it easier?"
If handling the bow is truly within physical reach, perhaps through more practice, a change in drawing method might help. If you are using the push-pull technique, try the rigid-arm draw with the bowarm held solidly out front, shoulder and elbow mildly locked. Also, try a change in the fistmele. There may be a "sweet spot" at which the bow draws a bit better. Begin by raising the brace height a half inch and trying that.

"I can't draw and hold the bow at anchor point, even though it is actually a light-drawing bow."
This is a case of target panic. Read the information in this chapter, and consider getting a clicker, like the Crick-It.

"I shoot low most of the time."
There are many possible reasons for this. A poor anchor point could be the problem. Try a different anchor to see if that helps. Also, time of day may be significant. Archers who practice after a hard day of work can be too fatigued for good shooting. Another cause of hitting low is a dropping bowarm. Have someone watch to see if your bowarm is dropping as the arrow gets away. Being overbowed can cause short drawing, giving the arrow less energy than it needs for a good trajectory. Plucking the string can also cause the arrow to fly low (or high). Also, the arrow may be too heavy for the bow, making it nose-dive.

"I shoot high most of the time."
Form may be the problem. An archer may draw his bow by raising it high first, then pulling back on the string while lowering the bow into shooting position, which may result in an early arrow release. Try drawing with a mildly rigid elbow and shoulder, or use the

pull-through method of releasing the arrow. Your anchor point might be too low for closer-range shooting. Plucking the string can also cause an arrow to go off course, either high or low. Overdrawing, although not common, can raise an arrow's arc of travel. An arrow that is too light can also fly high.

"I hit to the left (or right) most of the time."

The first thing to look at is arrow and bow compatibility, as discussed in chapter 10. If the arrow is either too stiff or too limber for the bow, it may fly to the left or right. Also, failure to gain a solid anchor point can be real trouble in keeping an arrow on course. For example, one archer's arrow, although matched to his bow as proved with a shooting machine, always flew wide of the mark. It turned out that this archer held his string hand to the right of his face, in midair, and not anchored at all. The value of a solid and consistent anchor point cannot be overlooked.

The millipede began to wonder about it. He didn't know. As he moved away he fell prostrate into a ditch, not knowing which leg came after which.

The conditioned reflex is vital to the process. After consciously learning how to do something, like riding a bicycle, the unconscious takes over. A practiced archer no longer has to think about hitting the target with his longbow or recurve. He just does it. When he stops to think about *how* he shoots, fluidness evaporates and he misses his mark. The successful bowman *internalizes* control. It becomes second nature. This is instinctive bowshooting.

Practice brings about the internalization process. My favorite practice is roving. It's far more interesting (to me) than shooting at the same bale every day. My backyard is filled with targets of different dimensions at varying distances, but after a while even these multiple aim points lose their charm and I have to go roving, or "stump-shooting," as it used to be called. Random shooting is not practice. Practice is the act of internalizing all the right moves. Practicing the wrong methods can produce the opposite of the desired effect—learning bad habits instead of good ones. That's why there are some days when putting the bow down makes more sense than shooting it. I've sat on the side of a hill for twenty minutes waiting for a mini-slump to go away. It usually does.

Practice is vital, but it must be structured. Shooting at the aerial targets can help. It's impossible to hit these without almost unconscious effort. A rolling disk or old basketball fired at with blunts works likewise. Practice

The game of 3-D promotes considerable arrow shooting, thereby providing considerable practice, which is vital to efficient instinctive marksmanship.These animal targets are prime examples of the sport.

brings up an interesting side-point. If barebow shooting were truly instinctive, we'd be born knowing how to do it. Practice may perfect our style, but that's all. There may be a little of this in us, but I don't think it's instinct. It may be a mental/physical ability that allows us to do a number of things. Dean Barrett, a brilliant engineer, was visiting one day. He wanted to try one of my stickbows on the backyard archery range. I said sure. With no previous training, Dean anchored the bow *at his chest*—and hit the target. Instinct? Or natural ability?

Newcomers to the sport sometimes get tangled up in the web of "professional advice" spun out by books, magazines, and videos. The beginner needs a starting place and veterans never stop learning; however, no expert should dictate how anyone should shoot a traditional bow. Ideally, the archer tries many different ways, then chooses the one that works best. A good coach, however, can point out the right and wrong of an archer's stance and delivery. By bringing attention to what the archer is doing right, those traits can be enhanced. By the same token, pointing out his bad habits can help him eliminate them. Every archer shooting with a buddy has a built-in coach. A partner can see a bowarm dropping or an anchor point floating or failing to reach home, or target panic setting in, or a rough release, or a plucked string, or an inconsistent stance. An instinctive archer doesn't want to stop the flow to examine his shooting. He wants all steps blended into one performance. Coaching is effective because the archer doesn't always know what he is doing wrong, and if he tries examining his own shooting, he can destroy his rhythm.

The shooting slump is real. If it's not a mind game, then jet airplanes aren't fast and skunks don't stink. Slumps occur in all sports. "He's in a batting slump." What is that? The guy was hitting like Hank Aaron two weeks ago and now he can't hit a beach ball. Unless the batter is physically injured, the only explanation is something going on between his ears. Likewise, an archer can be sharp one week and next week a 55-gallon oil drum at thirty paces is safe. The cause is difficult to assess. I suspect sometimes it's lack of interest. I was pretty good with my compound bow for quite some time. Then I slumped. My interest had waned. I gave archery up for quite some time, returning to the sport with the comeback of the stickbow.

Once an archer taps into his natural ability, releasing his mental and physical resources, instinctive shooting can be mastered. Trial and error precede success, of course, and the activity is learned, meaning it has to be practiced. But once internalized, the skill will never leave.

People coming back to traditional bows, having owned one in the past, perhaps in childhood, seldom have much trouble getting back into instinctive shooting. Although the comparison is overused, riding a bicycle does come to mind. When I began riding a mountain bike, after many years of never touching one, I peddled off on the first try. Naturally, the sophisticated bike required practice and learning, but the basic ability to stay upright on it was still there. Likewise instinctive bowshooting. Of all aiming methods, it's the best for today's traditional archer, regardless of the exact style he chooses.

A natural way to shoot a traditional instrument that has been with us from the beginning of history—that's traditional bowshooting. And it's still with us, giving us healthful exercise, enjoyment, recreation, and an interesting pastime in a busy world.

7

Tuning Longbows and Recurves

Modern archers will not abide any bow that doesn't perform well. Every time I see the 1938 film *Robin Hood*, I'm bitten all over again by the bug of ye Olde English longbow. So are thousands of bowmen turning to traditional sticks, all of them communing with the Spirit of Archery Past. But if these bows didn't shoot accurately with good speed, the rush back to traditionals would slow to a trickle. Today's bowshooter is a product of the computer age. He's too spoiled by high-tech gizmos to accept poor performance in anything, including longbows and recurves. He falls in love with the shapely lines and wonderful handling qualities of the simpler bow, and of course visions of Ishi, the last Yahi Indian befriended by Pope and Young, play on the cinema of his mind, but he stays with stickbows only when he learns how well they perform.

The untuned stick can sing a mighty sour tune. That's a shame, because once a longbow or recurve is properly tuned, it tends to remain that way for the life of the bow if the archer simply maintains the right brace height and nocking point and shoots the correct arrow. Physically tuning the bow is mainly a matter of adjusting fistmele (brace height) and nocking point, coupled with the use of correct arrow spine. The only tools needed are a bow square, nocking pliers, and a stringer. The method discussed here is not chiseled in granite; there are other ways to tune a stickbow. However, the following sequence works. Before tuning, the bow must be "set up," of course. This means string silencers, arrow rest, strike plate, and basic particulars, as discussed in chapter 8.

The bowshooter needs patience in bow tuning because there are many factors involved. The bow itself demands tuning only to three variables: arrow, brace height, and nocking point. But an archer's release style, chosen anchor point, choice of glove or tab, choice of arrow fletching, general overall shooting style, hold on the riser, even placement of his hand on the grip can also alter how the bow shoots a given arrow.

Unfortunately, although the three "little things" that make for a fine-tuned bow are mostly independent of each other, each may affect the other. Adjusting the fistmele, for example, alters the nocking point automatically as the string is lengthened or shortened; however, the change is generally too small to constitute a real part of tuning. In contrast, altering nock set position on the string does not change brace height at all, and switching arrow spine does nothing directly to either the brace height or nocking point. However, an arrow that won't shoot hot, straight, and true, because of either porpoising or fishtailing or both (these archery terms from the nautical world are discussed later), can be made to behave by altering brace height, nocking point, or both. Conversely, switching to an arrow with a different spine may fix the problem while leaving brace height and nocking point set just as they are.

The goal of tuning is balancing the three major factors to make the bow shoot right. Getting only one factor right will not tune a bow. Correct fistmele coupled with proper nocking point but wrong arrow spine equals poor arrow flight. Moreover, the cause of a problem may be difficult to discover at times. An arrow may fishtail or porpoise. Why? Maybe it's the wrong arrow for the bow. But the problem could also be incorrect fistmele, nocking point, or both. More rarely it might be an arrow rest or strike plate problem, or a combination of such factors.

Fistmele, an important part of bow tuning, is known as brace height. It's measured from the throat of the nock to the bow handle. A quick check to see if brace height has changed is accomplished by placing an arrow on the shelf to see that the feathers fall where they should. This longbow's brace height matches with a five and one-half inch feather.

Fortunately, there is a margin of forgiveness in most stickbows, so even though a bow is not tuned exactly right, the arrow still flies point forward. Fletching size and style can sometimes overcome a minor tuning problem. Ideally, however, the recurve or longbow is tuned like a Stradivarius; then when that forgiving arrow is matched to the bow, it shoots like a dream. The archer must experiment with his own longbow or recurve to make it shoot its best. There is no single brace height, nocking point, or arrow spine that is perfect for all bows or all bowshooters. Since bow tuning is shooting, what's the problem? We got into this game to fire arrows, so let's shoot away and have a good time as we tune our sticks.

Brace height, or fistmele (an older term, gone out of favor with many modern bowshooters), is the distance from the throat of the grip (handle) to the string. Other ways to measure fistmele have been proffered, including the distance from the front of the shelf to the string. The instruction sheet with a new bow will tell how that bow's fistmele is measured. Initially, it should be set according to the instructions, which may allow some leeway. One instruction sheet noted "eight to nine inches." So which is it? The archer has a choice. He can set brace height at nine inches and work down, or he can compromise with eight and a half inches, later raising or lowering that setting as necessary, or he can start at eight inches and work up.

A lower fistmele generally provides more arrow velocity, but initially, the bowman should opt for a higher brace height, which generally promotes quietness and good bow behavior. It's better to forsake a few feet per second rather than lowering brace height too much. How well the bow shoots is more important than a little arrow speed. So the bow with a suggested brace height of eight to nine inches is set at nine inches to begin with. Nothing more can be done with fistmele at this time until arrow flight is checked out. This is only a starting point, but we're on our way.

Fistmele is altered on a stickbow by twisting or untwisting the bow string. Strings are made with twist and can normally function safely with quite a number of revolutions. In fact, some strings may actually come apart if they do not have a sufficient number of twists to hold them together. (See chapter 9 for more on the subject of strings.) To raise or lower fistmele, unstring the bow (using a stringer for safety), and twist the string either to increase or decrease its length. Then restring the bow. Note: Strings can stretch a good deal. The new bow with new string should be left strung at least overnight before attempting to set fistmele, thereby taking some of the stretch out of the string. I've seen strings stretch as much as a half inch or more over a twenty-four-hour period. A string can be prestretched by shooting fifty or more arrows. There's also the "wax and wait" method. Heavily wax the string by hand using a standard bow wax, then string the bow and leave it

The author continues to favor the "old-fashioned" grip nock set that is squeezed onto the serving of the string with nocking pliers. A ring of plastic resides within the metal nock set shown here. Once squeezed onto the serving, this type of nock set stays put.

overnight. In the morning, check the fistmele. The string will probably have stretched in the night, lowering the fistmele automatically. So unstring the bow and give the string a few twists to shorten it to bring brace height back up. As noted, a bowstringer is used both to prevent a twisted limb and to save the archer from injury should the bow get away while he is attempting to hand string it. Optional: The archer can forego the wax and wait method and get into tuning right away, knowing that the string will stretch as he works, which will have to be reckoned with during the tuning process.

Next, the nock point is positioned. This is accomplished with a nock set. The *nocking point* is the location, while the *nock set* is the mechanical device that attaches to the string to create the nock point. There are many different kinds of nock sets, even movable types. Three fairly common nock sets are a brass unit with a rubber insert, dental floss wrapped around the serving on the string and heated to melt the wax in the floss, and serving thread wrapped into a little ball and glued in place. There are also shrink-on nock sets that slip over the string serving. A match or other source of heat shrinks them in place. I've tried all and prefer the commercial clamp-on brass unit attached with nocking pliers.

Of course, the nock set would have to be above the nock so that the arrow when "put on the string" will be aiming slightly point downward.

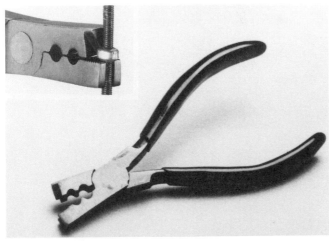

Although pliers can be used to squeeze a nock set onto the string, a specialized tool like these patented Adams E-Z Nock Pliers from the Pro Release Company makes the job really easy.

Clip the bow square onto the string so that the ruled portion lies on top of the bow's shelf. The markings on the square will help determine where to clamp the nock set in place. Place the nock set as high as one-half inch above square for starters, which gives the arrow a slight point-downward attitude when it is fixed onto the string. This assumes that the nock set is located above, not below, the arrow's nock. Some archers prefer the nock set underneath the arrow's nock, which is acceptable as long as the arrow is positioned on the string to attain the point-downward angle.

The goal is to move the nock set downward during tuning, ideally ending up about one-eighth inch above the horizontal when the bow is tuned, because some nock high is usually necessary to promote a clean takeoff of the arrow from the shelf. But that's not a perfect standard. The nock set must be placed where it works, not at some arbitrary point.

On this particular bow with straight grip, the bow square can be rested on the shelf, as shown here, to determine brace height. Otherwise, it would be placed directly on the deepest part of the handle.

A loose nock is used here for demonstration only. The center of the nock is aligned with the indicator mark on the bow square to determine proper nock set location.

The bow square is placed as shown here to determine nocking point location, another important factor in bow tuning.

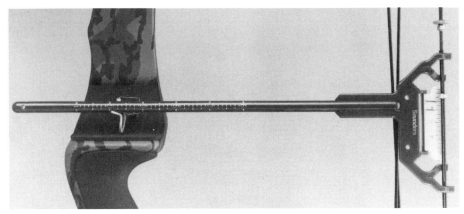

A Saunders bow square is set up here on a compound bow to place the nock set. It works likewise on longbows and recurves.

After setting initial brace height and nock point, gather experimental arrows. Wood, aluminum, fiberglass, and carbon arrows all shoot well from stickbows. Arrow choices are mostly personal preference. That's why arrows of various spine (stiffness) should be selected for trial tuning. Charts for aluminum and carbon arrows can help determine a specific shaft spine to begin with; however, it's wise to go above and below recommendations to see which arrow a particular bow and archer's shooting style "like" best. Wood arrows are spined in 5-pound increments to match bow draw weight. For example, for a 28-inch arrow, a 70-pound bow asks for either 65/70 spine or 70/75 spine.

Some longbow shooters prefer less arrow stiffness, shooting a 65/70 or even 60/65 spine wooden shaft in a 70-pound bow—with good arrow flight. On the other hand, a stiffer arrow seems better at "forgiving" fistmele and nock point problems. When the bow is tuned correctly, there is no need to use an extremely stiff wood arrow, but very few archers get away with wood arrows that exactly match their bow's draw weight, with even fewer able to use underspined shafts. Usually about ten pounds *over* normal spine is much preferred, with another five pounds of spine added per inch of arrow length over 28 inches. That goes for longbows and recurves.

I know an expert archer who uses 75/80 spine cedar arrows with extra large fletching in his 65-pound bow. His arrows go where he wants them to, which is all any archer can ask for. No one can argue with that archer's setup. He chooses to go with heavy spine and big fletching because they work for him with his bows. If he were forced to use an arrow with heavy spine and large feathers to make his bow shoot well, I would suspect a problem with bow tuning or archer shooting style. Generally, if a bow is tuned well with arrows of correct spine matched to it, overly large fletching is unnecessary for good arrow flight. In fact, a well-tuned bow will shoot an unfletched arrow fairly straight up to twenty yards or so. Although I don't think "bare shaft tuning" is vital, the process does have merits, one being that if an unfletched arrow flies point forward without too much wig-wag, it's probably a good match for that specific bow.

Let's look briefly at spine designations assigned to different kinds of arrows. Although there are various methods of designating spine, one factor holds true: Arrowmakers use specific means of categorizing shafts into ranges that match different bow draw weights. Standard for wood arrows, as we know, is spine measured in 5-pound increments. Other formulas have been used for wood arrows, but they are not as popular. In wood shafts, a specific deflection designates the bow weight, such as 55/60 pounds. Fiberglass, carbon, and aluminum shafts have their own designations. Fiberglass arrow shafts are hard to locate. They'll have their own spine chart.

The Gold Tip carbon arrow is a good example of uniqueness in gauging and designating spine. Gold Tip carbons come in only three different spines, XT3555, XT5575, and XT7595, each with a different diameter—.290 inches, .295 inches, and .300 inches, respectively. The first is for bows up to 90-pound draw for a 24-inch arrow, but only 55-pound draw for a 28-inch arrow. The second is recommended for bows up to 95-pound draw with a 28-inch pull, or 80-pound bows with a 30-inch draw. The last is spined to handle long-draw bows up to 95-pounds pull. The Gold Tip has a wide working range because only three spines are offered to handle all bow draw weights. This is not necessarily the case with carbon shafts from other companies.

Aluminum arrows have long used an easy-to-understand and precise spine value. A 2018 arrow, for example, is $\frac{20}{64}$ of an inch in diameter with a wall thickness of .018 inches. A particular 57-pound recurve I own "likes" 2216 aluminum shafts. This means the arrow is $\frac{22}{64}$ of an inch in diameter, with a wall thickness of .016 inches. In other words, the larger-diameter arrow with the thinner wall is a good spine match for that specific bow.

We know that the bow should be set up before serious tuning takes place. This means attaching not only string silencers, rest, and strike plate, but also a bow quiver if one will be attached to the test bow for general use. It's wise to tune the bow not only with the quiver in place, but also full of arrows minus one. This makes sense because the bow quiver is part of the bow itself now, and it will be fired, specifically, with the bow quiver full of arrows minus one—the one loaded in the bow. Of course, the bow can be tuned without the quiver attached, or with it on, but empty. But ideally the bow should be tuned as close to shooting readiness as possible, including tight limb bolts and bow quiver. That's the most realistic approach.

A bow quiver becomes a part of the bow itself, and that's why it's wise to tune with bow quiver in place, and filled with arrows.

Bare shaft tuning is important to include because it works well for many archers. Although it isn't necessary to tune a bow with an unfletched arrow, the process can be useful. The object is to arrive at fairly decent arrow flight at fifteen or twenty yards, where bare shafts are flying relatively true, ending up with the nock fairly straight out from the target. The shaft is left full length to begin with, be it wood, glass, aluminum, or carbon. It's fitted with a nock and a point, but no feathers. The overly long unfletched arrow is shot into a target at fifteen to twenty yards to check arrow flight. Slow-motion video, or the watchful eye of a careful onlooker, can detect problems such as porpoising or fishtailing (discussed later).

All arrows are subject to what is called the archer's paradox. When the arrow is released, inertia "tries" to keep it in place as the string delivers its energy to the nock, forcing the arrow to literally bend around the riser before it straightens out and flies its normal trajectory. That's why spine (arrow stiffness) is so important. The center-shot bow has its riser window cut away so that the arrow rests more in line with the middle of the limbs, and thus has much less need to bend around the riser in the archer's paradox. That's why the center-shot bow may get away with a wider range of shaft stiffness. There are many center-shot stickbows these days, but not all bowyers believe in the full center-shot design. As one bowyer put it, "I leave mine one-sixteenth inch or so off because I find that in true center-shot bows, we're always building the strike plate outward to make the arrow shoot better." Departure from the vertical plane is normal, even for a perfectly matched arrow. High-speed photography illustrates clearly that even a correct arrow for a bow does not fly in a straight line all the way to the target, staying

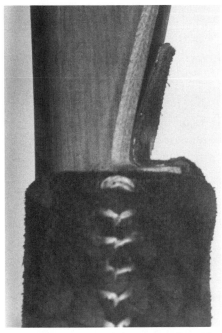

This bow is not entirely center-shot. The bowmaker in question prefers it this way. If cut true center-shot, the shelf of the window would line up with the centerline of the handle, which happens to be the stitching here.

This old bow is not center-shot; the arrow is shot off the side. Tuning this bow will require an arrow spined to warp around the riser in the archer's paradox.

neither completely in the horizontal plane due to normal trajectory, where the arrow must rise above the line of sight to "drop" into the target, nor in the vertical plane either. It stays near, but not exactly on, the "line of sight," an imaginary perfectly straight line from the point of the arrow to the target as the bow is aimed. So the arrow not only takes the usual parabola shape of trajectory, it also wags off line on the horizontal as well.

The arrow settles down as it progresses downrange. Of course, even though it does not fly in a perfectly straight line, if it's the right one for the bow, it will be *on course*. That's the difference between a proper arrow and a wrong one from a particular bow. Fishtailing arrows fly on the horizontal, but the nock is not lined up with the point; it is either left or right of the point as the arrow proceeds downrange. If the nock is left of point as the arrow flies, it's called "nock left," right of point is "nock right." Either sideways flight pattern is poor. Nock left means the arrow shaft is too limber. More spine is called for. Nock right means the shaft is too stiff. Less spine is necessary. But nock left and nock right can also be symptoms of wrong brace height, nock point, or both, as well as a poor archer's release.

Porpoising is movement of the arrow on the vertical in either a nock-low or nock-high condition. The nock of a porpoising arrow will end up either higher or lower than the point of the arrow in the target. High-speed photography can show exactly what's happening when an arrow is porpoising or fishtailing its way to the target; obviously, neither is what we want an arrow to do. We want it to fly hot, straight, and true from a short distance in front of the bow, after it stabilizes, all the way to its destination, where it hits the target with the nock straight out, neither high, low, left, or right.

How do we correct problems of fishtailing and porpoising? An obvious answer is "go to another arrow," but it's usually not that simple. After all, both brace height and nock point affect fishtailing and porpoising, because they alter the archer's paradox. If the arrow is porpoising, moving the nocking point downward a small distance on the string is a worthwhile early maneuver. I clamp a new nock set underneath the original nock set. Then I remove the original one, which changes the position of the new one just a little bit. Then it's time to trial-shoot the bow again. Although this method alters nock placement a little bit at a time, it can be enough to make a difference. The nock set was placed as much as one-half inch above horizontal to begin with and can be lowered until it is about one-eighth inch above horizontal. If nock replacement doesn't cure porpoising, the nock set is returned to its higher position and tuning continues.

If the arrow is fishtailing with a nock-left condition, stiffness of the arrow should immediately be altered. Recall that the arrow, no matter its material, was left full length for test purposes in the barebow tuning method. A long arrow is more limber than a short arrow, so reducing arrow length in half-inch increments increases spine, or stiffness. Cut the arrow back a half inch at this time. Taper the shortened shaft tip with a tapering tool (as described in chapter 11), and reattach the point using hot-melt cement, which requires only a few seconds to accomplish.

Continue testing. If the arrow ceases to fishtail badly at a 29-inch arrow length, flying relatively well, then cut the arrow no shorter. If the problem continues, then lop off another half inch. Never shorten the arrow beyond the normal draw length of the archer, of course. If shortening the arrow down to the archer's draw length, usually 28 inches, stops the nock-left problem, then lower the nocking point *slightly* a little at a time, remembering that some nock high is usually necessary to promote a clean takeoff of the arrow from the bow shelf.

The above pertains to the arrow fishtailing to the left only. By cutting it shorter, spine was increased. But what if the full-length arrow is flying nock right in its fishtailing pattern? Cutting the arrow shorter won't do any good because a nock-right condition means that the arrow is already too stiff. That shaft will have to be set aside in favor of another one with less spine. Although the process can eat up a few test arrows, it's worth it because once the bow is tuned, a supply of the right shafts can be purchased.

The tuning process so far has pertained to working with wood arrows, but the same procedure is followed with carbons, aluminums, and other shaft materials. The aluminum shaft can be cut back in the same fashion as the wood shaft was shortened by using a tube cutter, which, if not available at the archery shop, can be found at a hardware store or hobby house. Since inserts on aluminum arrows are installed with hot-melt cement, they can be removed easily with a little heat, leaving the point in place for two reasons: to offer a hold on the insert to pull it free, and to keep adhesive from melting into the threads of the insert. Carbon shafts are a little more troublesome, but can also be worked following directions for cutting shafts and installing inserts.

Bow tuning is slow going, but the end result is worth the effort. It's unfortunate that the three most important aspects of tuning cannot be accomplished simultaneously, because sometimes fistmele is altered when a change in nock point would have done more good, or the archer goes to another arrow when a combination of brace height and nocking point change would have improved arrow flight. Also, nocking point may have to be adjusted in various stages of bow tuning in order to cure porpoising.

After tuning with a bare shaft, feathers are installed. Plastic vanes are workable as long as the bow is set up with an elevated arrow rest, but these days shooting off the shelf is far more popular, which demands feathers because they fold back as the arrow glides off the arrow rest and strike plate. A well-tuned bow handles a variety of fletching sizes and styles. I find it unnecessary to use a high-profile feather in my longbows and recurves for clean arrow flight. Nor do I set my arrows up with helical fletching, although such a spiral is perfectly fine and I have nothing against it. I prefer a five and one-half inch standard or low-profile feather mounted straight, not helically, but with an offset pitch. I use left-wing feathers because I find them easier to get. Right-wings are more popular because a number of bowshooters mistakenly think that if they're right-handed, they must shoot right-wing feathers.

How an arrow behaves out of the bow is affected by its length, spine, weight, fletching, size and spiral, plus the type of point used. Spine and weight are not the same, because even with wood arrows it's possible to have a light-weight shaft that is stiff. I have a number of lightweight shafts that have lots of spine. The reverse can also be true: A flexible shaft can be heavy. The carbon shaft is a perfect example of an arrow that can be stiff but light in weight. The latest Gold Tip carbons, for example, work in stickbows, their crisscross pattern making them strong. Added weights (installed within the shaft) can be used to bring final arrow mass up for those who prefer more heft in the arrow.

The specific physics of the bow, its exact design and construction, plus the type of materials used to build it, as well as the weight and individual shooting style of the archer, allow some bows to shoot a wider variety of arrows than others. I have one recurve that, with 63-pound limbs attached, shoots tapered cedar arrows of 55/60, 60/65, and 65/70 spine—all extremely well. They fly out to fifty yards beautifully, landing in the target with nock straight out. Then there are bows that shoot one particular arrow type and spine best, handling others not nearly so well. But that's not a problem; once the right arrow is found for a certain bow, the archer buys a supply of them.

After the arrow is flying fairly well, it's time to look at fine-tuning. Although a bare shaft may have stabilized at 29 inches, the archer may wish to try his finished, fletched arrows at a slightly different length. This is not going against the findings of the bare shaft test, because it was the bare shaft that showed the way to a proper arrow. However, it does allow the archer to custom fit the arrow to his own draw length. I cut my arrows to 28 inches. My draw length used to be much longer, but the compressed style of instinctive shooting prompted me to shorten arrow length considerably. I know that if my bow shoots a 29-inch arrow well in bare bow tuning, then it will shoot that same arrow at 28 inches when it is fixed up with feathers.

Various points must be mounted and tested on different arrows in bow tuning. Sometimes a heavier or lighter point improves arrow flight. A 160-grain field point may fly better on a given arrow from a particular bow than a 125-grain field point, or vice versa. It's worth trying several different kinds because some may shoot true and others may not. For example, an arrow may handle a certain blunt, while failing to shoot another blunt well. Fortunately, the JUDO point, the most important head in roving, works on any arrow that functions with a target or field point, because they are well made and finely balanced. (See chapter 14 for a short story of JUDO point development.) Heads must be mounted true, of course, especially on the wooden shaft where there may be a chance of offsetting at an angle. Spinning the finished arrow with point in place tells the story. Provided the head is symmetrically built, as points are today, and mounted true, the arrow will spin true.

Fine-tuning searches for the "sweet spot" where all aspects of the bow are in harmony. Extremely minor adjustments in brace height and nock point should be made while shooting the finished arrow. Although not entirely necessary,

Intended strictly for carbon arrows, the 3-D Tunable Point System from the Game Tracker Company is "adjustable" by weight.

fine-tuning with the point the archer intends to use with that arrow is never a mistake, although tuning with a field point is all right, too. Sometimes the nocking point has to be raised or lowered to shoot specific points better, too. One good thing about bare shaft tuning is that once a bow is shooting fairly well with a featherless shaft, fine-tuning with a finished arrow is a lot easier, including inducing bow quietness. For example, one aspect of bow quietness is brace height. Extremely low brace height on a recurve may cause the string to slap noisily against the recurve section of the forelimbs. Type of arrow and fletching are also important to bow quietness, as are string silencers. A bow well tuned with a bare shaft doesn't go out of whack with a minor brace height adjustment or other minor alterations.

Part of bow tuning lies in accessory choices. Even an arm guard, as well as a shooting glove or tab, can make a difference in shooting. I used a glove for years, but found that the tab allowed a bit smoother arrow release for me. A bow quiver can alter how a bow behaves, too. Some archers find that a bow quiver stabilizes the bow. Others feel it causes imbalance. I prefer them on recurves, but they seem to upset the balance of cloud-light longbows. The archer must tune himself as well as his bow, but that's a discussion for another campfire. We do know, however, that mere hand pressure on the grip of the bow can alter arrow flight, especially with a recurve.

Once a bow is tuned, it's time for the archer to make a permanent record of all pertinent information. A little booklet with each bow registered in it is helpful. Record the name of the bow, proper brace height, nocking point, arrow, and all other particulars. Notes on tuning are never a bad idea because the archer won't remember all the details. Did a small blunt work well on arrows for a particular longbow? Check the record book on the bow to find out. If only a few bows are owned, the archer's bow square can be marked with indelible ink—a line for brace height and another for nocking point location.

Proper stickbow tuning brings confidence in equipment. The archer knows his arrows are flying true. He also knows that if he does his part, his bow will perform flawlessly. A straight-flying arrow hits the target reliably, which is the goal of every shot. That arrow also flies farther than a wig-wagging shaft, and it's more enjoyable to watch in flight. There's something extra special about watching a smooth-gliding arrow fly toward the target than a fishtailing or porpoising shaft that spans the gulf between archer and target awkwardly. For every reason, the tuned stickbow is best, but trial and error is necessary in order to achieve that happy condition. The well-tuned bow is a compromise between fistmele, nocking point, and arrow, and as promised at the outset of this chapter, once tuned, the stickbow stays that way. That's the good part.

8

Setting Up
Stickbow Tackle

The beauty of longbows and recurves, aside from pure shooting enjoyment, is simplicity. There are no wheels on longbow or recurve tips, no cables, no scooplike overdraw rests for short arrows. Few carry sights. Target bows may wear stabilizers and various devices to promote arrow placement on the target, but the grassroots bowman doesn't use these paraphernalia either.

In spite of how clean and pure the traditional bow is, it still has to be set up. Tuning was covered in the previous chapter because that knowledge should be in mind first, before we think about how to set up a stickbow. Now, with an understanding of what we are going to do with it when finished, it's time to get the longbow or recurve ready for action.

It's fun to tinker with the bow until it's properly ready for good shooting. A first consideration for stickbow setup is the guidance system of the arrow—which means feathers the vast majority of time. The business of arranging strike plate and arrow rest is conducted because our arrows have feathers. Plastic vanes require an entirely different setup, namely, an elevated arrow rest. There is nothing wrong with an elevated rest, by the way, and there are dozens of different kinds on the market, most with stick-on backing so they can be put on in seconds. A few traditional archers prefer these so they can shoot vanes if they want to. Scant others even favor them over feathers.

Vanes are waterproof, but the feather is so forgiving in nature that it allows shooting off the shelf, the way it's done these days. In the 1950s, our stickbows wore elevated arrow rests, in spite of the fact that we all used feather fletching. True traditionalists of that decade didn't bother with these devices, and even fewer do today. Regardless, many good elevated rests are available, including the Bear Weather Rest, a soft rubber unit that attaches via a self-adhesive backing. A concave flipper holds the arrow on the rest, reducing shaft surface contact for less friction. The Saber elevated rest, made of rubber with a flipper, can be used with a cushion plunger by target archers.

Feathers are a definite part of setting up. Different styles include helical parabolics, far left, smaller shields on a carbon arrow, parabolics mounted straight offset, and on the far right, shield helicals.

Black Widow sells it. The Brush Rest from the same company has what looks like a mascara brush for the arrow to ride on.

Here we're interested in getting arrows to fly cleanly from the shelf of the bow without an elevated arrow rest. Bowmen of the past have actually rested the arrow across a knuckle when they shot, disregarding the arrow rest. There were bows that had no shelf at all, in fact, so the hand itself becomes the arrow rest. Today, several different materials are used to make workable arrow rests and strike plates. One is Velcro , purchased at a fabric store in two parts; the hook and the loop.

The two parts mate to form the locking action of Velcro; however, the loop part of the Velcro strip works fine for both strike plates and rests. (The

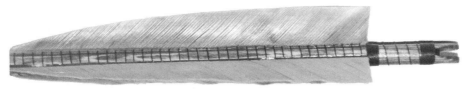

These special gray goose feathers are tied on using a fine silk thread. While the style is old, the long, low-profile look works as well today as ever.

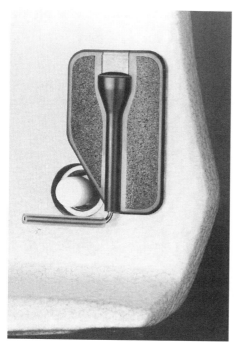

Longbows and recurves (especially the latter when they have large windows) can use an elevated arrow rest like this Flipper Rest from New Archery Products; however, shooting off the shelf is preferred by most traditional archers today.

other part of the strip is not used.) To create an arrow rest and strike plate, cut the Velcro loop strip to size and shape and stick it in place. Some archers may prefer a solid piece of Velcro, folding it into the corner of the shelf, but most use two separate pieces of loop section, one for the strike plate on the side of the riser, the other directly on the shelf as an arrow rest. The fuzzy, yet stiff, construction of Velcro allows an arrow shaft to glide across its surface slickly and smoothly, which is exactly what we want.

Other shelf materials are equally workable. McMahon Traditional Archery Company sells excellent leather side plate and leather shelf rest stick-ons. These die-cut pieces, made of top grade leather in black or brown, provide a slick surface with reduced friction for the shaft to glide along, and their self-adhesive backing makes them easy to install. The side plate, another term for strike plate, is precut to shape and can be attached as is, or trimmed with sharp scissors to suit the archer's personal bow. The shelf rest material can be cut down to fit various shelf sizes and shapes. If in doubt, you can first make a template, a paper cutout that is cut to fit the shelf and the strike plate of the bow. When satisfied with the shape and size of the templates, place them on the arrow rest and strike plate materials and cut around each to get the same size and shape. Strike plate and arrow rest should look neat when fixed in place; neither should be overly large or small. They should be large enough to make total surface contact with the arrow shaft during shooting. When setting up to "shoot through the gap" (explained below), the arrangement of strike plate and arrow rest is crucial. In this setup, the arrow rest is generally quite small, because it fits only to the outside of the shelf, leaving a bare passage (the gap) in the corner of the shelf covered with neither strike plate nor arrow rest material.

Velcro and leather are only two types of arrow rest/strike plate materials. There are many others. Bear Archery has long offered its Bear Hair Rest, for example, which consists of a thick rug for an arrow rest, that is noted for quietness, along with a side plate. This is another self-adhesive arrow rest/strike plate combination that is easy to install. Calf hair side plates are very slick, making a low-friction surface for the arrow shaft. There are also separate rug arrow rests and riser rug strike plates that have self-adhesive backs and are simple to install. There is also a one-piece leather rest and side plate that serves both purposes by folding into the corner of the shelf with stick-on backing.

The setup for shooting throught the gap is accomplished by placing the arrow rest and strike plate on the shelf and riser with a space between them, running as large as a quarter inch wide, at the inside corner of the shelf. It also requires a specific arrangement of the three feathers on the shaft so that

Two different materials used for arrow rests and strike plates are Velcro, as shown on the left, and leather, on the right. Both are stick-ons.

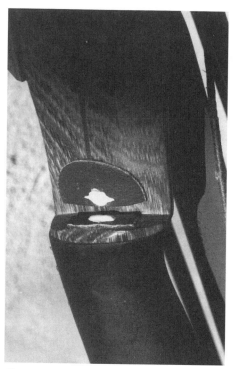

One way to establish an arrow rest and strike plate is with a dot of epoxy for each, as shown here. These should be broken in by firing a number of arrows before doing any serious shooting.

one hen feather shoots through the gap with minimal shelf contact. This is easily accomplished during arrow assembly (as described in chapter 12). The nock is only pinched on the nock taper while the arrow is fitted with feathers. Then the fletched arrow is placed on the bowstring and rotated so that a hen feather aims toward the gap. Only then is the nock glued in place. In this way, a hen feather is always aimed toward the gap in the shelf when the arrow is nocked and shot. I further modify the system by placing a dot of epoxy about the size of a kitchen match head on the lower portion of the strike plate so that the arrow shaft will make contact with it. This does two things. First, the dot creates a very small contact point for the arrow shaft, reducing drag. Second, the raised epoxy lump forces the arrow shaft slightly out from the strike plate, which creates an even wider path for the hen feather to follow through the gap. Once the epoxy has a fairly deep groove in it from use, the dot can be touched up with another drop of epoxy and allowed to dry overnight.

Shooting through the gap reduces friction, which is always desirable, and spares the hen feather some wear, which may be even more important. What shooting through the gap doesn't do is change arrow flight. This is easy to prove by shooting six arrows. Place the first three on the string in the normal fashion with the cock feather facing outward and fire them at the target. Place the next three arrows on the string and fire them with the cock feather up against the strike plate. The archer will find all six arrows in the target as usual. The arrows with cock feathers pointed inward did not go astray, because of the forgiveness of the feather, which collapses out of the way. On a sensitive arrow, the hard base of a cock feather may make contact with and push away from the riser. However, this condition is fairly rare.

Shooting through the gap is not a panacea, but it is one, and only one, way of setting up the arrow rest/strike plate on the longbow and recurve.

Another aspect of setting up traditional tackle is quieting the bow. Whereas the hum of an arrow, like the buzz of a swift bumblebee, is a joy to the ear, rattling, whooshing, and twanging noises coming from a longbow or recurve are unpleasant. Untuned bows can be noisy. (Refer to chapter 7 for fine-tuning principles.) Low fistmele normally increases bow performance, but it can also create noise by causing the string to slap against the limb of a recurve. Better to forsake a couple feet per second in arrow speed than to put up with such disharmony in a bow. Simple experimenting with brace height is the answer to this noise problem. (How to change fistmele is discussed in chapter 6).

The wrong arrow can also produce unwanted noise in a traditional bow. This may be a simple matter of a very light shaft that does not absorb a good share of the energy from the string—somewhat akin to dry firing a bow, which is not only dangerous, but noisy. Another potential noisemaker is the arrowpoint. Loose screw-in points on carbon or aluminum arrows are especially prone to humming a tune. The obvious cure is tightening points from time to time during a shooting session. Tightening by hand is sufficient; no need for pliers. Fletching may also cause noise. Although feathers are known

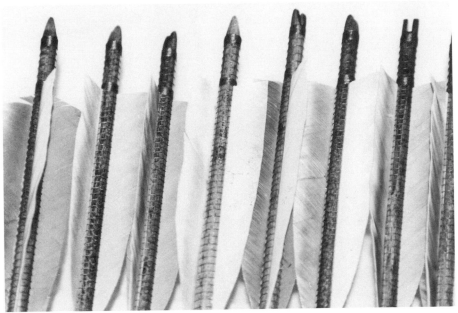

Fletching is part of bowshooting sound. The larger the fletching, the more noise. These medium-sized gray goose feathers are on the quiet side.

for quietness, radical helicals can be noisy. Also, the larger the feather, the more vocal. The very noisy flu-flu arrow has a lot of feather surface to purposely create drag, slowing the arrow down for short-range shooting. Flu-flu arrows with JUDO points are easy to locate after shooting, because they normally don't go far. Large fletching not of the flu-flu type still provide plenty of surface area for drag and can make a good deal of noise. As with so many other things in archery, there are tradeoffs. Fletching must only be large enough to guide the arrow, unless the archer prefers more fletching, which some do. The special sound that only an arrow makes can be enjoyable.

Another noisemaker can be the bow quiver. Bow quivers that have arrow grippers placed close to the hood leave a lot of the lower arrow shaft unsupported. When the bow is shot, the hanging shafts vibrate and cannot help but make contact with each other. If possible, increase the distance between the hood and the arrow gripper. When this can't be done, at least arrange the arrows in the quiver so that the feathers make the least possible contact when the bow is shot. A loose bow quiver or one without washers between quiver

Setting up tackle includes the correct mounting of a bow quiver. This custom bow is set up with a bolt-on quiver using a spacer for proper alignment.

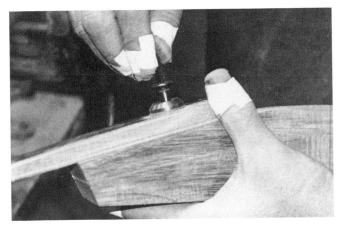

The fitting between limb and riser on fine bows like this custom model is very close. However, a squeaking sound can come from this area when the bow is drawn. It's easy to fix with a little lubricant between limb and riser.

and bow riser will rattle when the bow is shot. Tighten a loose quiver with the appropriate wrench, and use lock washers or rubber washers between quiver and riser on the quiver bolts to keep a bow quiver tightly in place.

On the takedown longbow or recurve, contact between the base of the limb and the riser platform where the limb bolts on can create a creaking sound when the bow is drawn. This noise does not at all indicate a badly built bow. It's simply the nature of two solid points flexing together, if ever so little. Some bowyers now design stronger limb wedges to prevent this noise. The bowyer can install a flexible cork pad in between the base of the bow limb risers, which is often sufficient to squelch creaking when the bow is drawn. The problem may also be easily fixed by placing certain substances between riser platform and limb base. Ordinary bowstring wax can do wonders for a creaking bow, and I've found that a light coating of lubrication used in muzzle-loaders works especially well. Called Ultra-Score, from Big Bore Express Company, it can be found at black powder shops or ordered from the company. The very lightest coating of this lubricating gel stops all creaking in my bows.

Everything must be well attached and tight on a bow for quietness, including limb bolts, the little screws that hold a bow quiver hood in place, arrow rests, and strike plates. How the feathers meet the shelf can also make a difference in noise, albeit slight. Shooting through the gap may have a small quieting effect, since it reduces feather contact with the arrow rest and strike plate. Another minor consideration is string construction. I can't prove that Fast Flight strings are noisier than the older Dacrons, because Fast Flights may actually have a higher pitch, rather than more decibels of sound. But a lighter-weight string should make a bit more noise than a heavier string, so the new strings probably are noisier, but also better. Fortunately, string noise can be corrected, if not entirely, at least significantly.

Quieting the string is vital to quieting the bow. Releasing the string causes a boowang! noise, and the string doesn't have to slap a limb to make that sound. I find such string noise disconcerting, much preferring not to hear it. Fortunately, there are a number of good string silencers on the market, including Tarantulas, Puff Silencers, Beaver Balls, and Cat Whiskers. The idea of all string silencers is the same: to dampen (absorb) noise. My personal choice is the Cat Whisker, which is a simple collection of narrow rubber strips that come in a sheet and are separated into individual segments after attachment to the string. Properly fixed in place, these do a fine job of quieting the string and they last a long time.

The first thing to do with Cat Whiskers is to cut the slab of rubber down the middle, making two equal parts. If full-length Cat Whiskers are attached, they whip more and wear out faster. So instead of one pair of full-length Cat Whiskers, one on the lower end of the string and another on the upper end, use two pairs of half-length Cat Whiskers, two on the string below the riser, two on the string above the riser. These can be spaced in various ways and still be effective. For example, the topmost Cat Whisker can be placed a few inches past the curve on the recurve bow, or a few inches below the bow nock on the longbow, with the next one attached six inches or so below that one. Do the same on the bottom part of the string. I've placed Cat Whiskers only a couple inches apart in both sections above and below the riser with excellent results.

How the Cat Whiskers are attached is more important than their exact location on the string. Tied on the outside of the string, they may work fine, but they won't last as long and they look lousy. Instead, thread each short Cat Whisker—remember these are standards cut in half—through the string. This is easily done because strings are generally bicolored. Thread the Cat Whisker between the two string colors, with equal portions protruding on both sides of the string. I do the whole operation with the string off the bow and stretched between two chairs using rubber bands on the loops to keep the string taught, but not so tight that the strands cannot be easily separated.

Have a helper tug on both ends of the Cat Whisker to stretch it out, keeping it equally spaced on the string so that the same amount protrudes on either side, while you tie it in place firmly with nylon thread in a crisscross pattern, back and forth a couple times until it is knotted firmly on the string. A drop of superglue on the knot will keep the Cat Whisker from coming off, most likely, for the life of the string. Tip: Use a long piece of nylon thread so that it can be handled and tied easily. Cut off the long ends after the final knot is tied and a drop of superglue has been applied to the knot.

When finished, the bowstring will have four short Cat Whiskers in place, centered between the string strands, tied on with strong nylon thread, and

These Spider Legs are mounted in between string strands. A wrap-around of nylon thread secured with a dot of superglue helps hold the silencers in place.

secured with a drop of superglue. I have no way of measuring the effectiveness of Cat Whiskers; however, my ears tell me that they definitely arrest unwanted string noise. All my traditional bows wear at least one Cat Whisker, depending on how many it takes to silence the string. For example, I have a Pronghorn Three-Piece Takedown Longbow that was quieted with only one short Cat Whisker placed midway between the lower bow nock and the center of the riser. That bow was already so quiet that one short piece of Cat Whisker was sufficient.

Let's talk a bit about using traditional bows and arrows in wet weather. If it has been well finished, the bow itself requires no special attention. And most strike plates and arrow rests are weatherproof. Finishes are relatively rainproof, and have been for many moons. Fullerplast, a finish used by many bowyers, is a catalyzed product that even defies solvent, let alone water. Warning: Although modern bow finishes are extremely tough and weather resistant, they will not stand up to insect repellent, which can eat through the finish. One bowshooter at a meet found this out the hard way. It was summertime and gnats were bad. The archer doused himself with bug repellent, incidentally transferring a good amount to his bow riser and limbs as he handled his longbow. His bow had to be refinished.

Bows with leather-covered handles don't show much problem in wet weather. I own a recurve with a kangaroo hide handle, and it's been soaked several times, being none the worse for the drenching. I do treat leather riser handles with Filson's Original Oil Finish Wax, which is intended for leather garments, or a similar product, such as Lexol Leather Conditioner. The modern synthetic string defies bad weather, too. String wax helps, and it should be applied in dry as well as wet weather.

So the bow is generally safe in wet weather, as long as the archer properly maintains the arrow rest and strike plate and keeps his leather handles well cared for. But what about the arrow? Carbon and aluminum shafts laugh at moisture, and the well-finished wooden shaft, although not as defiant of the elements, doesn't warp unless it's really drenched by rain and left wet. For those who like to shoot regardless of the weather, it's wise to seal even the nock and point tapers of the wooden arrow to prevent moisture from entering these areas.

The feather fetching used on traditional bows is susceptible to soaking. One cure is turning away from feathers to plastic vanes with elevated arrow rests, which most traditional bowbenders are not about to do. So what can be done to keep feathers dry in wet weather?

Setting them up to defy moisture begins with the dressing fly fishermen use to keep dry flies from getting soggy. Brush this liquid into the feather. Normally, the bottle cap itself contains a small brush that's just right for the job. After the fly dressing is entirely dry on the feather, dust it with a waterproofing powder sold at archery shops, such as Fletch-Dry. Apply it carefully. It's so light that if it gets away, it stays airborne a long time, in which case, try not to breath the stuff in. The treated feathers, painted with "duck oil" (as fly dressing is sometimes called) and dusted well with dry powder, will repel most water. In addition, for arrows carried in a bow quiver, standard back quiver, or regular side quiver, cover the fletching with a plastic bag. The most certain way to keep feathers dry is to give them the oil/powder treatment, and then secure them in a Catquiver, St. Charles back quiver, or similar covered arrow carrier.

Setting up a traditional bow can mean the addition of what many think of as gadgets, which may be an unfair assessment. Sights are the first consideration. I once had a Bear Kodiak recurve bow with sights. I shot it "straight up" like a compound and the sights worked perfectly. When I sold the bow, the sights of course went with it, and I have never again attached sights to another traditional bow. Why not? Because I got back into the flow of instinctive shooting and found that I could actually hit more accurately under field circumstances without sights. I never had to guesstimate the range before deciding how to aim my bow. Nonetheless, for those who want to mount sights on a traditional bow, it's a matter of personal choice, and no one has the right to say longbows or recurves should not wear them.

The same goes for stabilizers. They are perfectly at home on traditional target bows and certainly should be used, whereas they seem out of place on a standard field longbow or recurve. The projecting stabilizer poking out from a standard traditional bow makes it look like it belongs with the compound clan. Although I wouldn't have one on a regular bow, there's no doubt that stabilizers suit other archers, for they can be installed readily on these bows. Black Widow, for example, offers an optional insert for a stabilizer. The cushion plunger falls into the same kettle with the stabilizer. For those who like them, or on target bows, they're fine. However, the natural off-the-shelf shooting style of the traditional bow does not require a cushion plunger, and my bows will never wear one. Arrows fly so well from the arrow rest/strike plate setup described above that a cushion plunger would be superfluous.

Setting up traditional tackle is absolutely essential to reliable bowshooting. It's not difficult and quite inexpensive to attach the right arrow rests and strike plates for shooting off the shelf or through the gap; align feathers correctly, use the right arrows and treat them for water resistance, put string silencers correctly in place, select the correct feathers to stabilize an arrow without undue noise, tighten all limb and quiver bolts, place arrows in a bow quiver spaced for maximum quietness, lubricate the contact point between riser and low limbs, and, of course, if desired, add bowsights, stabilizers, and cushion plungers to a longbow or recurve. Doing these things enhances bow tuning and produces the most performance from traditional tackle.

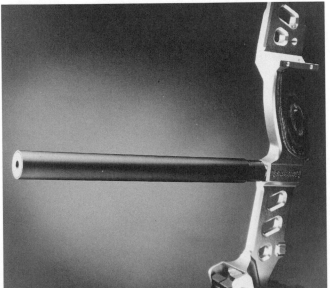

A stabilizer like this one is generally found on target bows. It has a dampening effect on the bow.

9

Bowstrings

The bowstring is truly a wonder. Without it, there would have been no bow at all. It is no incidental accessory, but the very life of the "strung stick." As with all inventions, it's difficult to imagine the first string or rope coming to life: Someone sits holding loose parallel fibers, vegetable or animal, twisting them together into a single ply cord. Internal friction prevents the fibers from slipping past each other as long as the cord remains strained, unable to untwist back into individual fibers. This basic form of string may have served for bows, but it's likely that a more sophisticated cordage followed that would not unravel so easily, possibly one made of long, thin fibers, that made a stronger string than fewer, thicker ones.

Students in a bowmaking class, such as Art Hunter's in Colorado, marvel at the crafting of a self-bow, but when it comes to making a bowstring, the act resembles pure magic. It's difficult to believe that right before your eyes a batch of loose fibers as fragile-looking as hair suddenly becomes a string sufficiently strong to withstand the drawing of a bow and casting of an arrow. The student knows it's a skill he will never master—until he actually does.

It turns out that the string is much more than a device to hold the bow in a ready position, for it has much to do with arrow cast. Tim Baker, expert primitive bowmaker, discussed this fact in volume 2 of *The Traditional Bowyer's Bible*. A self-bow wasn't living up to expectations. The string was suspected, proved to be the culprit, changed, and the cast of the bow improved significantly.

Well into the 1940s, preparing strings was considered a home task performed by the individual archer. Adolph Shane, in his 1936 book *Archery Tackle, How to Make & How to Use It*, explained the making of a string from No. 12 linen thread: thirty threads for a 45-pound bow, twenty-one for a 30-pound bow. The work was accomplished with a smooth board over seven feet long, with two small finishing nails set one foot greater than the full bow length measured tip to tip. In other words, for a six-foot bow the nails were

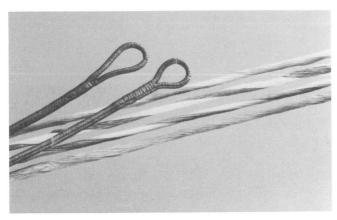

Strings can be overlooked by traditional archers, but they are, obviously, among the most important parts of the bow. There are many different types of strings on the market today, each with specific characteristics.

set seven feet apart. The thread was tied to one nail, then wrapped around the other, back and forth, taut, until ten strands were set. These were cut with a sharp knife into ten individual threads of equal length.

The remaining procedure included waxing the individual threads with each end extending beyond the other successfully at half-inch intervals. These were waxed together into a single strand. Two more groups of ten strands were made likewise, for a total of thirty threads. This is not a forum for string-making, since the traditional archer seldom does this for himself any longer; however, it's interesting to know that three strands were united as a single bowstring with an "eye" that was later fitted with serving. Reading about the process, or attending a bowmaking class (which is very enjoyable and rewarding), gives the traditional bowshooter an appreciation for the grassroots beginnings of this great sport, even though he will stay with traditional tackle, rather than going to primitive bows and arrows.

Many different types of bowstrings, including endless, Flemish, rawhide, and gut, have been made of an assortment of materials. Flax, hemp, ramie, dogbane, nettle, milkweed, iris, yucca, bamboo, sisal (agave), palm, abaca, and silk are among the vegetable fibers used, whereas sinew, rawhide, and gut were useful animal fibers for bowstrings. Each material had its own properties of stretching and strength. Saxton Pope did his own study of fibers, printed in 1923. He ranked horsehair at 15-pounds breaking strength, cotton at eighteen, catgut at twenty, silk at twenty-three, Irish linen at twenty-eight, and Chinese grass fiber, also known as ramie, at thirty-two pounds. String making has long been a study unto itself from ancient times to the present, with new strings appearing regularly.

Today's traditional archer may not study strings; he leaves that up to the scientist and technologist. He is also unlikely to make one himself, but the string remains absolutely vital to longbow and recurve performance,

Although building a string may never become part of the "average" traditional bowshooter's game, having some notion of the process promotes understanding of this important piece of tackle. Here, spools of Fast Flight and S4 string await action.

especially as new bow designs take advantage of space age materials now used in strings. The Fast Flight string is a perfect example of the trend. It is considered a high-performance bowstring because it commonly gives longbows and recurves greater arrow cast. Initially, the low stretching tolerance of Fast Flight (rated at 1.5 percent stretch) was credited for increased performance levels, since it stretched less than Dacron (4 percent), linen (2 percent), or silk (4 percent).

This rather slight difference in stretch, while helpful, did not account for Fast Flight performance as much as another factor: low mass. The lighterweight Fast Flight string used up less energy when it functioned. The new string also was so strong that it could break a bow. The problem was cured by making stronger bow nocks to withstand the added shock of the lowstretch, lightweight Fast Flight string. For example, Pronghorn custom bows are built with supertough micarta overlays for extra strength in the bow nock, and the Fast Flight string will not break or cut it. Today most bows are constructed with Fast Flight in mind, so these bows last just as long using the newer string as they do using older string materials. The latest strings are superstrong, with even less stretch than the original Fast Flight—and they're light in weight.

Fast Flight S4 is such a string, being created with "no stretch or creep." Original Fast Flight strings, as good as they are, do creep. If a bow was strung with one for a year, the string would continue to stretch during that time, if only by tens of thousandths of an inch. Fast Flight S4 simply does not stretch. It is also abrasion resistant. Whereas other strings may fray from rubbing against brush, for example, Fast Flight S4 takes a lot more of this type of punishment before fuzzing up. It's also considered far stronger than the already strong standard Fast Flight string. It lasts a long time, in part because of its inherent single-strand strength, but also because of a special "hot-melt coating" that prolongs its life. In short, Fast Flight S4 is a remarkable string the likes of which have never been seen before.

But it's not the only great contemporary bowstring. Brownell's Fast Flight 2000 string is 25 percent stronger than the original Fast Flight, with all the speed and durability credited to that string but with less creep. At the same time, Brownell's Fast Flight 2000 is no heavier than original Fast Flight, and it comes in the same diameter strands. Technology never comes to a standstill, not even in bowstrings. Another new string, the 450 Plus bowstring from BCY is called "the best bowstring material in the world without question! It is the strongest, has no creep, and is very fast." Furthermore, the 450 Plus bowstring is considered to give "more arrow speed, more durability and no fuzziness."

BCY didn't stop with its 450 Plus, coming out with a DynaFlight 97 bowstring, announced as the company's "new generation" product. DynaFlight 97 has 50 percent more strength, better abrasive resistance, and less creep and stretch than original DynaFlight, which was already known as a good product. The battle for market share in the world of bowstrings is hot and getting hotter. Demand runs so high for strings that one Colorado archery concern had to triple its string-making crew in only one year. While the bowstring operation remains only one part of that full-service pro shop, the string-making part of the business has eclipsed the rest of the store's sales, with strings shipped to all parts of the country. Bowstring technology will continue to advance because bowstrings are so vital to many aspects of archery, including ballistic performance.

The string, as part of the bow "machine," is subject to hysteresis (hiss-ter-re-sis). More or less, hysteresis is the internal friction at work in any system. It means the bowstring absorbs some of the energy that would otherwise go into doing work. Where string is concerned, weight, as explained earlier, makes a difference in arrow speed. I don't like rules of thumb because they generally don't hold up across the board, but we can say, only as a general gauge, that for each 20-grain increase in a bowstring's total weight, there is a one foot-per-second arrow speed loss. Whether this is completely accurate or not isn't important. The *concept* is, however, which is to say that light strings absorb less energy from the bow than heavy ones. This is why Fast Flight and other high-tech, lightweight strings have improved bow speeds.

It would seem that the string is under most stress when the bow is taken to full draw; however, all evidence points to the string's collapse toward the limbs as its most stressful period. This is due in part to the fact that the string is traveling at about the same speed that the tips of the bow are moving when the bow is fired. So bowstrings break most often when the limbs leap forward after release.

Why wouldn't a string with a lot of "give" put more power into the arrow? If the string stretches out like an elastic band, it should store energy in doing so, imparting this energy to the arrow nock. But it doesn't work that way, because the string is under most tension when it comes down on the bow nock (tip of the bow) after release. A stretchy string would act as a shock absorber at this point, actually soaking up some of the energy in the system (hysteresis again), whereas a nonstretchy string delivers the most energy from the limbs to the nock. Also, whereas it is appropriate, and even necessary to twist a string a few times, the string that is twisted many times is like a coil that absorbs energy, resulting in a very slight loss of energy in a highly twisted string over one that is less twisted. Purists will therefore want to buy a string that truly fits the bow, rather than a longer one that has to be twisted many times to gain the correct fistmele.

Because the string is so crucial not only to the performance of the bow, but also to the safety of the archer as well, ordering one is serious business. A broken string can not only break a bow, but also put a limb tip in the bowman's forehead, or worse. So how is a string ordered? The string must match the bow, of course. I have a bow, built within the past six years, whose maker says that under no circumstances is Fast Flight string to be used. He does not guarantee that his bow tips will survive with Fast Flight string, and he's not the least bit ashamed of the fact, because he believes the few feet per second gained by the new string is meaningless. Whether or not I agree, his dictate must be followed. The warning sounded about older bows bears repeating. Many older bows have come out of the closet with the current rush to traditional bows. These vintage models were not built to withstand a no-stretch string that does not act like a shock absorber when the limb collapses during shooting. There was no Fast Flight string around when they were built. Although a few do have heavy limb tips, and will withstand a new string, most will not.

After selecting the correct string material to match the bow, choose the right string length next. Remember that although a string can be twisted (and must be to keep it intact), overtwisting to shorten a long string makes it an energy absorber, causing a loss, no matter how small, in arrow speed. Also, overtwisting may weaken the string, depending on the material it's made of. In severe cases, a string can actually cut into itself when overtwisted. On the other hand, a string that is too short produces an overly high fistmele.

To help archers get the right string length, the Archery Manufacturers Organization (AMO), a standardization agency of sorts, came up with a formula called the "AMO string length." A 60-inch bow, for example, takes an AMO 60-inch string, which in fact runs perhaps 56 inches in length. The string package shows both figures: the length of the bow, in this case AMO 60 inches, plus the length of the string. Another way to get the correct string length is by measuring the existing string on the bow, assuming it is correct to begin with. This is done by slipping one loop over something to hold it, then stretching the string out to full length using a tape measure to determine inches from one loop end to the other loop end. Suppose the measurement comes out to 64¼ inches. Then a 64¼-inch string is ordered from a custom string-maker, bowyer, or archery company.

Winding a bundle of "threads" for a Flemish-style bowstring.

Here, the string maker is getting ready to cut the bundle of threads to form the parts of the future Flemish Bowstring.

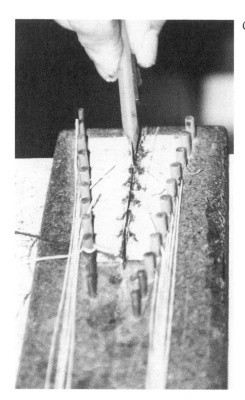

Cutting the bundle of strands.

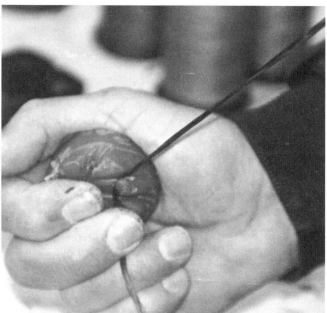

Waxing the bundle of strands into a unit.

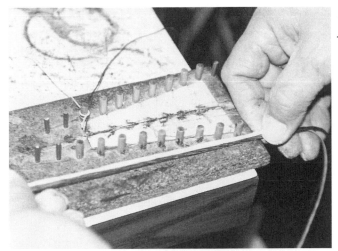

Measuring the length for the exact spot to start the loop.

One loop is prepared for twisting.

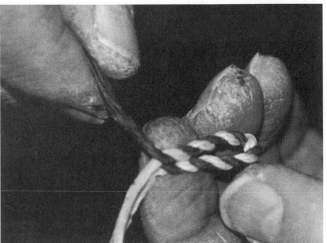

Twisting a loop.

A complete Flemish twist loop.

Winding a center serving.

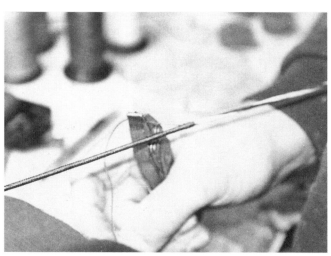

Tying off a center serving.

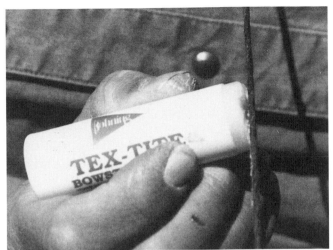

Wax and relax—that's the bowman's motto. Wax helps retain the integrity of the string.

And all this time you thought a string was simply a piece of twine that looped on the ends of the bow to keep it "cocked," when in fact it turns out to be a much more sophisticated element than you imagined, and far more important than you may have thought.

Strings have been a favorite topic of archers over the ages. Colonel Walrond, in his book *Archery*, coauthored by C. J. Longman in the late 1800s, said, "The string is made of hemp treated in a particular way with some preparation of glue, the composition of which was a secret possessed only by a maker named Mules, who lived in Belgium, in whose family it had been for generations. He died without revealing the secret; consequently, it was lost, and for some years no truly good strings have been procurable, new ones frequently breaking without any apparent cause."

This quote certainly gives insight to the state of archery in England during that period. The author explains that the string should be three-stranded, round, smooth, and even of size throughout, gradually thickening towards the ends so as to be strong enough for the eye and the loop." Longman further explains that the string should be thick enough for safety, while he understood that a "thin string undoubtedly gives a better cast." The *eye* of the string, as it was called, slipped over the upper bow nock, while the *loop* fitted on the lower bow nock. So even certain string nomenclature has changed. An unknown French author of the fourteenth century wrote, "The string should be made of silk and nothing else, for three reasons," citing strength and long life, with silk being "so stiff and hard that it will drive an arrow or bolt farther," and because it can be made in whatever size "pleaseth" the archer.

In 1515, another French writer said, "Strings should be made of silk or fine female hemp, which is finer than male hemp. They should be gummed and not glued." Roger Ascham, author of *Toxophilus*, said in 1545, "Now what a stringe oughte to be made of, whether of good hempe, as they do nowe a dayes, or of flaxe, or of silke, I leave that to the judgement of stringers, of whom we must buy them." That's an interesting statement from so long ago, because it fits so aptly today. We, too, count on "stringers" to tell us what we should buy. In 1830, the United Bowmen of Philadelphia said that "The Bow String is made of catgut, hemp or silk." Now, well over 105 years later, our strings are composed of synthetic materials. They're the finest the world has ever known, a perfect match for the best longbows and recurves ever made.

10

Gloves, Tabs, and Arm Guards

Gloves, finger stalls, and tabs have been around for ages. We know no more of their origins than we do the dawning of the bow; however, it's clear that at least two of these finger-saving implements have never become outdated. They're as valuable today as ever. The mechanical release is king among compound shooters, who seem to think it's a recent invention, when in fact there was a patent on one in the 1940s. The mechanical release makes sense with the newest compounds because of super letoff. The new bows may have as high as 80 percent drop in draw weight after breakover. This is good . . . and bad.

In the main, two types of finger protection are popular today, the glove and the tab. Both work equally well, although some archers prefer one over the other for personal reasons.

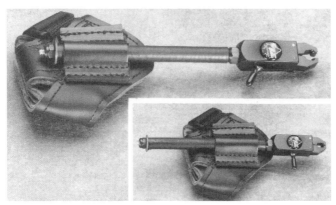

The mechanical release, shown here for comparison, is an old idea returned to help compound shooters with high letoff bows.

Tabs can be far more sophisticated in design than imagined. This Saunders Fab Tab has a screw-in finger separator, plus a finger ring, plus special stiff walls that prevent up/down pressure on the nock when the bow is drawn.

It's good because once a powerful compound is drawn past about the halfway mark, it becomes a breeze to hold at full draw.

On the other hand, release of the string is like running your fingers through mush. The string curls away from the glove or tab and release is soft, rather than sharp and crisp. The mechanical release overcomes the problem, allowing a clean, sharp release with the pulling of a trigger. Such releases are fine for compounds but absolutely out of place on longbows and recurves. Whereas stalls are all but dead, several kinds of gloves and various tabs provide excellent finger protection. The archer must try both before deciding, because these little items are extremely important to the release, and how the arrow gets away from the string can mean a hit or a miss. That's how vital finger coverings are to stickbow shooting success.

It's only fair to begin an assessment of gloves and tabs by admitting that some people use neither. My archery partner, Ted Walter, disliked every glove he tried, and considered the tab a fumbling bit of leather. His favorite finger protection was a simple Band-Aid. He stuck two on each shooting finger and he was set for the day. He had no problem roving for hours, firing dozens of arrows. That's because his fingers were toughened up. The Band-

Aids didn't really offer full protection—calluses did. Another friend wraps his fingers with surgical tape, following the same practice my bowshooting partner did years ago. One acquaintance uses nothing—never has, never will. He prefers to feel the string with bare fingers, and his digits are apparently used to it, because I've never heard Bud complain about soreness even after shooting a 70-pound longbow.

Most of us need something to protect our fingers from the ravages of the bowstring. There's nothing new about that. Maurice Thompson, cofather of modern archery, wrote in the nineteenth century that "the shooting glove is made to protect the three first fingers of the right hand from the wearing effect of the bowstring in shooting. It is formed of three thimbles of stiff, smooth leather, having elastic stitches to allow them to perfectly conform to the size of the fingers." Thompson went on to say, "If your fingers can stand it, shoot without gloves." That was his advice in 1878. The reason for going without a glove was feeling the string with bare fingers, which can provide a supersmooth release if the archer can stand it.

Thompson's finger protectors were true gloves, not finger stalls, for they had straps that met at the wrist band. Finger stalls were composed of single slip-over leather cups for each shooting finger. They probably worked fine when made to fit correctly. I've never used stalls and very few modern archers do. I suspect most bowshooters of Thompson's time, and several decades later, were glove people, although the tab does have ancient roots. Here is what Saxton Pope had to say about finger protection in 1925: "Doubtless the ancient yeoman, a horny-handed son of toil, needed no glove. But we know that even in those days a tab of leather was held in the hand to prevent the string from hurting." Pope explains his own "leather finger tips" in a

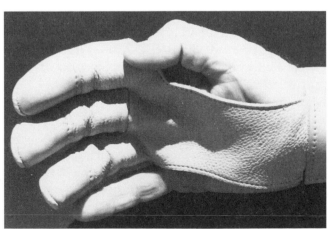

Some traditional archers will prefer a glove like this one with bold wrist strap and palm cover. Others will opt for the older-style glove without palm or back-of-hand cover.

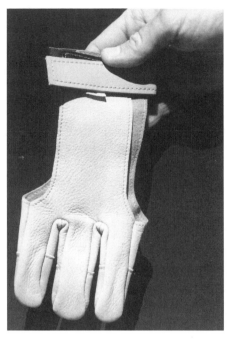

The glove draped over the hand is patterned after one used by Howard Hill. This one comes from the Jerry Hill Longbow company. It has open fingertips. The tab held in the right hand shows the finger ring that retains tab in hand, plus finger separator (nonpinch style), that prevents pinching the nock.

Off of the hand, this glove's design is easier to see. It offers protection for the first three fingers of the hand, along with back-of-hand plus palm covering, and it closes with a Velcro wrist band.

somewhat medical manner, indicative of his profession, saying that the "tips enclose the finger on the palmar surface up to the second joint."

Pope's "glove," however, was not a glove, but rather, fingertip protectors—perhaps not stalls, exactly, but close. He called them "finger tips." They were made of leather, shaped to fit the forepart of the fingers only, stitched on top with a hole for the knuckle to protrude through. I've never tried a fingertip, nor have I even seen one. I'd fear for it taking off with the arrow upon release, but it must have worked fine for Pope and friends. Note that Pope mentions a tab of leather used by the bowman of ancient times. Today's tab is generally more sophisticated than a little piece of leather.

Moving on to 1953, the great Howard Hill had his chance to talk about finger protection. "The protectors, or stalls, for the fingertips should be selected with care. A shooting glove works well, but when worn all day it often becomes uncomfortable, especially when the weather is hot." Hill may have believed that a glove was not always comfortable, but he did not suggest a tab. He said, "A shooting tab, as used by many target archers, does not allow

Famous archer Fred Bear preferred a glove over a tab. The choice is personal. It's a matter of what feels right to the individual bowshooter.

the hand enough freedom of movement." Hill wore an archery glove with finger protectors joined with straps to a wristband. He alludes to stalls being fingertips, as Pope called them, but these are actually a true glove for him, with wrist strap to hold the "fingertips" firmly in place. This type of shooting glove remains with us today, with many variations on the theme.

Coming forward to 1968, the unforgettable Fred Bear talks about finger protection. "It is actually the skeleton of a glove, with but three finger stalls for the first three fingers of the drawing hand," he says. While Bear mentions the tab, he does not truly recommend it, especially for beginning archers. In the photos I've seen, Bear is using a standard archery glove, the glove sold today by many archery concerns in numerous variations, including the moccasin glove with small openings at the fingertips, the closed-end glove, which has a piece of leather folded and sewn over the fingertips, and the traditional glove. This last glove differs from the first two by lacking the elastic band between the finger covers and the wrist strap. Instead, there are long pieces of leather extending from each finger cover back to a wrist band. As well as these three types of gloves, there is also the Damascus model in various versions. This glove is quite unlike the moccasin, closed-end, or traditional types. It looks like a leather glove that has been only slightly cut away on the sides. It comes in thin or thick leather versions.

These are some of the archery gloves sold today, but certainly not all of them. There are a number of proprietary gloves made by or for specific companies. There's also the ordinary glove, very much like those used for driving a car, usually made of fine tanned leather. I've had a pair of pigskin gloves for decades that have served me well and are now about finished. I've sewn the fingers closed many times until there's very little material left to stitch up. These are special gloves in that they have extra leather reinforcement sewn in place on the appropriate three fingertips. This glove keeps the hand a bit warmer on a cold day, at the same time offering finger protection. This sort of glove is coming back with the current rush toward traditional archery, and it can be made up using a standard tanned leather glove. A shoemaker or other leather worker can add additional leather to the three fingertips for protection against string burn.

The values of the glove are many. The glove is traditional, and if you will, historical. Not that the tab isn't both of these things if you consider the "bit of leather" in the hands of long-ago archers. However, the glove is associated with many archery greats, while tabs are not. One advantage of the glove is that it's always ready for action, firmly on the hand. Unlike the tab, which you hold in your hand, the glove stays put. It is, after all, strapped in place around the wrist. On the down side, the glove supposedly gives a less smooth release than the tab, because the fingers may pinch together tightly around the nock, which doesn't readily happen with a tab. The theory is correct, but I've never had a problem with glove release, nor do my friends. Admittedly, I've seen newcomers to the glove pinch the nock so hard that the arrow actually bent downward against the riser of the bow, but that habit can be unlearned.

That's a glance at shooting gloves, along with a mention of fingertips and finger stalls. Although there are many types of gloves, their number doesn't come close to the number of different tabs available. Jack of Jack's Traditional Archery considers tabs, in general, "much more practical and accurate" than the shooting glove "because they are simple, cost less and except for speed shooting are more efficient." His Shooter's Tab has no finger separator or spacer. It "works well wet or dry" with a simple toggle tension system that amounts to a draw cord with a locking device. This tab is said to prevent plucking of the string (see chapter 11).

In contrast to the Shooter's Tab from Jack's, the Super Archery Mitt Tab is a complicated design (as studying its folds reveals) that even has an adjustable wrist strap and loops of leather to separate the fingers. The Black Widow Wilson Tab is also starkly different from the basic tab. This one goes back to the late 1950s when the Wilson brothers owned Black Widow Custom Bows. It still comes in readily identifiable red and black, and can be chosen in smooth leather or with a calf hair covering. There are several tabs that have similar shapes, although made by different companies. These are somewhat

This Saunders tab is yet another model of this "simple" finger protector. The securing ring is integral to the body of the tab and it can be used as shown here or built up with extra padding.

standardized in form and usually have finger separators, unlike the Shooter's Tab or Wilson Tab.

The Marshall Tab is noted for being quite thin. This die-cut tab is considered correct for light-draw bows, but in fact is appreciated by any archer who wants to feel the string while still getting some finger protection. Because the Marshall is a flat piece of leather without a finger separator, it can be worn on either hand, unlike tabs with finger separators, which come in right- or left-handed models. The Pinch Free Tab deserves mention. A standard tab design, it always has a finger spacer, generally made of plastic. Finally, there are various types of leathers used in tabs that set them apart. Kangaroo leather is considered to last a lifetime, for example, while cordovan is thought to be the finest leather in the world by some archers. Others still like "everyday leathers of the type found in old oil-treated logging boots," to quote Jack's Traditional Archery; they're considered "consistent shot after shot."

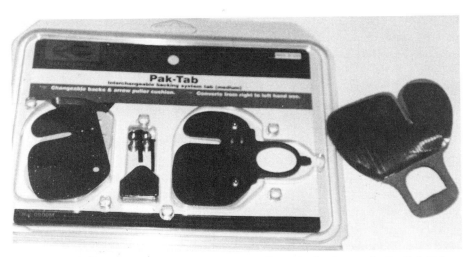

Proof that the modern tab is offered in many different styles is seen in the Pak-Tab from Saunders, which is a modular approach to finger protection. The archer can mix and match parts to suit himself. On the right is a tab made of special space age material for an extra-slick surface.

Along with leather tabs come synthetic types that do a wonderful job. They don't readily take a groove and they're so slick that getting an arrow away is nothing but clean and swift. At the moment the best known of these synthetic tabs is the Fab Tab from Saunders Archery. It comes in many different styles, including a versatile model Fab Tab with interchangeable parts. If there is anything slicker than the synthetic material in the Fab Tab, I don't know of it. Of course, the traditional archer who prefers old-time materials and appearance will probably shy away from synthetic tabs; they remain excellent all the same.

Whereas the glove is loved for its close fit to the hand, the tab is versatile because it is cool to wear no matter how warm it is outdoors, and at the same time, it is warmer than a shooting glove. How? It can be worn right over a regular glove, as long as the glove is not too thick. The tab is noted for providing a clean release. It doesn't bind the string unless badly grooved. Once gotten used to, it doesn't feel like a lump in the hand, and it can be turned to the outside until the archer is ready to nock an arrow. In this position, it simply rests against the back of the hand; then it's turned around for use. It only takes seconds to put it into shooting position.

Some archers feel that the standard shooting glove takes a groove rather easily. Is this a problem? Not for the glove-using shooters I know, unless the groove is very deep. One of my archery associates has a glove he bought as a young bowman. He's now in his fifties and he's shooting the same glove. It is grooved, but my friend likes it that way. If the groove hurts his shooting, I've seen no sign of it. Others feel that the groove catches the string and impedes a clean release. Tabs can groove, too, depending on type of leather and design. The Shooter's Tab is known for not taking a groove, which some archers greatly admire. Whereas one of the finest tabs I've ever used, made of cordovan, can take a groove, and will. If deep, the groove can cause problems, but if it is slight it hurts nothing.

In fact, a slight groove acts as a kind of locator, forcing the archer to take the same hold every time. But a deep groove in a glove or a tab destroys any chance of a good release, since the string has to jump out of the groove for the arrow to get away. A slight groove in tab or glove never hurt my shooting, nor that of any archer I ever shot with. Some archers, though, do have severe problems when this happens. One showed me a cordovan tab, many years old, that was deeply grooved. He proved to me that getting a clean release with that old tab was impossible. The only way to get the string to "let go" of the arrow was to pluck it. The same archer showed me an old glove, made of heavy leather, that was just as badly grooved and caused the same trouble. So let's leave it at this: A modest string groove in tab or glove is not bad, but deep grooves can cause trouble. Remedy? Throw a badly grooved glove or tab away and get a new one.

Much of the work of traditional archery is getting used to a piece of equipment. I had nothing but trouble trying to shoot a tab without a separator to keep the index finger and second finger apart so they couldn't pinch the nock, but I finally got used to a Shooter's Tab, after shooting with it quite a bit. It's a matter of practice. So although no one can tell an archer he should go with a tab or a glove, everyone should try each, not just in passing, but seriously, to see which he prefers, and more importantly, which he uses best. That's the smart way to go with all traditional archery tackle because not one piece of equipment that has withstood the test of time is useless, or it would have perished years ago. Traditional bowshooters are too wise and practical to put up with nonfunctioning equipment.

The buyer's guide in appendix A includes several companies that sell archery gloves and shooting tabs. The following is a more complete description of some gloves and tabs to give the reader an idea of what's available.

The Western Style Finger Tab from Jack Howard Archery Company is made of double-thickness cordovan leather with a hard, slick surface that takes glove powder (talcum) well, making an even slicker surface for a clean release, and it feels cool and light in the hand. The Fab Tab is a product of modern technology that works extremely well for the traditional archer. The Neet PRO-2000 Finger Tab is another absolutely unique tab with what the company calls a "touch and close hook and loop finger adjustment strap" for proper individual fit. This tab can be disassembled for parts replacement. It's made essentially of cordovan leather. The Neet PFT-H Pinch Free Tab, also from Neet products, is an all-time favorite that comes in different styles, including the R. T. F. Rib Tab Facing, which makes less contact with the string for reduced friction. There is also a Super Leather option that is soft for good string feel, but slick for a good release.

The Damascus Shooting Glove from Butler's Traditional Archery Supply proves that when it comes to gloves, variety is the rule. A well-made and interesting glove, it's made of tanned deerskin, with reinforced goat skin tips and Velcro fasteners to ensure a snug fit. The Super Archery Mitt Tab, from the McMahon Traditional Archery Company is unique in design, adjustable in quarter-inch increments to accommodate different finger sizes, but cleverly constructed of a single piece of leather that looks like multiple pieces sewn together without stitches.

The Mega Glove from VISTA is a spin-off of their Comfort Glove. It's made of Cordura backing with optional facings, including what the company calls Mega Hide tips. A wide elastic wristband and flexible knuckle area are other features. The Black Widow Wilson Tab, previously mentioned, has a unique design. Made of a product called Superleather that's virtually weatherproof, it features what the company calls "finger fenders" that protect against string burn. The Wyandotte Glove from Three Rivers Archery Company differs from other gloves with a flexible band between the finger covers and the wristband. It's made of tanned leather with closed fingertips. The Batemen Three Fingers Under from Little Jon's Archery is designed for those who do not use the English-style draw. Instead of two fingers below and one finger above the string, all three fingers are placed underneath the nock. These are just some of the wide variety of gloves and tabs for the traditional archer.

In the same camp with the archery glove and tab is the bracer, or as it is called today, the arm guard. It does similar work of protection and it can also make a huge difference in shooting. It both protects the forearm from abrasions that may be caused by the string slapping that part of the archer's body, and it keeps shirt and coat sleeves out of the way for a clean arrow release. A string striking a sleeve can force the arrow way off course, so far away from hot, straight, and true that it may miss a straw bale entirely at only twenty paces. Because of these two important factors—protection of the bowarm and true flight of the arrow—the simple arm guard becomes one of the more important pieces of tackle in the traditional bowshooter's kit.

It will come as no surprise to the reader to learn that there are dozens of different arm guards for sale these days, not to mention countless personal homemade styles. Most are made of leather, but there are also synthetic models. These are extremely light, and usually skeletonized so they are also cool to wear. They offer full protection for the forearm, while keeping sleeves out of the way of the bowstring. Since its concept and design are so simple, the arm guard won't receive a lot of attention here. Along with different materials, the major differences among bracers are two: length and attachment.

For example, McMahon's offers a thirteen-inch leather arm guard that truly is thirteen inches long, and Neet has a traditional arm guard that is about one-half that length. There are many ways to attach arm guards. One is with crossover adjustable elastic stretch cords, loops that run across the arm, attaching to hooks on the opposite side. There are also arm guards with leather lacing that runs back and forth into hooks to secure the guard to the arm, and arm guards that attach with elastic cord and buttons, such as the No. 204 Latigo Leather Arm Guard from Black Widow, six and three quarter inches long with a single elastic cord that rolls into three elk antler buttons, making it fast getting on or off.

The bowshooter should consider length first, which will be based on two things: his build and what feels right for him. Long-armed shooters may

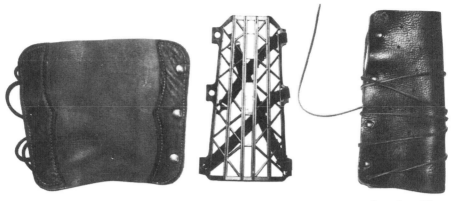

The arm guard on the left secures with stretch straps that loop around eyelets. The middle guard, designed especially for warm weather, is made of space age plastic, with adjustable stretch straps. The arm guard on the right is one-piece leather with eyelets. A long leather thong wraps into the eyelets to hold this guard in place.

have a foot between wrist and elbow. A short arm guard may not work for this person, because it doesn't pinch down enough sleeve. As with gloves and tabs, some archers don't need arm guards at all. Their crooked-elbow stance keeps the string away from arm and clothing perfectly. The next factor to consider is how the arm guard attaches. The lace-up type easily adapts to whatever the shooter is wearing, from short-sleeved shirt to heavy coat. In the first situation, a bare forearm, extra lacing is wrapped around and tied, while the extra lacing is used up getting around the coat sleeve.

That's a look at three basic, yet vital, pieces of archery tackle: shooting gloves, tabs, and arm guards. These accessories must be carefully chosen, because if ill-fitting or annoying, they may actually be a hindrance to shooting instead of a help. On the other hand, good-fitting gloves and tabs can lead to comfortable shooting with protected fingers, plus that all-important clean arrow release, and arm guards can prevent severe string burn on the forearm, while holding garments out of the path of the bowstring. These are obviously important functions that cannot be ignored.

11

Matching Traditional Tackle

Compatibility, the answer to uniform performance, means matching traditional tackle for best results—not only arrows to bows, but tackle to the individual archer as well. Fortunately, longbows and recurves aren't especially finicky; each handles aluminum, carbon, fiberglass, wood, even steel-tube arrows. Further, bowshooters can learn to handle equipment that at first doesn't seem to "fit" them.

Many traditional archers expressed concern a few years ago when a shortage of Port Orford-cedar was reported. Luckily, more cedar was located, cut, and shipped, and having traditional archery's number-one arrow wood readily available again brought smiles to cedar lovers. As this is written, cedar shafts can be readily purchased for $15 a dozen in spines from 30/35 to 75/80 matched to within 20, or even 10 grains of weight. Compressed tapered cedar shafts run just about double that figure. Barreled cedar arrows taper on both ends, rather than at the nock end only. They are also expensive—and excellent.

Many different arrow materials have been used over the years, including aluminum, steel, various fiberglass formulas, graphite, and carbon, to name some. Furthermore, we can expect to see innovative shaft construction appear at any time. For example, Easton's A/C (aluminum/carbon) shaft is a precision aluminum tube combined with carbon fibers. All these shafts work well in stickbows. Today, with the resurgence of traditional archery, bowbenders are once again shooting arrows of various materials, but they always return to wood, because wood arrows and traditional bows blend like cream in coffee. Modern manufacturers know that. That's why we see more wood types used today for arrows than ever before. In the past, a first-class wooden arrow meant cedar but that's not necessarily true today. Cedar is still king, and with good reason, but it doesn't stand alone. Is wood used only because it's traditional? Not entirely. In longbows, for example, where the archer's paradox is

130

prominent, it's difficult to find a better material than wood for warping around the riser of the longbow, then springing back on track to the target.

Today's traditional archer owes it to himself to look at shafts made of different woods, but he may not find one that he likes better than the ever-popular, but not always easy-to-find, cedar. It may still be, overall, the best arrow wood on the planet. Port Orford-cedar, named for a town on the Oregon coast, the only area where it may be found, is actually more closely related to cypress. Cedar makes a strong, medium-weight arrow that readily matches draw weights in the popular 55- to 65-pound range. Air-dried, cedar "cures" beautifully. I've located arrows in the spring that were lost in winter snow and they were still shootable with a new set of feathers. If a cedar shaft warps, it can be straightened by hand. Cedar is wonderful wood; it even smells good.

The temporary shortage of cedar prompted a serious look at many other woods by today's traditionalists. After all, not every archer of the ancient world used Port Orford-cedar for his arrow shafts. They were content with what they had on hand in their vicinity or could trade for, as Gabriela Cosgrove, an expert arrowsmith, explains in volume 3 of *The Traditional Bowyer's Bible*: "Throughout history, many types of wood have been employed to make arrows. We use Port Orford White Cedar but are always experimenting with alternatives."

Ramin has long been used by archers, especially when cedar has been hard to find or too expensive. It's basically the hardwood dowelling sold in hardwood stores, a bit on the heavy side and not always straight. (It is not, by the way, Forgewood—sometimes the two are confused. Forgewood is highly compressed cedar, making a strong, heavy shaft.) Ramin arrows are especially good for roving and plinking because they are cheap. Of course, dowelling must be sorted and straightened before becoming arrows. The advantages of Ramin are strength, economy, and weight when more mass is desired. Since Ramin arrows weigh more, spine for spine, than cedar arrows, they may nose-dive out of lighter-draw bows. Those of us who began our archery careers a number of years ago know Ramin shafts well. In the decades before video games and twenty-four-hour TV movie channels, most boys, and some girls, took up the bow as part of their maturation process. Many were made by hand, misshapen little sticks to everyone except the bowmaker himself. Kids got their arrows for four for a buck at the archery shop, and they seemed to break easily. Or a young bowyer made his own darts, sometimes with hardwood (Ramin) dowels. I built mine with reeds I found across from my grandfather's house, and fletched them with chicken feathers. My arrows were no better than my stick-and-string bow. Nevertheless, hits were common, which happens when you work with a tool every day. Reeds, dowels from the hardware store, store-bought cedars—all our arrows were made of wood. Fiberglass and aluminum came later.

Shafts made of woods other than cedar prevailed long ago and are still viable today. The Ice Man, subject of chapter 5, died about 5300 years ago in the Italian Alps. He had a bow made of yew, but the arrows he carried in a quiver were built of laburnum, an Old World tree with dark, hard wood, the seeds yielding a poisonous alkaloid. Douglas fir, red spruce, Chundoo, Sitka spruce, ash, Norway pine, and many birch woods are also arrow worthy. Sometimes two different woods are spliced together into "footed arrows." These beautiful darts, well known in the forties and fifties, are again available. Butler's Traditional Archery Supply offers footed arrows made of compressed parallel cedar shafts with purpleheart spliced into the tip.

Slow growth pine is another arrow wood we should know. Blue Mountain Arrow Shafts, of British Columbia, offers slow growth pine shafts $^{23}/_{64}$ of an inch in diameter. This proud company includes a Certificate of Origin with orders of one hundred shafts or more, indicating confidence in their product. Slow growth pine is also heavier, spine for spine, than cedar—and stronger. These shafts come from pines in the far north that truly do grow slowly, one of the better areas being north central British Columbia. Harsh winters retard maturity, which in turn produces tight growth rings for a denser shaft material. The shafts come bundled together in fifty-packs if ordered by the hundred, and should be kept bundled until the arrow is built to help keep them straight. Some slow growth pine shafts require hand straightening, which is not difficult. Instructions for this process come from Blue Mountain. The strength advantage of slow growth pine is especially appreciated for roving, where arrows can really take a beating.

The slow growth pine arrow, marginally heavier than a cedar one, may cause a looping trajectory in lighter-draw bows. The Blue Mountain slow growth shafts I tested in 65/70 spine averaged about 450 grains, resulting in a finished arrow weight of around 600 grains. Some of these shafts may have a light, waxy coating of pitch. Blue Mountain recommends wiping these shafts clean with a cloth, then allowing the shaft to rest a while. If more pitch shows up, a little paint thinner will dissolve it. Also, pine shafts should be stored for a few days before making arrows so that the wood can adjust to the ambient humidity. Chundoo is another cedar alternative that comes with high marks. It grows at higher elevations, especially in northern British Columbia. It's reported to have higher elasticity than pine, with a smoother final finish. Chundoo is also easy to work and to straighten.

Douglas fir is another tough shaft material, similar to slow growth pine in strength and weight. Allegheny Mountain Arrow Woods offers premium grade Douglas fir priced with cedar. Grain is quite straight in this wood, which makes a sturdy arrow. Fir normally sells for slightly less than cedar, and the ones I tested turned into arrows of medium weight. Larch, a deciduous conifer, is another strong, durable arrow wood. Ash, cherry, and poplar also turn into viable arrows. Ash makes lighter-weight arrows, at least in my experience, than arrows of pine. The wood seems more elastic, too, and quite tough. Some archers consider ash an ideal arrow wood, due to its straight grain and toughness. Cherry, of the rose family, is also a strong wood. The cherry shafts I tested were a bit lighter weight than pine of similar spine. The wood of poplar and aspen, both of the willow family, also turns into a useful arrow.

We can't leave the subject of arrow woods without talking about hickory. I tested barreled hickory shafts from Butler's Traditional Archery Supply and found them to be exceedingly strong, smooth, and straight. Unfortunately, they cost considerably more than the best cedar shafts and they are heavy. Hickory arrows can sink like a stone out of a lighter-draw bow, which is enough to put them down the list when considering good arrow woods. But for close-range shooting, even from lighter-drawing bows, hickory makes a long-lasting roving dart.

Sitka spruce is also a superb arrow wood. In my tests, it proved to be an arrow weighing much like cedar and responding likewise in flight. It's my favorite arrow—after cedar. I appreciate both cedar and spruce for their weight-to-spine ratios. Either arrow at 500 grains shoots great out of most longbows and recurves.

Knowing the characteristics of different arrow woods gives the archer the ability to match them to different bows, shooting conditions—and archers. One of these characteristics is the spine-to-weight ratio. It's not a difficult subject. Heavy-drawing bows mate with stiffer (higher spine) arrows that are

Although wood is certainly the more traditional material for arrows that match up with longbows and recurves, it is certainly not the only viable one.

This riser includes a locator grip, a notch resting just below the shelf of the bow. The web of the hand fits into this notch in the same place every time— hence "locator."

often, but not always, heavy. If an arrow is stiff, it must be heavy, some archers think. That is not true. The latest carbon shafts, for example, may have spine in the 90-pound range, yet weigh less than wood arrows spined for 45-pound bows. In other words, spine and weight do not have a linear relationship. That's an important bit of knowledge for the traditional archer who wants to extend his range by using a lighter arrow in a fairly heavy-drawing bow. Although gauging arrow speed by "eyeballing" is usually not possible, the difference a carbon arrow makes in speed is visibly evident.

A certain amount of spine, or stiffness of an arrow, is vital to correct arrow flight in traditional bows, mainly to resist the archer's paradox, whereby the arrow must bend around the riser of the bow before taking a straight course to the target. At release, inertia works to keep the arrow at rest while the string pushes against it via the nock, fairly collapsing the shaft in the middle. Longbows are generally more prone to the archer's paradox than recurves because they are not usually as center-shot. Not all recurves are fully center-shot, either, nor should they be. Some bowyers have found that recurves shoot best with the riser window cut to leave a sixteenth-inch offset of the shaft. In other words, the string is not lined up perfectly with the tip of the arrow, the front angling off slightly to the left on a right-handed bow. This angle increases out to the end of the arrow so that a mere offset of one-sixteenth inch at the riser puts the point of the arrow several times that far to the left of the bow's center. Longbows generally being even less center- shot than recurves, may offset the shaft from dead center as much as three-sixteenths inch at the riser, which translates to an even greater left-hand offset of the arrow's point for a right-handed bow. This is not "academic stuff." It's an important principle to understand before we can correctly choose an arrow that matches our bow in spine. Fortunately, there is some leeway; a bow will usually handle a *range* of spine.

Arrow weight is obviously important, too. It may seem ideal to go with the lightest-weight arrow possible for the thrill of sending the flyweight dart a long distance. But it's not exactly that simple. At least in theory, an arrow could be so light that the bow would essentially be dry fired. So a very light arrow can be hard on a bow. This is one reason to consider the little grain-weight-per-pound-of-draw formula put out by the AMO (Archery Manufacturers Organization), which tries to standardize the industry as much as feasible. The AMO considers 9 grains of arrow weight to each pound of draw force a good rule.

Using this formula, a 50-pound bow would shoot a 450-grain arrow. Remember that this is a testing standard, not a prescription, used to give archers an idea of comparative bow performance. How fast does a bow shoot? It shoots at such and such velocity with an arrow weighing 9 grains per pound of draw weight. That's how fast. The formula makes for a good comparison from one bow to the next. Even the Gold Tip carbon arrow that shoots so well from one of my recurves comes quite close to matching the formula. Yes, these are normally lightweight arrows; however, mine are weighted slightly to bring their mass up a bit.

So much for spine and arrow weight, except for one other important point: Wood weight may vary within a species as much as between species, meaning two cedar arrows of 55/60 spine may not weigh the same. An arrow spine chart, such as one from Easton Technical Products (see appendix A) is a good start. Charts aren't perfect, because bows differ in what they "like," as do archers. A friend of mine who is an excellent archer shoots arrows spined twenty pounds greater than the draw weight of his bow. I prefer the middle ground in arrow weight. My bows, with me shooting, "like" arrows spined close to draw weight. Hickory arrows, for example, although beautifully straight and strong, are too heavy for my bows, whereas cedars, Sitka spruce, some carbons, various aluminums, and some other arrows fly "just right."

Now, how about a matchup of fletching to the shaft. No fletching forgives like a feather; it sweeps over the shelves and strike plates of our longbows and recurves without throwing the arrow off track. They're so

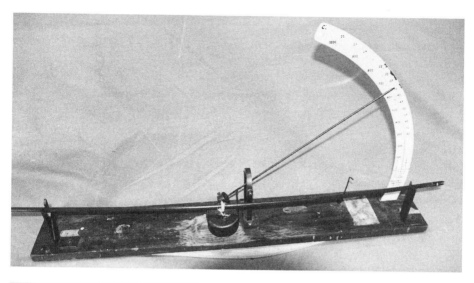

Although this is an old spine tester, it proved to work perfectly by using a specific weight to apply pressure to the arrow shaft, deflecting it a certain degree.

forgiving that the cock feather can be turned in against the riser and the dart still flies true, as easily proved on the range. Also, because of their amazing structure, feathers return to shape if they get ruffled. The vane, also known as the web, is composed of barbs interlocked with barbules, which interlock with barbicels. When they come unattached, these can be connected up again by running the fingers along the vane. Feathers are also tough and light-weight, plus they continue to guide arrows even when tattered. Using

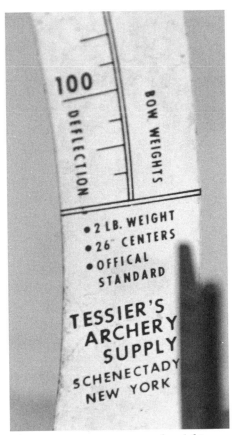

This tester uses a two-pound weight, with the shaft supported on twenty-six-inch centers as a standard.

feathers for fletching is an ancient practice. The Ice Man used three parallel-mounted feathers on his arrows. Certain African tribes used feathers. Native American archers certainly did, the Plains Indian often having but two on his arrows. Ishi, the Yahi Indian who taught Dr. Saxton Pope about archery, preferred three feathers secured by sinew. They were generally taken from eagles, hawks, turkey vultures, and flickers. Japanese and Chinese arrows could be dressed with fine feathers from fish hawks. Roger Ascham (1515–68), author of a work on archery called *Toxophilus*, believed that "there is no feather but only of a goose that hath all commodities in it." Pheasants, peacocks, swans, blue herons, and many sea birds also donated plumage to the archer's cause, but today the white turkey feather dominates.

In medieval England, the king's fletchers sometimes worked twenty-four-hour shifts, whereas bowyers were not allowed to work after dark, lest they prepare a faulty bow. Records reveal a 1369 royal command ordering 850,000 arrows delivered to the Tower of London arsenal, incorporating 2,550,000 feathers! In 1418, the English government demanded 1,190,000 grey goose feathers—and got them.

Feathers remain popular today, not only turkey, but goose as well. They're still with us not for the sake of tradition, but because they stabilize arrows magnificently. They do it in two ways: by drag and rotation. When mounted in parallel in the shaft, feathers promote drag, whereas, feathers mounted helically or straight offset promote arrow rotation, and rotation promotes stable arrow flight. Straight offset mounting means the feather itself is not twisted, but is attached at an angle to the shaft, whereas helical fletching is twisted.

Helical mounting is most popular because of its great stabilizing ability, and the slight resulting loss in arrow speed due to drag is not of practical concern. Straight, or parallel, fletching works on some arrows shot from some bows, but is not always reliable and is seldom seen today. The majority of my own arrows wear straight offset feathers, which means no helical twist in the feather itself, but feather cocked at the same angle, either left or right, to match the right or left wing. (As we know, arrow flight does not hinge on a right-handed archer shooting right-wing feathers, or vice versa.)

Varying the number of feathers on the shaft alters total square inches of surface area. Increased feather surface means more air drag and can also provide greater arrow rotation because of an increased area for the atmosphere to affect. For example, three five-inch tapered shield-style feathers ½-inch high at the back yield *roughly* three and three quarter square inches of surface area. Four tapered shield-style (most four-fletched arrows actually use parabolics) feathers one-half-inch high at the back yield *roughly* four square inches of surface area. The value of a four-fletched arrow supposedly is either-way arrow nocking, because there is no cock feather. But a three-fletched arrow can be shot with the cock feather against the strike plate without harming flight. So the only practical difference between the two lies in more feather surface area for the four-fletched arrow.

For whatever reason, I don't require tall feathers for my arrows to fly straight from my bows. An archer friend of mine not only prefers a radical helical twist to his feathers, but he also likes them large. Why are there so many different feather shapes and sizes? For individual matchup. In his book

Feather matchup is crucial to proper arrow flight. Here are a few feathers from Trueflight. The parabolics, on the left, vary in length from two and one-half to five and one-half inches, which means a vast difference in air drag.

Toxophilus, Ascham listed many of the shapes popular in his day: triangular, square-shorn, round, swine-backed, and saddle-backed. Two of the most common feather shapes over recent years have been shield and parabolic. A shield-shaped feather has a squarish back end; a parabolic is rounded on the back. Both work perfectly well. The parabolic may be a little quieter than the shield, but I've never been able to prove it. Parabolics in low profile suit me fine; however, I have arrows bearing shield and other-style feathers mainly for the sake of appearance.

Appearance is important, no matter how little it has to do with performance. The Pope and Young cut is chosen by some archers because of its stylish looks. On the other hand, specific feather height and length do alter arrow flight. Obviously, the higher feather produces more drag, which may be important to the flight of a particular arrow from a specific bow shot by a given archer. The banana feather was created for those who want the arrow to get on track fast. In other words, this high-profile feather offers more drag than smaller ones, which whips the arrow onto a straight path soon after it leaves the bow. This is especially important when shooting at ten or twenty yards, or even closer.

The larger feather also slows the arrow faster than a smaller one, again because of drag. In roving for short-range targets, the large-fletched arrow, especially when fitted with a JUDO point, "stays found" better than an arrow with less drag. Staying found is the whole idea behind flu-flu fletching, where the feather is mounted to give maximum air drag. The middle ground is occupied by standard shields and parabolics, but there are high profiles in both of these shapes, too. The banana or Maxi-Fletch feather takes high profile another step—it's a really big feather. The larger feather not only straightens an arrow out faster at close range, but also tends to control a damaged, ill-mounted, or extra large point, such as a big blunt. The downside of the big fletch is speed loss and noise. Drag increases both of these factors.

In the "old days" we didn't know tuning from tuna, so our arrows were "standards," including feathers—one size and shape fits all. Now there are dozens of different feather sizes and shapes, including proprietaries. Using a Young Feather Burner, an archer can even create his own. The Little Chopper, which die cuts feathers to shape, comes in many styles by popular demand. Trial and error is an ideal way to test feather types, remembering that fletching must match not only the bow and the archer's shooting style, but also the arrow. A heavyweight arrow may require a little more "rear end ballast" than a lighter one. Matching must also include the point. Feather shape and size can be vital in controlling arrows with certain heads.

There are many other factors regarding feathers. Three are: source, natural barred versus artificial barred or solid color, and color variation.

Most of our feathers come from the barnyard white turkey these days, only the strongest wing feathers being good for arrow fletching. Many other birds also yield usable feathers. Eagle feathers worked well in the past; however, it is now against federal law to own these without a special permit. One craftsman, who prided himself in creating authentic Native American bows and arrows, recently paid the price for having eagle feathers in his possession. He lost his precious bows and arrows, his life savings as well, and he may face a jail term. So the source of the feather—the bird that gave it—is important.

It is not a crime, however, to use goose feathers for arrow fletching—or duck, or even crane or raven. Goose feathers are currently sold by a few traditional archery supply houses, usually advertised in traditional archery magazines. Feathers seem to hold a fascination for many anyway. I can't recall ever stepping over one without picking it up, unless it was from a hawk, eagle or other protected species, or one that I simply didn't recognize and wouldn't take a chance touching. I have even used natural barred feathers from wild turkeys (totally legal). White turkey feathers, however, are far and away the most common fletching used in our sport today.

Turkey feathers are dyed various colors, even artificially barred. Natural barred feathers can drain the wallet in no time—I've seen some for a buck each. But are they really better than feathers from white turkeys? Gray-barred feathers are a bit stronger than those from white birds, and they contain a little more natural oil. However, I've constructed test sets of a dozen arrows, six fletched with dyed barred feathers, six with natural gray-barred feathers, and the shooting machine has yet to show a difference between the two in actual performance, including target grouping. Further, recent tests conducted for a company that deals only in feathers concluded with results favoring the white turkey feather for strength. I think we're lucky to have dyed feathers in so many different colors, but does color truly matter? Yes, in three ways.

Color is important because we see in color and appreciate the different hues. We even have favorite colors and those we don't care for so much. It is the color, as well as the texture pattern, of feathers that causes us to bend

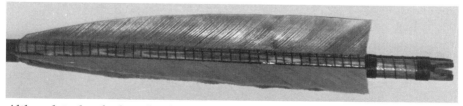

Although turkey feathers dominate, they are not the only good ones for traditional bows. These are gray goose feathers, which have a high oil line, making them less vulnerable to moisture than many other feather types.

down and pick them up on a trail in the woods. Feather color is also important to finding arrows. In the great sport of roving, this is especially true. Drab fletching does nothing to help the archer find his arrow, while bright colors do. Bright-colored fletching can help the archer follow, with his eye, the flight of his arrow. As with a tracer bullet, which leaves a visible trail behind it, certain feather colors are easy to track to the target. Eye-tracking an arrow is useful to finding it later, but just as importantly, it helps the archer see any inconsistencies in the flight of his shaft.

Fishtailing and porpoising, for example, are far easier to detect when the fletching of the arrow can be followed in flight. So what colors are best for this tracer effect? White has to rank near, or at, the top. White fletching shows up vividly as the arrow makes its way to the target.

Fluorescent orange is very noticeable, and so are other bright colors, but all in all, it's hard to beat white. Does this mean that every archer should buy all-white feathers immediately? Most certainly not. I make arrows with colored feathers and will always do so. It's part of the wonderful variety afforded by traditional archery. Also, certain show-off arrows simply look a lot better with specific feather colors, rather than all white.

High-tech bowshooters feel that plastic fletching makes the most accurate arrow, and this point needs to be addressed. Perhaps this is true if one is shooting at dime-sized targets on the archery range, although I know of no one who has proved the point. However, feathers provide terrific accuracy when properly matched to the arrow. A sliced plastic vane can whistle in the air and even fly off the mark, whereas a feather has to be nearly destroyed before it fails to guide an arrow to the target. I've shot arrows with tattered feathers that flew hot, straight, and true to a McKenzie 3-D target or a pine cone on the ground thirty, even forty yards away. Concern about inaccuracy with feather fletching is a waste of time. It simply doesn't happen.

There is also controversy about arrow velocity with feathers versus vanes. I've chronographed downrange with both, and it's tough to get truly error-free results because there are so many extraneous variables that get in the way of accuracy. Sometimes, I have actually ended up testing bows, not fletching, in these little excursions. On the one hand, feathers, being lighter, may have a slight advantage over plastic vanes in arrow speed, but, on the other hand, slicker-surfaced vanes probably have less drag. One thing is true, however, about arrow velocity and fletching. Great big feathers slow an arrow down sooner than little feathers. Even this, however, is moot. After all, the arrow, like Mozart's music, which required only so many notes, no more and no less, demands only so much fletching for stabilization, no more and no less. And if the arrow is slowed down because it needs larger fletching to make it fly right, the trade-off is well worth a few feet per second in speed.

Arrows of bygone years had self-nocks; that is, the nock was cut directly into the butt of the shaft, as seen on this primitive arrow.

It's difficult to get away from arrows when talking matchups in traditional archery, because putting the right arrow with the right bow is paramount to good shooting. Even choosing the nock for the arrow is important. Many nock styles have emerged over the years, from the primitive self-nock, which works just fine by the way, to the latest snap-on. Generally speaking, nocks have different personalities based mainly on throat configuration and string hold. Deep-throated nocks can give the archer a sense of confidence as he draws his bow. They hold the string securely until the bowman turns the arrow loose. Short-throated nocks work extremely well, too, giving the archer the feeling, if not fact, that the arrow leaves the string extra cleanly. I have no preference, finding both deep- and shallow-throated nocks equally responsive.

When it comes to string hold, however, I have my opinions. Lousy nock-to-string matching must be avoided. A nock that hangs onto the string with a death grip can cause poor arrow flight, as can a nock that slops onto the serving loosely. My favorite nock is the soft-snap-on, because when it fits correctly, it holds the string securely without strangling it. But the hard-snap-on nock, unless it holds unmercifully onto the string, is just as good at providing a clean release. It's much wiser, however, to choose a nock based on how it fits the individual string serving, rather than its hard- or soft-snap-on characteristics.

Indexed nocks have a bump on them that the archer can feel so that he does not have to look to see if his arrow is nocked with cock feather out. As far as flight goes, it doesn't matter whether the arrow is nocked cock feather out or in, but it's best to keep it outward for reasons of wear. Many different kinds of indexes are available. Black Widow offered a fine nock that had a

The nock on the left is a mild snap-on. The one of the right is open throat. The one on the left has no indexing bump, and the one on the right has a pronounced raised indexing tab. Which one to choose is a matchup question best answered by the individual archer.

little raised dot on it. Though the dot was small, it was easy to feel. Some nocks, such as the Mercury, wear a fin. There are also many nocks that have no index. The archer glances down, checking the cock feather to see which way to nock the arrow.

Nock color is important mainly to matching the scheme of the arrow, but bright nocks are easier to see when an arrow is hiding in the grass and when it's in flight.

Nocks can be altered a little. A tight nock can be opened up slightly by immersing it in very hot water, then wedging a flat stick (such as from an ice cream bar) into the throat. Similarly, a loose nock can be heated with the ends pinched inward to narrow the throat. Altering the nocks, however, is not an entirely satisfactory process. Ideally, the archer picks the nock that fits his string. That's how a correct match is made.

String fit on the bow is another vital matchup. A longbow strung with a recurve string ended up with a delaminated bow limb because the string's loops were too large and let the limb go. Longbow strings normally have smaller loops than recurve strings. One look at the average longbow string nock compared with the average recurve string nock clearly shows why strings cannot be swapped from one to the other. Using plucking to release the string—flicking the fingers outward wildly—besides being bad shooting form, can cause the string to come off the bow nock if the string is not a proper fit.

The handle, or grip, of the bow should also match the shooter because grips can affect shooting accuracy. Today the high-wrist hold is fashionable.

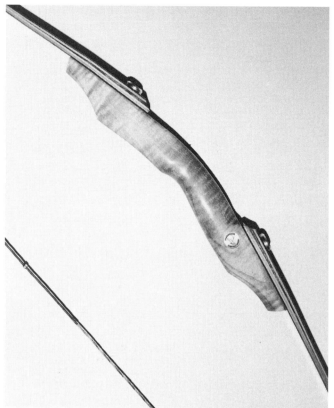

Bows match with archers on a highly individual basis. This Three-Piece Takedown Pronghorn Longbow is light with sleek lines. It has a low-wrist grip with mild indicator indentation.

To get the high-wrist profile, handles were made with deeply cut throats that were common on the target range. In the high-wrist archery hold, fingers point downward, which means the wrist bends downward as well. In the low-wrist hold, the fingers of the grip hand make a somewhat loose fist with the wrist straight. Deeply cut risers, usually associated with recurves, promote high-wrist shooting. Broom handle risers take a low wrist hold, which usually goes with longbows.

However, some of us prefer the low-wrist grip, so our recurves have broom handles, which seem especially suitable for shooting off the shelf, almost as if shooting off the fist. This does not imply that locators are out. They are not. A locator is any sort of indentation in the grip that allows the archer to place his hand in the same spot every time. On a couple of my bows I had the bowyer cut a smooth notch for my pinky. When that little finger falls into the notch, I know I'm gripping the bow right where I held it the last time I shot, and the time before that. The more traditional grip style is the broom handle, but the archer should choose the high-wrist or low-wrist grip style as he does so many other things in this sport, by shooting both types. Or the archer can do both. It's no big trick to shoot both high-wrist and low-wrist holds. The former usually calls for light hand pressure, the latter for a more firm hold.

Another important matching is archer to draw length and draw weight. A "try arrow" is ideal for finding draw length. There are at least two types. One is a full-length (usually 34 inches long) arrow marked off in inches. The bowman draws repeatedly while someone else reads off the distance he draws to. The other type of try arrow is simple to make and it works perfectly. Push a piece of cardboard about two inches square with a hole in its center onto a full-length arrow to about midway along the shaft. Now draw your bow. The cardboard will hit the riser and be pushed forward, stopping when you reach full draw. The distance between the throat of the nock and the piece of cardboard is the correct draw length. The arrow should be finished perhaps an inch longer.

Draw weight is a little more difficult to assess for several reasons. First, archers who work out correctly can actually increase draw weight ability if they want to. Second, just because a strong person can draw a 75-pound bow is no reason to own one of that weight. It all depends on the use of the bow and the desires of the individual. That archer may much prefer a 50-pound model. Third, some bows do draw easier than others of like draw weight. I realize this seems to be an impossibility. After all, two 55-pound bows both draw 55 pounds; how could one draw easier than the other? Stacking, where draw weight increases out of proportion to draw length, is one response to the question.

Also, a bow with limbs mounted behind the riser (inboard limbs), such as the Black Widow featured on the cover of this book, is easier to draw than a bow with limbs mounted in front of the riser (outboard limbs). Consider bow length, too. A 60-inch longbow with 50-pound draw at 28 inches comes to its limit around 28 inches. A 64-inch longbow with the same 50-pound draw at 28 inches can be drawn farther back and is generally smoother drawing, although we have to be careful here because our best 60-inch longbows, such as the Pronghorn, draw very smoothly. So it's not merely a matter of how many pounds a bow draws, but also how that bow comes to full draw that counts. There are two easy ways for an archer to decide on a bow draw weight. The first is by shooting, especially on 3-D targets, or by roving or plinking, where many shots are fired. If fatigue sets in before the shooter is ready to rest up, the bow is probably too heavy.

A second means of testing for draw weight is with the Crick-It. This little device fits on the top bow limb belly and attaches to the string. It's set up for a specific draw length. When the bow is pulled, the Crick-It sounds off, when full draw is just slightly overreached. If the Crick-It is quiet, the archer is not coming to full draw for that bow. He is short drawing. Is that bad? On the one hand, short drawing does not allow the full potential of the bow's draw weight. On the other hand, I've watched some excellent archers short drawing their bows with super accuracy. They may still have an anchor point, but it's often the back of the hand or even the wrist, not the fingertips. All in all, the best method is a full draw, not only to realize the potential of the bow, but also for consistency. Therefore, the traditional archer should select a bow weight he can truly master.

The matching game is not as hard to play as it seems at first. Yes, there are a number of factors involved, but as stated at the beginning of this chapter, traditional bows are adaptable. The archer has to remember that he, too, is adaptable. Some go through literally dozens of bows trying to find the one that shoots perfectly, as well as arrow after arrow, looking for the shaft material that will do it all, when a few alterations in shooting style, plus practice, could correct all problems.

12

Assembling Arrows

Hand-assembling high-grade arrows is one of the pure joys of archery. They can be made to shoot in primitive, traditional, or high-tech bows, but when they're crafted for longbows and recurves, traditional or primitive, they take on a special quality, uplifting the archer's sense of aesthetic appreciation. Arrows for compounds are often unicolored darts that shoot great, but have no life beyond utility, whereas hand-assembled arrows for stickbows are usually beautiful as well as true flying. We're not talking here about making arrows. That's another process altogether, a step beyond what most of us have time for, or interest in. This chapter is about arrow assembly—putting store-bought components together to build high-class arrows that also look wonderful.

The art of arrowcrafting is easy to learn, enjoyable, inexpensive to get into, money-saving, and rewarding. The reward lies in watching a hand-assembled arrow speed true to the target. Making arrows is reminiscent of ammunition reloading. Factory ammo is so excellent these days that it's a wonder anyone bothers putting handmade fodder together, but handloads are personal. So it is with arrows. Factory products are superb, but handmades are unique. Since purists will say we only "put ours together," rather than building each one from scratch, let's take a look at making arrows versus assembling them. Then we'll know the difference. Handmade arrows require a lot of work if they're done correctly. That's the first big difference. Assembling arrows is not difficult or time-consuming. It's a purely enjoyable pastime. The true arrowsmith making his from scratch must first decide on a wood. Dozens of different woods have been used over the centuries to hand make arrows, including Ishi's favorite hazel, Pope and Young's birch, the medieval Englishman's ash, and the Native American's dogwood. Wood selection wasn't a mere matter of whim, nor simply choosing what was readily available. The late Jay Massey, who successfully popularized primitive archery, pointed out that wood decisions were based on long-term experience.

The mounted Mongol or Hun archer, for example, shooting a composite bow made of wood, bone, sinew, and horn glued into a powerful shooting instrument, was the light artillery of his day. Hordes of these soldiers rode dashingly toward the enemy, firing arrows from their powerful bows from a great distance. Their weapons were long-range for their day. A heavy arrow would not have flown as far from their bows. Medium-weight shafts went the distance, and so they chose woods that made medium-heft darts. Roger Ascham, author of a sixteenth-century archery classic, *Toxophilus*, said that ash was the best arrow wood because it was "hevye to geve a great stripe [a hard hit]." From the English archer's 80- to 150-pound bow, this was absolutely the correct missile.

Today's archer has dozens of different woods to choose from for hand making arrows, far too many to comfortably list here. Self-arrows (those made of only one shaft material) can be handmade in several ways. Shafts can be gathered "in the round," meaning living saplings or reeds are cut, trimmed, and dried. They can be made from long rectangular pieces of wood that are turned or trimmed into roundness, and sanded until smooth. Also, split shakes of wood can be planed to a semblance of roundness, then finished by hand. Softer woods can be used if they are "footed," which means adding a harder piece to the forepart of the shaft, an ancient process known to arrowsmiths of prehistoric times. If broken, the forward portion could be replaced, rather than building a whole new arrow.

After the shafts are made, the rest of the truly handcrafted arrow is a matter of stripping feathers and burning or chopping the vane into form. These self-arrows have self-nocks, which are essentially notches cut directly into the butt of the shaft for the string. (For more details on arrowmaking, see volume 1 of *The Traditional Bowyers Bible*, which is listed in appendix C.) Hand making arrows is interesting, but we're going to assemble arrows from ready-made components. This process is far from automatic, and assembling truly high-grade arrows requires a degree of manual skill, a modicum of care, and some definite know-how.

The primitive archery fan builds his arrows of wood. However, traditionalists have a wide range of materials to choose from. Longbows and recurves of the '40s, '50s, and '60s, the subjects of this book, fired arrows made of aluminum, fiberglass, even steel tubing, as well as wood. Today acceptable materials include carbon as well. The latest Gold Tip carbon shafts have come a long way to promote strength with their spiral fiber construction, and can be weighted to make a shaft of reasonable heft. I see no reason to shun them, or other carbons, for traditional arrows. On the other hand, we all have favorites. I lean toward Port Orford-cedar, preferring the compressed, tapered shaft or compressed, barreled shaft over any other.

A number of basic tools are required to put arrows together. These vary in price according to sophistication. High-class implements work either better, faster, or both, over simpler ones, but there are many modestly priced tools that do the job more than adequately. Let the arrowsmith's wallet be his guide. *Pliers* are used to hold points when attaching them to the shaft with hot-melt cement. An *alcohol burner* is ideal for heating points and melting cement. A *tapering tool* is necessary for turning the ends of the shaft to accept points and nocks. The Woodchuck Taper Grinder is an electric machine that cuts tapers fast (for about $135), and a True-Center tool works well by hand.

I use a Martin Archery *hobby saw* to cut wood and carbon shafts to size. An *aluminum tubing cutter*, available from hardware stores, is essential for cutting metal shafts to length; a cutoff saw does the same job, albeit much faster. A cartridge case *deburring tool* is perfect for smoothing the cut ends of aluminum shafts. A reloader's powder/bullet *scale* to weigh the finished product is nice to have. The last two items are sold through many sporting goods shops. Martin's Grain Scale is handier than an ammunition reloader's scale; it's listed in many archery catalogs. A *fletching jig* is indispensable, and a *knife* is helpful.

The arrowsmith may elect to build "painted" or plain sealed darts. The fully finished arrow, stained, dipped, and crested, requires other tools. The gasket lacquer method of finishing arrows is my favorite because it's fast, simple, and does a good job. *Dip tubes* and *dip tanks* are needed, as well as *arrow holders* of some sort. So is a *crester* (cresting machine) with *paint brushes*. The arrow crester should be a good one, for it will provide many hours of quiet pleasure, plus professional results. It's not impossible for a good crester to pay for itself should the traditional archer make finished arrows that he can sell for a profit, usually on consignment through local archery shops. A model that I highly recommend is the Arrow Specialties Arrow Crester (see appendix A). An arrowcrafter may wish to add a *feather trimmer* to make his own feather fletching design. The Young Feather Burner uses a hot metal ribbon that can be bent to various shapes. The Little Chopper is a die-cutter that with one blow chops full-length feathers to shape. It comes in various shapes, including standard shield and parabolic.

Supplies must be chemically friendly. There are specific dyes and lacquers that are compatible with various arrow shaft materials, whereas others are not. Instructions on containers usually relate matchups. Even fletching glues must be right. Fletch-Tite and similar products are correct for Fletch-Tite lacquers, while Duco cement is better for gasket lacquers. Along with fletching cement, other supplies include feathers, shafts, nocks, various points and heads, hot-melt cement for installing points, a little wax, alcohol for the alcohol burner, and a metal conditioner, such as Prep-Rite Surface

Conditioner from Bohning, which cleans the surface of aluminum and carbon shafts for both gluing and finishing (painting/cresting). Follow instructions carefully. Surfaces need to be "squeaky clean" and free of any agent that may prevent bonding, or fletching may fall off and paint may not stick to the arrow. Bohning also offers Instant Fletch-Tite Remover, which is excellent for taking off excess glue, especially from the carbon shaft. Scraping glue free from a carbon shaft can damage it.

Although many shaft materials have been used for arrows, including stainless steel, various woods, fiberglass, carbon, and numerous other products, our interest here is in three: wood, aluminum, and carbon. Though our main arrowmaking interest is wood, the other materials are just as good, and for some applications, better. If a scientist set out to invent a fantastic product to shoot out of stickbows he'd be hard-pressed to beat the right wood. Wood is compressible, tough, can be straightened, is light in weight, can be spined for heavy bows, and is easy to work with. The problem with some woods lies in cost; high-grade cedar shafts are expensive. Aluminum is tough, resilient, comes in numerous precise spines, and is exact in dimensions and weight; it can also be less expensive than wood. I have yet to come across a lousy aluminum shaft. If the tube came from Easton Technical Products, that's all the guarantee I need that it's a topflight product. Carbon shafts are strong, often outlasting either wood or aluminum arrows, also light in weight, forgiving in spine, and highly uniform.

A final factor to consider when choosing between the three popular arrow shaft materials is function. Carbon arrows fly like lightning from longbows and recurves, making them good possibilities for 3-D shooting. Aluminum shoots perfectly well from longbows, too, and is a first-choice material for many recurve shooters who like their precision. Wood seems especially at home in longbows, where it functions ideally in the archer's paradox. I'm also happy with woods in my recurve bows. I ask for no better arrow performance than "homemade" woods provide in my traditional bows, especially Port Orford-cedar and Sitka spruce arrows.

Buying shafts is the easiest thing in the world to do if aluminums or carbons are materials of choice. Any archery shop is loaded with these. Purchasing cedar shafts is also simple, but where I live it means mail-ordering them. Archery shops in my neighborhood are just now realizing that a full 50 percent of my archery club shoots longbows and recurves. There are two broad choices in considering cedar shafts: bulk or custom. Bulk orders of a hundred-count and higher are available from traditional supply houses. I buy shafts by bulk, but never for making top-grade arrows, preferring matched shafts, straight-walled, tapered, or barreled for special arrows. I order my custom shafts from J. K. Chastain, of Wapiti Archery Company (see appendix C).

These are carefully matched and graded, tapered, or parallel cedars. The last batch I ordered—forty-eight shafts—varied only 10 grains in weight, the lightest shaft being 420 grains, the heaviest 430 grains. The custom shaft comes ready to build into an arrow. A lot of preparation makes this so. The custom shaft is expensive, as it must be, considering its quality, but the expense of a high-grade cedar arrow that performs so remarkably from longbows and recurves, is soon forgotten. The shafts I buy from Wapiti Archery are spined within a five-pound range, such as 70/75, and as already noted, matched for weight. They are straight as a ramrod and the nock end comes perfectly and accurately tapered. These arrow shafts are fast approaching $3 each as this is written. That's for compressed tapered cedars that run $^{23}\!/_{64}$ of an inch in diameter with nine inches of taper to $^{5}\!/_{16}$ on the nock end.

Some experts feel that tapered shafts are useful only from a longbow that is not center-shot, because of the archer's paradox. These archers further contend that a parallel shaft is every bit as good as a tapered shaft from a bow that has its sight window cut center-shot. Others feel that the tapered shaft pays off no matter the style of the riser, because the back of the arrow is smaller than the front, allowing a cleaner "getaway" from the arrow rest and strike plate. Furthermore, they like the strength of the compressed aft section of the tapered cedar arrow.

A fine custom shaft, such as those prepared by Cedarsmith and sold through Wapiti Archery, begins as a three-eighths-inch Port Orford-cedar dowel, hand sanded to remove splinters and surface imperfections. The sanded shaft is cleaned and then compressed by a series of dies to achieve a reduced and uniform diameter, resulting in a compressed-wood shaft. Each shaft is then inspected for grain direction and overall appearance. Shafts with erratic grain structure or blemishes are discarded or sold as seconds. Sound, but not perfectly straight, shafts are straightened by hand. Then each arrow shaft is categorized by weight and spine. The end result is a shaft that falls into a weight bracket varying by no more than 10 grains, and a spine range varying by no more than five pounds. The compressed shaft is less susceptible to warpage, and is stronger than an uncompressed cedar shaft. Its surface is smooth and hard, almost slick, resulting in reduced friction in the bow.

Cedar arrows for practice and roving do not have to be made of expensive shafts, of course. Sitka spruce, for example, costs a little less than cedar and makes a wonderful arrow. Bulk cedars also save money and they're fine for daily shooting. Bulks must be processed by the archer. They come ready-matched for weight, and even though they are generally close in spine when ordered by the hundred count, rechecking is wise. This work is easy and a fine arrow results, although not of the grade associated with the compressed custom shaft. Here's how to work with bulk shafts: a hundred arrive. They're matched by spine and weight, but not hand sorted, so variation can be considerable, especially in weight, where a 100-grain difference is not unlikely.

The serious arrowmaker who intends to build hundreds over a long period of time should consider a professional spine tester. Archery supply houses sell these tools, including the Adams Spine Tester, for around $125. A simple way to test for approximate stiffness is with a homemade spine tester consisting of two wood blocks set twenty-four inches apart. A prespined shaft is placed across the blocks, supported by its ends, and a two-pound weight is suspended (as with a string) from its middle. Amount of sag in inches is noted. Each arrow from the bulk set is now placed, one at a time, across the blocks and tested with the two-pound weight for matchup. For heavier-spined arrows a heavier weight may be used, although this is not necessary until arrows for 80-pound to 90-pound-plus bows are considered. In this way, many shafts can be quickly spined. The handmade unit supplies an approximation only. The resulting groupings will not be in perfect five-pound increments, but are good enough for most shooting. Only a little time and effort is required to sort bulk arrows by spine using this method, and by weight using one of the grain scales mentioned above. It's wise to order shafts heavier in spine than the draw weight of the bow to keep lighter-spined samples from the batch of bulk shafts from flying totally wild from that bow. As mentioned before, most stickbows tolerate heavier-than-called-for spine better than a spine that is too weak.

Wooden shafts can be hand straightened to a fine degree of uniformity. Straighten the shafts by sighting down each one and bending it to get the warp out. (Refer to chapter 15 which describes the process more fully.) Shafts can be sorted in seconds by rolling them on a table; crooked ones can be immediately spotted and straightened. I like to heat the shaft by wrapping a clean cloth around it and polishing rapidly, creating friction. Then the warm shaft is bent in the opposite direction from its warpage, producing a counterwarpage. Arrow straighteners, as mentioned in chapter 15, are sold through archery supply houses, and yes, there are models that work with wood shafts. A cedar arrow that is not perfectly straight still shoots well enough for informal use, such as roving and plinking (although I may not go to Archer's Heaven for saying so). Of course, for competition only the straightest arrow is allowable.

Next, check the ends of the shaft to see if one is better than the other, which is usually the case. Cut off the less perfect end, which may even have a little crack in it; the better end becomes the nock taper. In some cases, both ends will be rough in bulk shafts, requiring cutting back each. If an archer shoots a traditional bow instinctively, his arrow will not be overly long, because he uses a compressed style. I have a "reach" from fingertip to fingertip

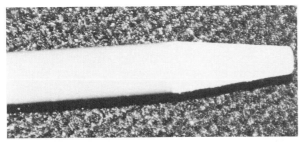

The wooden arrow shaft requires tapers on either end. This is the point taper, which is 5 degrees. Some companies, like Raven, will cut and taper shafts for a customer.

The nock taper is cut at 11.5 degrees. This arrow is tapered from $\frac{23}{64}$ inch down to $\frac{5}{16}$ inch over 9 inches, so it requires a $\frac{5}{16}$-inch nock.

Arrow shafts are squared up by the nock end before marking for stain.

of well over six feet, but a 28-inch arrow is plenty long enough for me. Since raw shafts normally run 32 inches in length, this leaves quite a bit that can be lopped off.

Tapering is accomplished in seconds with a handheld taper tool, which puts points on both tips of the shaft just like sharpening a pencil. Small, inexpensive plastic devices are workable, but larger ones, like the Tru-Center Taper Tool, are not too expensive, and are well worth the investment of about $30. After tapering the nock end of the arrow at 11.5 degrees, visually inspect the taper. It should be clean and free of splinters, chips, or voids. If it's not entirely solid, saw off the taper squarely and cut another. Twist a nock into place to see how it fits, but *do not* glue it on at this time.

If you are going to dye an arrow, now is the time. Tandy leather dye has been working well for me (I especially like the red). Color the bare shaft by dipping a cloth in the dye and stroking it onto the wood. Use plastic gloves since the dye will also color the hands. Set the colored shafts aside to dry for a few moments. The colored shaft can be crown dipped later to give it a second color. Various color combinations can be used to personalize the arrow. I like black and red—red for the body, black for the cap. Where the colors meet, a crest can be applied. The Arrow Specialties cresting tool mentioned above will crest a fletched arrow, or cresting can be done before fletching, after the arrow is sealed, which is the next step. The colored (dyed) arrow requires a lacquer finish to seal it. Gasket lacquer works great and it's applied by dipping. (It's called gasket lacquer because it works with a dip tube that is capped with a rubber gasket with a hole in it.) Dippers expressly for gasket lacquer can be purchased from archery shops or traditional supply houses, such as McMahon's (see appendix A).

After pouring lacquer into the dipper, run the colored shaft through the small hole in the gasket and down into the liquid. Then pull the shaft back up out of the dipper; it will come out almost dry. Set it aside in some sort of arrow holder, such as a couple of suspended clothes pins pinched onto the tip of the shaft. Do a dozen shafts; by the time the twelfth one is treated, the first one will be dry enough to coat again. In buying a dipper, it's important to note that it's for gasket lacquer, so that it will be provided with the correct top having a rubber gasket and hole in its center. Three coatings are enough for utility arrows, nine to twelve for fancy sets.

Fortunately, gasket lacquer is in good supply, as seen here, along with dip tubes.

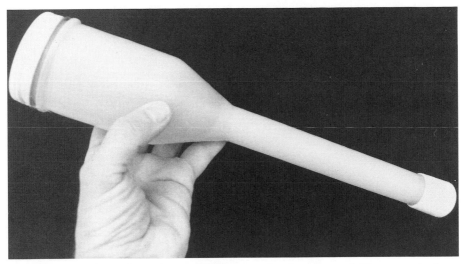

The short dip tube is shown here with lower cap in place as a seal. Upper cap is also screwed on, which retains the gasket.

Sealing the shaft with gasket lacquer requires a smooth stroke; the shaft is run through the gasket down into the dip tube and right back out, all in one continuous motion.

The wooden arrow is made of very few components—basically a shaft, feathers, point, and nock. Shown here is a set of a dozen tapered cedar shafts with appropriate feathers and nocks to assemble a fine set of arrows.

Now it's time to fletch the finished wooden shaft. Fletching aluminum or carbon shafts is the same process as for wood ones. Both require different prep, however, to get them ready for fletching. Instructions come with these shafts, so details are not necessary here, although I may mention some in the following discussion about fletching wood shafts. Suffice it to say that aluminum must be cleaned with a special solvent so that fletching remains bonded after gluing, whereas wood arrows demand only a clean, dry surface. A light touch-up of woods with fine sandpaper is an acceptable practice, but not necessary.

After deciding on a feather, match it to a particular fletching clamp. The Bitzenburger fletcher comes with various clamp options: straight, right helical, and left helical. The straight clamp is used for left-wing or right-wing feathers to mount them offset to the left or right as appropriate. The left-wing helical is for left-wing feathers and the right-wing helical clamp is for right-wing feathers. As for which shoots best, left-wing or right-wing, it makes no difference, as tests prove. Right-handed archers do not have to use right-wing feathers on their arrows, and vice versa. I have stated this several times in the book, because of a widespread, but false, belief to the contrary. The Bitzenburger jig, which is the one I use, has settings for three-fletching or four-fletching. Most of my arrows wear three feathers, mounted with the

The Bitzenburger is considered the Cadillac of jigs. It offers a wide range of adjustments to accommodate different feather angles, along with various clamps, such as straight, left-wing helical, right-wing helical, and so forth.

straight clamp, but pitched offset. Straight fletching, where the feather lies parallel along the shaft with no pitch, is workable, but straight offset or helical are preferable for arrow stabilization.

Twist a nock on the nock taper of the shaft, then place the nock end of the arrow in the throat of the jig. The nock should be pinched on the taper so that it will not revolve, but it is not glued at this time.

The shaft has been dipped and a nock is firmly twisted on the end taper. Set the desired fletching position, say, 120 degrees, whereby three feathers will be unidistant on the shaft. Position the feather properly in the clamp using the index marker. Choose an index line on the clamp that allows a little room in front of the nock for the fingers, but keeps the front of the arrow from contacting the shelf of the bow. I mark one of these with a lead pencil so I won't have a problem remembering where the back end of the feather is supposed to rest in the jig clamp. Consecutive feathers will be positioned at the same scale mark so that when the set of arrows is complete, fletching will be uniform. Place the clamp on the jig now (the clamp on the Bitzenburger is held in place magnetically). Adjust the jig so that the base of the feather fits properly on the arrow shaft. To do this, use an Allen wrench to loosen and turn the two adjusting wheels, which moves the jig clamp, then reset them when the feather base is properly aligned on the arrow shaft.

To get a better view, hold the jig up in the air with the unglued feather clamped in place. It's easy to see from underneath if the base of the feather is making full contact with the shaft, or is off of the shaft at any point. In offsetting a feather using the straight clamp this is especially important because the feather base can be offset so much that it runs off the shaft and hangs in midair. Helicals are less a problem, because the twist is in the feather itself and the base line of the jig clamp rests parallel with the shaft. We're told to align the nock so that the throat runs with the grain of the shaft, but I have found this to be unnecessary. I suspect it's as hangover from self-nock days, when it was important to cut the throat of the nock with the grain so that the nock itself did not break out.

Of course, if the archer wishes to position the nock so that when it's finally glued in place it rests across the shelf of the bow with the grain opposed to the shelf, that's okay. During the archer's paradox, the grain in the shaft will run horizontally. Again, I've not found grain direction to be a provable concern, but watching grain direction does render the most stiffness horizontally.

Before putting glue on the feather, which is clamped tightly in place, scratch the base lightly with a fingernail to rough it up ever so slightly. This provides a good contact surface for the fletching cement. Try to use an extremely thin bead of cement on the base of the feather; no prizes will be won for arrows that have a sloppy glue line. Excess glue is squeezed out of the way when the clamp is set in place on the jig. Since fletching cement dries clear and hard, a *little* extra along the base sides of the feather isn't unsightly, plus this sort of glue joint is strong, the edges of the feather base having a slight glue buildup. One way to ensure a neat glue line is to run a finger along the base edges of the feather after glue has been applied. This picks up excess cement and distributes the glue neatly along the feather base.

Some glues come with a screw-on cap that has a fine tube-nozzle. These are excellent. The glue tube comes sealed and must be punctured to start the flow. I use the tip of a paper clip to puncture a small hole in the seal, then screw the dispenser cap in place. Duco cement comes unsealed. It has a rather large exit hole in the nozzle. Using a pair of needle-nose pliers, squeeze the tip down to make a smaller orifice so glue runs out in a thin line.

The feather remains clamped in place for a full thirty minutes. Of course, the glue dries far faster than this, but the business of arrow assembly is not a race. The feather, especially one in a helical clamp, must also conform to a new shape, so the glue line is given plenty of time to dry. Naturally, the arrowcrafter does not sit there watching the glue dry; he's off doing something else while the feather bonds.

If the jig clamp tends to stick, this means too much glue has been applied to the base of the feather. A little regular bowstring wax applied along the edge of the jig clamp helps to create a barrier between glue and clamp. Don't press

The use of glue requires covering the work surface, especially if it happens to be a kitchen table, where many thousands of arrows are fletched. Since these arrows were dipped with gasket lacquer, Duco cement is used for compatibility.

the feather in the clamp down on the shaft too hard, which will force too much cement out. The clamp should be fully, but lightly, set to rest on the shaft.

After the feather in the jig clamp has been set in place, it's wise to check and see that it remains in place. Sometimes it's necessary to use a sharp-pointed object, such as a pencil or a straight pin, to poke a small section of fletching back in place against the surface of the shaft. Sometimes the very front of the feather may tend to slip free of contact with the shaft, so it's simply, and gently, nudged back in place for full contact. An aid to getting good contact between a tapered shaft and the fletching is to place a toothpick or even a small wooden match in between the shaft and the front cradle of the jig before setting the clamp in place. This lifts the shaft up a little at that point so that it aligns better with the base of the fletching in the clamp.

After thirty minutes, it's time to set another feather in place. Gently release tension on the clamp and lift it away, leaving the feather bonded on the shaft. Rotate the knob on the jig slowly and carefully to align it for its next feather. *Recall that the nock is not glued in place.* Quick turning of the knob may cause the nock to slip in its taper on the shaft, misaligning it badly. If glue sticks to the clamp even though it has been waxed, a little Bohning Instant Fletch-Tite Remover will get rid of it. Excess glue can also be removed, gently, with a flat piece of wood—a knife edge or other sharp instrument could damage the clamp. After the arrow is fully fletched, remove it from the jig. Place a tiny drop of glue on the forward edge of the feather, making a little bead that dries hard. This bead prevents damage to the forward part of the feather, which can take a beating if the arrow passes completely through a target. For arrows going into the field, add an additional dot of glue after the first drop dries and shrinks in place on the forepart of the feather. This will dry rock hard as a protector when the leading end of the fletching takes a beating. Adding a tiny drop at the back part of the feather is less necessary, but doesn't hurt anything.

Now it's time to glue our nock in place. But first, fit the arrow on the string of the bow and rotate it to find where the feathers are best aligned to clear the shelf of the bow. Then glue the nock in place. If the bow is set up to shoot through the gap (as described in chapter 7), gluing the nock after fletching is especially important. Rotate the nock of the arrow into position so that one of the hen feathers aligns with the gap. Then when the arrow flies over the shelf, the hard base quill of the feather passes through the gap.

Before cutting the point taper, cut the shaft to length, taking into consideration the type of head to be installed. Leave the shaft one inch longer than the desired finished length of the arrow, because the point taper is about an inch long. Use the tapering tool to cut a standard taper angle of 5 degrees, which will allow any point with a 5-degree angle to be attached directly to the taper with hot-melt cement. The nock was tapered at 11.5 degrees, incidentally, while the point taper is 5 degrees. If desired, install a wood point adapter at this time. The adapter has a female thread that accepts screw-in points of many different types. It's called Change-A-Point and is sold through archery shops and catalogs.

Heat hot-melt cement with the alcohol burner and smear a dab on the taper of the arrow. Hold the point or adapter (with point screwed in to keep cement out) with pliers and heat it, then rotate it into place on the tip (taper) of the shaft. The heat from point or adapter softens and distributes the hot-melt cement. To ensure a true fit, press the point or adapter against a hard surface for a moment to expel any trapped air from within. If allowed to remain between the point or adapter and the taper on the shaft, a pocket of air can force either off the shaft. Naturally, no point taper is cut onto the aluminum or carbon shaft. Instead, a converta-point insert is installed. When attaching an insert with epoxy to an aluminum or carbon shaft, screw a target point into the insert first to keep the epoxy from running down into the threads of the insert. Even with care, a touch of epoxy may find its way onto the threads of the point and the insert, bonding the two together. A little wax rubbed beforehand on the threads of the target point shank will act as a release agent should the epoxy make contact.

Spinning the arrow after a point is fixed in place is a good way to check alignment. If the arrow wobbles, remove the point with heat and glue it back in place. If this does not fix the problem, a new taper may have to be cut, but use restraint or the arrow will be shorter than its brothers in the set. The wooden point adapter, which is used to take screw-in points, can be difficult to align and may require reheating and coaxing with offset pressure to line it up. Aluminum and carbon shafts are almost assured of alignment, provided the inserts are correctly installed. In making arrows from bulk cedar shafts, there will always be some arrows that aren't perfect. These make fine plinkers.

That's the homemade arrow. The entire process is simple, and if the archer pays attention to the smaller details, it makes the operation fairly foolproof. I make arrows—aluminum and carbon as well as wood—for all my bows because I enjoy this hobby. It's relaxing, restful, satisfying, and fun. I also like the results, with specific arrows handcrafted for specific traditional bows. Handmade arrows also allow a lot of shooting at a modest expense, especially with bulk shafts picked up a hundred at a time. They also allow personalization in color schemes and cresting. There's no mistaking someone else's arrows for yours. These reasons, I think, are sufficient for anyone interested in the stickbow to tool up for arrowcrafting.

Arrow Painting with Gasket Lacquer

1. Mark each arrow shaft with a lead pencil 9 or 10 inches from the tip of the nock taper. This part of the shaft will be the cap dip and will receive lacquer in step 9 below.

2. Wrap masking tape around the shaft above the pencil line (considering the nock end as the top). This protects the 9- or 10-inch area at the nock end from being stained; it will receive the cap dip later.   (continued)

3. Use a rag to rub leather dye into the forepart of the shaft up to the masking tape. *Always wear rubber gloves to protect your hands from the stain.* Tandy's and similar stores sell leather dye. A popular brand is Fiebing's *alcohol-based, not oil-based,* leather dye.

4. Immediately after applying the stain, remove excess dye with a clean dry cloth.

5. Pour clear gasket lacquer into a dip tube to within about 2 inches of the top. Screw the top with the gasket, which has a small hole in its center, into place on the dip tube and secure the tube upright. (Gasket lacquer can be purchased from Butler Traditional Archery Supply; see appendix A.)

(continued)

6. Wipe down the shaft one time with a tack rag before the next step. (Tack rags are sold at building supply or hardware stores.)

7. Dip the forepart of the shaft into the gasket lacquer through the small hole in the rubber gasket. The shaft is dipped only to the middle of the masking tape. Since there is lacquer held in the gasket hole, that hole is used as a marker. The shaft stops when the middle of the masking tape is in the gasket hole.

8. Apply three coats of clear gasket lacquer to the shaft from the forepart up to the middle of the masking tape. Gasket lacquer, applied with the dip tube and gasket, dries so quickly that by the time shaft number twelve is finished,

shaft number one is more than ready to dip again.

9. Remove the masking tape and turn each shaft around and dip three more times fully from the nock end all the way down to the forepart of the shaft. This now puts clear lacquer over the cap dip section of the arrow.

10. Wipe the nock taper clean with a rag to remove excess gasket lacquer. Otherwise, the lacquer will dry and cause a problem with fitting the nock properly later.

11. Now using a shorter dip tube and colored gasket lacquer, apply the cap dip only from the tip of the nock taper forward 9 or 10 inches. Apply a piece of masking tape so that the cap dip will not run onto the body of the shaft. (continued)

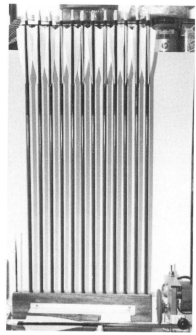

12. Set up the shaft in the crester and apply a large cresting stripe where the colored cap dip and dyed body of the shaft meet. Use gasket lacquer in small containers for this operation. Thin it with acetone to form a runny paint that can be applied in hairline stripes.

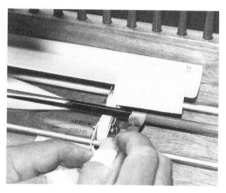

13. Apply the rest of the cresting, such as a band where the feathers will go. Hairline stripes are painted on top of these bands to complete the cresting process. This dresses the arrow up beautifully.

14. Now fletch the shaft with nock and point fixed in place, and the arrow is ready to shoot.

Cleanup

1. Drain the gasket lacquer from the dip tubes back into their containers. Make sure the cans are well sealed, with their lids firmly pressed into placed.

2. Clean the gasket itself with lacquer thinner and wipe it dry with a rag.

3. Clean the dip tubes with lacquer thinner and allow them to drain upside down.

Ordering a Custom Arrow

"For good shooting, everything depends upon the arrow. No matter how true your aim, how staunch your bow, or how steady your hand, you cannot hit regularly without perfect arrows." That's what Maurice Thompson said in his book, *The Witchery of Archery*, written in 1878, and the same holds true today. Although traditional archers assemble their own, there's nothing quite like a set of "store boughts," although some archers are capable of making darts that look like customs.

Arrowmakers are skilled craftsmen, their trade going back centuries. Peoples of many tribes in many places counted on the expertise of arrowsmiths to produce quality projectiles, and the tradition has never died. "Tru-Flite Arrow Company has produced its 100 millionth arrow," John Gooding, vice president of the fifty-seven-year-old firm, reported not long ago. While Tru-Flite is the largest arrowmaker in the world, there are many smaller companies building beautiful custom arrows as well.

Handmade arrows can be expensive. They always were. Maurice Thompson paid $9 a dozen for custom arrows in the late 1800s, at a time when skilled tradesmen might earn $3 or $4 a day. Stoeger's sold a dozen arrows for $16 in 1950; a Winchester 22 single-shot rifle cost the same. Today expect to lay out four or five times that sum for high-quality customs. So what does a traditional archer get for his money when he buys handmade arrows?

Straight grain configuration is one criterion for a top grade professional arrow. Straightness, correct spine, perfect nock alignment on the shaft in relation to the grain, consistency of crest pattern and placement, consistency of striping, point alignment on the shaft, and perfection of fletching, including glue line, are others.

Expert arrowcrafters begin by grading shafts for natural straightness and lateral grain structure; then the shafts are spread out to promote further seasoning (drying), because low moisture content promotes consistency of spine. Seasoned shafts are sorted into groups by spine and weight to create matched sets, and then they're cut to length selecting the best section of the shaft for true nock and point tapers. Tapered shafts are reduced in diameter for 9 inches from $\frac{23}{64}$ inch down to $\frac{5}{16}$ inch, then sanded lightly and hand straightened if necessary. Straightening is done throughout the entire arrowmaking process so that the arrow finishes up straight. The entire prepared shaft is given a lacquer finish and cap dipped for contrasting color if desired by the customer. Straightening occurs once again after the final coat of finish is dry enough to handle the shaft.

Tapers for nock and point are cut next. A final finish before attaching nock or point ensures that the shaft is sealed from end to end. Now the shaft is crested, the hair lines in the crest applied uniformly in width and evenly spaced. Nocks are attached now. Feathers are fixed in place with a smooth glue line. Ideally, only enough glue is used to cement feather to shaft, without excess showing on the sides of the feather base. Also, the back of each feather must be equidistant from the nock end of the arrow. The quill at the forepart of the feather is tapered close to the shaft with a trace of glue where it meets the shaft for a good bond. Finally, the head is set in place with hot-melt cement.

Ordering custom arrows begins with the wood. The customer should never compromise on wood because in the long run it's not the most expensive part of good custom arrows—the labor is. Tapering or barreling are not necessary, but for the modest added cost should be considered. At extra cost, some companies build arrows to the customer's personal specifications. If there's an arrow worksheet, such as the one provided by Allegheny Mountain Arrow Woods, it should be used. It helps the arrowmaker keep all particulars straight, including bow make, draw weight and length, Fast Flight string—yes or no—weight of intended point, desired feather shape and color, stain, tapering option, cap dip color, art-barring, shaft material, and more.

13

Carrying Arrows

Henry VIII was an archer. Imagine him on the range, mutton-fed and pastry-toned, wielding his longbow. Beside him is a "cocker," an Old English word for quiver. This one rests on the ground, securing the king's arrows for rapid and facile shooting. Although bows were coveted in the past, a situation reborn in our times with the return of traditional tackle, it's somewhat of a surprise to learn that quivers were also highly valued. Henry VIII included one in his will, as did other notables of that era. In the book *Archery* by Longman and Walrond, originally written in 1885, the authors cite wills that contained not only bows, but also accessories: "These bequests often include quivers. They are generally of leather; but John Smallwood, in 1578 leaves 'an arrow case of strawe with lock and key,' while one John Billingham, in 1577, includes 'one quiver, one arrow bagge, and a sheafe of arrows.'"

Logically, soon after the ancient archer contrived a bow, he had to have something in which to carry arrows. Back quivers are so ancient that one was found with the Ice Man, the 5300-year-old mummified bowhunter found frozen in the ice of the Italian Alps and honored in chapter 5. The quiver could have preceded the bow for carrying the longer darts associated with the atlatl, although the length of those "arrows" makes even carrying them in a quiver questionable. We'll never know. We do know that arrows were generally carried on the upper part of the back in some sort of quiver, or on the lower back or side in a belt quiver of one type or another, and much later, on the bow itself in a bow quiver. Today, all three methods are still used, along with ground quivers to corral arrows for target shooting on the range. One method is no better than the others; one being favored is mainly by the personal choice of the individual archer.

Through the years, arrow carriers have been made from many different materials. Leather has long been favored for back and belt quivers, some with metal liners to stiffen them, others with heavy leather bottoms. Animal hides were used, sometimes intact with fur. Some archers still make these

Carrying arrows was probably one of the first problems that had to be solved by early archers. By the nineteenth century there were many ways to do the job. This illustration of a nineteenth century archer shows him wearing a sort of belt quiver.

Quivers have been both functional and decorative over the years. The one shown here with two longbows is made of high-grade leather and has an extralarge accessory pouch.

ancient arrow-carrying pouches, which are usually worn on the back. Plastic and other synthetics go into all kinds of quivers these days, especially bow quivers, but into other types as well. Polar fleece is also popular. Brass, painted canvas, carved wood, and other materials are no longer with us commercially. Primitive archery fans build authentic Plains Indian quivers, which hold both bows and arrows, functioning in a particularly unique manner from horseback.

Here is a belt quiver in which only the point ends of the arrows are held in place—ideal for getting an arrow out during a 3-D shoot like this one.

Some Plains Indians had a unique method of carrying bows and arrows. A large sheath contained both, but arrows were also held in a separate leather tube, as shown here. A stick attached to the tube so that when it was pulled, out came the entire bundle of arrows.

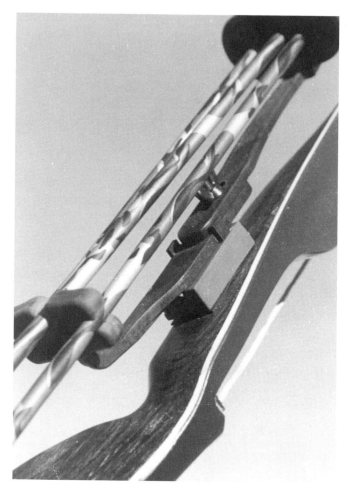

*A Kwikee Kwiver
on the bow.*

Quivers on the open market include dozens of different varieties, from fancy leather models worn on the back or side, to slip-on types that clip onto the riser of the bow (the Kwikee Kwiver). Some of the finest quivers ever made are handbuilt today by custom bowyers or in commercial shops. They may be of tooled leather or snakeskin, adorned with fringe or tassel, personalized with initialing, beaded, or dolled up in some other fashion. Back quivers with accessory pockets remain popular. One way or another, however, arrows have to be carried in something. The variations don't come close to those of the past, but there are still plenty to choose from.

Ancient Egyptians used bows, and so they probably had quivers. Ramses II, circa 1300 B.C., had his bows entombed with him. These were first incorrectly classified as musical instruments, but soon identified as war bows. (I suppose archeologists thought they were played like a string instrument—a

Two back quivers are seen here, one hand-made from a pelt, and a medium-sized commercial model.

single-string "guitar?") Since the use of the chariot was common in the time, some sort of container may have been placed directly into the war chariot it-self. We do know that Egyptians carried arrows on their backs, indicating a back quiver, especially when shooting from a horse. A report on Amenhotep II cited the king entering the northern end of his garden on horseback, riding up to four targets, and "as he rode northward, shooting at them . . . his arrows had come out of the back."

A rendition of an ancient Greek archer from a painting on a vase shows him clearly shooting his bow with a left-hand hold on the riser, while extract-ing arrows from a quiver worn at his waist in front, and held in place by a shoulder strap. A pen and ink drawing by Andrew Goddes (1789–1884) shows a Tarter archer with a large quiver strapped on so that it rests beneath his right arm. An original watercolor of a Circassian chief decked out in

Hand making quivers certainly goes back to ancient times. Here is one made of a pelt.

Asiatic armor with a recurve composite bow resting in his left hand includes a quiver tucked under his right arm so that the arrows' feathers protrude rearward. The ancient Ainu archers of Japan had yet another means of carrying arrows. A clear silk scroll painting by Toyosuke Nagasaki shows an Ainu from Cape Soya, Hokkaido, wearing his bark costume "with the distinctive quiver of arrows slung from his forehead." Further information from E. G. Heath's book *The Grey Goose Wing* states that "quivers used by the Ainu today are carved of wood, with a curious pair of wing-like projections designed to keep the quiver in place when carried on the back."

Samurai bowmen of the twelfth century were known for their bravery and ability. An author of the era said that "Their ponderous bows are *San-nin-bari* (a bow needing three ordinary men to bend it) or *Go-nin-bari* (five-man bow); their quivers, which match their bows, hold fourteen or fifteen bundles of arrows."

Native Americans of the eastern prairies carried arrows differently from their horse-mounted brothers of the western plains. One superb rendition of Chippewa Indians from the great grasslands of Canada shows two braves in a birchbark canoe, a large quiver of arrows on the back of one.

As always, time brings change. In 1885, Longman and Walrond wrote: "The use of the belt and quiver has quite disappeared among men, the arrow-pocket in the coat having superseded it; and when the garment is doffed, the trouser-pocket acts as a substitute. With ladies, however, it is still required, as the quiver is their only means of carrying arrows." Although the back quiver was king for decades, the bow quiver came on fast. Early photos of well-known archer Fred Bear already include the bow quiver. Hip quivers, also called side or belt quivers, have never gone out of vogue, some of the finest ever crafted being made today, such as those from Jack's

The Neet quiver is small . . . neat. It holds a dozen or so regular wood arrows and twice that many narrow carbons.

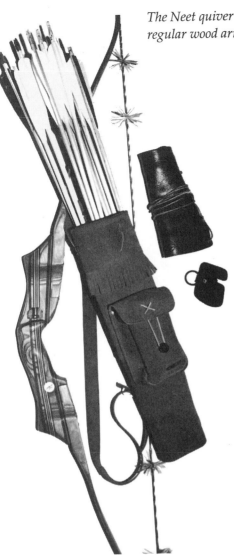

Traditional Archery (see appendix A). These are professionally handcrafted from heavy leather with a fleece covering to protect fletching. By first covering them with a plastic bag, then the fleece top, feathers are highly protected against not only the elements, but also contact with brush, limbs, and other hazards.

Well-known archers like Will and Maurice Thompson, as well as Pope and Young, had cylindrical arrow carriers that looked like they belonged on their backs, but in fact these four carried their quivers at the side. Howard Hill carried arrows in a back quiver. The various types of quivers have their good and bad features, of course. The popular bow quiver is useful because it turns bow and arrow carrier into a single unit with arrows always handy. On one long rove into the mountains a year ago, I had along a Herb Meland Ferret recurve bow with bow quiver attached, giving me seven arrows to plink with. By choosing targets carefully, I returned after three days and two nights with these arrows left unbroken. Obviously, a large back quiver holds far more than seven arrows, and had I not picked targets with soft backstops, I would have been arrowless the first day of my outing.

Smaller back quivers, like Neet's T-BQ-3 also have merit. They're easy to carry, they still hold more arrows than bow quivers, and they keep the bow clean. A lightweight longbow is a feather in the hand but stick a bow quiver on it and that feather can become lopsided and ungainly. Whereas the small back quiver is handy for target practice, as well as for informal "stump shooting," large back quivers hold a lot more arrows—thirty-six plus. Roving, especially, can eat up lots of arrows. The back quiver is easy to use. After a little getting used to, it's second nature to reach back, get your fingers on a nock, pull an arrow out, and load it on the string. You don't have to be blessed with manual dexterity to rapidly load and fire arrows from a back quiver.

Although bow quivers make sense because they attach to the shooting instrument itself, side quivers and back quivers are good because they *don't*. Many times, I've slipped back or side quiver free, setting it on the ground as I fired arrow after arrow at a distant target. It was nice to shoot unencumbered by a quiver and at the same time, have a bow that was equally free of an arrow carrier. Strap-on bow quivers offer a similar advantage, plus they can be used or left home at will. These do as their name suggests: They attach via nylon straps with Velcro closures.

The return to traditional bows brought with it a number of excellent quivers, including high-class models made to work hard, but also look good. The Selway is a perfect example of this class. It comes in several models, including the original slide-on with special limb grippers. Selway offers bolt-on models, too. My own Black Widow bow wears one. Great Northern also makes a quiver built for looks as well as service. Instead of the stitched rawhide hood of the Selway, the Great Northern uses a more rectangular-shaped, smooth leather hood. Both Selway and Great Northern bow quivers are carefully handmade by experts for looks as well as function.

Along with the many different kinds of quivers available, there's another way to carry extra arrows, and that's in a pack. I bought my

Bow quivers can be mounted in various ways. This is a bolt-on model on a custom recurve.

Remington pack not only because it was the right size for my carrying ability in the outback, but also because it has sleeves on either side of the pack. These sleeves hold several extra arrows each, without points attached. Aluminum or carbon arrows with converta-points are ideal for carrying in this pack. It's a simple matter of slipping the points into a container and the container into another pocket of the pack. Then when a camp is reached, arrows are removed from the pack sleeves and points are simply screwed in place. Wooden arrows without points also fit into the sleeves. A little hot-melt cement by the campfire and a pair of pliers are the only things needed to fix points on these arrows.

I like the bolt-on bow quiver because it becomes part of the bow. Although I don't believe that bow quivers promote the appearance or handling characteristics of any bow (some archers like the added weight), I do think they make a great deal of sense. However, aside from unbalancing a bow, their biggest drawback is the lack of protection they give feathers. Bow quivers leave fletching sticking out for brush and limbs to attack, whereas other types of quivers protect fletching, two being the Glenn St. Charles and the Catquiver. Both of these rest in the center of the back with arrows riding point downward and fletching well-protected under hoods.

The St. Charles is a back quiver, and the Catquiver is a combination quiver and daypack that comes in four models. Catquiver I is the smallest of the clan, with a pouch section measuring seven by nine inches, and three inches deep. Catquiver II has the same main compartment, along with two additional compartments, one on each side. Catquiver III has a main bag that runs fifteen by eighteen by eight inches, along with a 14-by-14 inch compartment and six D-rings for tying equipment on. Catquiver IV is the largest, with a big main pocket and three pouches, plus padded hip strap with two more compartments and six D-rings. Catquiver choice obviously depends on how much gear the archer wishes to carry in the field.

Back quivers are as functional as they are traditional, fitting the recurve or longbow image while remaining modern in utility. On one trip, I got forty slender carbon darts into a Jerry Hill back quiver. That's a lot of ammo. Another good point about both back and side quiver is that neither changes bow balance as arrows are fired away, whereas the bow quiver does. A seven-arrow bow quiver carries one-half pound of arrows (at 500 grains each)—all on one side of the bow. Furthermore, as each arrow is loaded on the string and fired away, the bow's weight is reduced by 500 grains until it's a full half-pound lighter. Most archers handle this changing imbalance without a problem, but some are annoyed by what they call lopsidedness when the bow quiver is loaded. They prefer back and hip quivers.

There are so many good quivers these days in all general categories that the archer is bound to find one he likes and that fits his style of bow and shooting. The following are points to consider in quiver selection.

Capacity. Since some back quivers hold thirty-six regular arrows and even more carbons, it's clear that this is the type to go with if carrying a lot of arrows is desirable. There are bow quivers and hip quivers with good capacity, too, but in this category, the back quiver is the clear winner.

Versatility. The back quiver wins again because of its capacity, and the fact that it can be used successfully with any type of bow. In one back quiver, an archer can carry various arrow types, reaching for the one of his choice through feel. The back quiver is the rover's delight, while functioning equally well on the target range or on backyard straw bales. Furthermore, large capacity back quivers make reasonably good storage containers. Arrows are fairly well protected in a back quiver, too, especially in the Glenn St. Charles type or a Catquiver.

Bow balance. Back and hip quivers stay off the bow, so they cannot in any way interfere with its balance. This is ideal from the standpoint not only of shooting, but also of carrying the bow. A loaded bow quiver can so unbalance a bow in the hand that it feels lopsided as it's toted along. Also, as a bow quiver is emptied, bow balance changes. This factor may be of little consequence to some, but annoying to others. As noted, lightweight longbows are no doubt affected more than heavier recurves by the weight of a bow quiver.

Bow accuracy. Attaching a quiver to a bow may reduce accuracy potential, at least in theory. When a bow is "locked up" in a shooting machine, this factor does not seem to play a role. But specific bow shooting styles may be altered by attaching a quiver to a bow. Obviously, the hip quiver and back quiver have no effect here.

Easy access to arrows. Hip quivers put arrows at the bowshooter's fingertips. Practice with a back quiver makes that arrow carrier fast, too. Either is probably a little faster than a bow quiver for repeat shots, which may be of some consequence for a few of the games played at archery clubs and shoots, such as one game that included running a course of targets, shooting at each for a shot before moving on to the next. Since there were ten targets, the bow quiver was not the best choice. Nor were contestants allowed to hand carry arrows for safety reasons. Hip quivers and especially back quivers ruled the day at this little competition in terms of easy access to a lot of arrows.

Storage for accessories. The back quiver wins the show here. All four models of the Catquiver stow away plenty of gear. Standard back quivers wear pouches quite well, too. Bow quivers don't normally have storage capacity, whereas hip quivers may or may not. Some side or hip quivers have decent-sized storage compartments, some as large as those found on back quivers.

Arrow protection. Most quivers are uncovered and leave fletching hanging out in the breeze and unprotected, although the center-worn back quiver protects arrows quite well, actually, without regard to rain or snow. The covered Catquiver and Glenn St. Charles protect fletching against rain, brush, limbs—whatever might scrape against an arrow. Although bow quivers don't cover fletching, the bow can usually be maneuvered out of the way to save arrow damage, except in thick brush where it's impossible to save fletching from the attack of foliage.

Overall quietness. Bowshooting with traditionals is a peaceful game. The archer wants his bow to be quiet, of course, but also his tackle. Loading a pound or so of oatmeal into the standard back quiver will quiet it by keeping the fletching from rubbing together. Bow quivers, which hold each arrow firmly in place, are dead quiet, except in brush, where it's impossible to prevent feathers from rubbing. Hip quivers are quiet, too, especially when the bowman learns exactly how to wear them. All in all, however, the bow quiver receives highest marks for quietness.

Specific bow quietness. This is entirely another matter, not how quiet the quiver itself is, but how quiet the bow shoots with the quiver attached. The bow quiver can cause bow noise during shooting if fletching vibrates or if the quiver itself

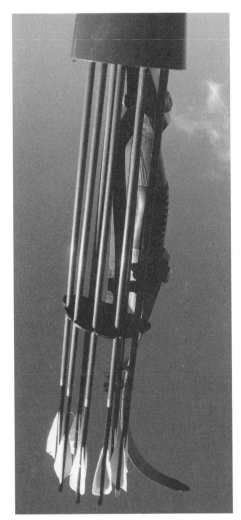

The bow quiver is handy and always ready. It can be noisy if the arrows are not gripped down low enough. If too much arrow is uncontrolled, the feathers may vibrate against each other when the bow is shot.

hums. The first is easy to fix. Arrows are arranged in the bow quiver carefully to prevent fletching from acting like cricket's legs. Also, the shaft gripper should be far enough from the hood so that arrows are held stiffly in
place. When the gripper is too close to the hood, arrows can vibrate because
they stick out so far that they're flexible. All bow quivers should be attached
firmly with the proper bolts, and checked often for tightness. A tight bow
quiver with a properly-distanced shaft gripper will keep the bow quiver
quiet. Also, as part of maintenance, a bow quiver hood should be checked for
cracks. A cracked hood can hum when the bow is fired. Back quivers and hip
quivers can't cause bow noise because they are not on the bow.

Compactness. The bow quiver, because it creates a single unit of bow
and arrow holder, is more compact than back quivers, which are separate
pieces of equipment.

Arrow removal noise. For those who care, the bow quiver is totally
quiet during arrow withdrawals, although side quivers and back quivers
that offer downward arrow removal are also quiet. The top-loaded back
quiver can be a little noisy when its arrows are withdrawn up and out.

Arrow removal motion. For those archers who like the slickest possible
arrow removal, the bow quiver is probably the leader, although the St.
Charles and Catquiver's down and out movement is smooth, as is arrow
withdrawal from the hip quiver.

Comfort. On warm summer days, a heavy leather back quiver can make
an archer sweat. Back quivers can get a little heavy at times, too. Bow quivers are obviously comfortable as far as wearing is concerned, since archers
don't wear them, but they can make a bow bulky and even unbalanced. The
hip quiver is the most comfortable. It's worn out of the way, off of the bow,
but also not really against the body.

Safety. All quivers are safe when used in a safe manner. In the unlikely
event that the archer takes a tumble while wearing a back quiver, the arrows
might fly out and could puncture him. Bow quivers and hip quivers, as well
as St. Charles and Catquivers, lock arrows up securely, making these models
ultrasafe for carrying arrows.

Point protection. Arrow points are safely out of the way in all quivers,
but especially in any type that locks the point in place, such as a bow quiver
with a foam-loaded hood that points actually stick into.

Convenience. If convenience means having a lot of arrows handy, then
the archer will want the standard back quiver. However, under other conditions the bow quiver probably edges out other types for arrow-carrying convenience, because once loaded, it holds shafts out of the archer's way until he
wants one.

Quiver weight. The back quiver is without a doubt the heaviest of the bunch. Whereas the bow quiver doesn't add weight on the body, but can add a half-pound of arrows and another half- pound for the quiver itself. The hip quiver can be ultralight, so it wins this category.

Size. Large-capacity back quivers are not small, although there are back quivers that are quite compact; of course, they don't hold as many arrows as their bigger brothers. Some bow quivers are pretty large, too, adding bulk even though they fit on the bow and not on the archer's body. The side or hip quiver, however, can be quite small.

Aesthetics. Traditional archery is a lot more than shooting arrows out of longbows and recurves. It's a quiet, relaxing hobby that brings with it an appreciation for equipment as art. Although Selway and Great Northern bow quivers are definitely handsome, and the fine hip quiver carries clean lines, the leather back quiver can be made with graceful lines, and also any degree of tasteful embellishment.

Durability and maintenance. All bow quivers can last a lifetime, and all are nearly maintenance free. Leather models should be cleaned up now and then, as well as treated to a little preservative. Rawhide and leather bow quivers deserve a rare cleaning, too, along with a touch of wax. A bow quiver may eventually require a new gripper should it wear to the point that arrows are no longer firmly held in place.

As traditional archery grows in popularity, more tackle will be created for the bowbender. Among those pieces of tackle there will be new and different arrow-carrying devices; however, the old standbys can be counted on to stay around for a good long while, certainly well into the next century. That's because they're time tested, and each model is appreciated by its own following.

14

Roving with the Stickbow

Recreational bowshooting can happen wherever there's a safe place to launch a dart. My own backyard range is one of my prized possessions, even though it amounts to no more than three McKenzie 3-D targets and a half dozen straw bales set up for different kinds of shots. Of course, before setting up a backyard range, a telephone call is required, because it's against the law to shoot bows within most city limits and in some other neighborhoods as well. Local law enforcement authorities must be consulted before an archery range goes in—for legal reasons. Indoor ranges are ideal for wintertime shooting where the weather is bad, which includes, if we're honest, most of the USA during the colder months of the year. Archery clubs all over the United States and Canada have 3-D ranges where members can shoot informally or in competition. Shooting 3-D has become a specialty within the sport of archery, grown to such popularity that there are hundreds of gatherings for bowbenders interested in trying their skill throwing arrows at synthetic animal targets. Some are serious 3-D tournaments. There are even magazines devoted just to this archery game. In a way, 3-D is related to roving, where targets are generally arranged over the larger landscape with a trail leading to each one. Usually, 3-D targets are numbered so a shooter can follow them in sequence. They also have scoring rings for shooting matches.

Walking the 3-D range is fun with any bow, but I think longbows and recurves are more interesting than compounds in this game, especially when the targets are cleverly set up. Recently, I shot a 3-D course designed strictly for stickbows. The archer had to send arrows through "holes" in the brush on some shots, while kneeling for others, sitting, standing—you name it. One target, a 3-D javelina, was placed so that an arrow had to be launched over a bush for a hit. When the game is played with compound bows, it becomes much more precise and businesslike most of the time. There are experts who shoot all over the country on 3-D courses using wheel-and-pulley bows, and

Getting ready for a rove means stringing up the longbow and hitting the trail, this one is a scenic wooded area.

their scores are stupendous, far higher than the vast majority of longbow or recurve fans could hope for. But for fun, the stick and string is hard to beat.

Several companies now make 3-D targets, including Timberline Targets, sold through Martin Archery. They're made of Duraflex foam, a blend of polyurethane resins, for long life and easy arrow removal. Timberline's synthetic animals include elk, caribou, antelope, moose, whitetail and mule deer, black bear, coyote, and javelina. Although there are excellent 3-Ds from various companies, McKenzie Targets of North Carolina remains so well known that often 3-Ds are called "McKenzies," just as facial tissues are known as Kleenex and gelatin is called Jell-O. While the compound bow remains most popular in 3-D tournament shooting, more longbows and recurves are showing up. That's no surprise, since the stickbow is gaining ground every day, everywhere.

There are also paper targets of every description to shoot at. Martin Archery offers a full line of what the company calls "MAT" targets that have animal pictures on them, not only the larger species, but also fox, turkey, raccoon, and squirrel. There are numerous target faces as well, including regulation standards in specific sizes and colors, used in tourneys. For example, there's the No. 4362 Vegas 3-Spot, which is specifically for the Las Vegas Indoor Tournament, as well as the No. 4369 Official NFAA (National Field and

Archery Association) Indoor 40 cm face, both of these from Martin Archery. Along with 3-Ds and tournament targets, there are dozens of other targets to shoot arrows at with stickbows, such as balloons, old golf balls, used-up bowling ball pins, and so forth, limited only by the imagination of the bow-bender. Aerial discs, for example, can be made with just about any material that can take a beating, while old basketballs or soccer balls make good moving targets for blunt-tipped arrows.

McMahon Traditional Archery sells many superb targets that are interesting and well designed. The Saunders Indian Cord Matt, introduced in 1944, remains one of the best. I've owned one for several years and it's still going strong. Morrel Eternity targets with weatherproof polypropylene faces are also excellent. Bracklynn's Dura-Stop is another good target. It's light in weight for portability, water resistant, and it lasts for hundreds of shots. Made of polypropylene, the Stumper kick target is easy to carry along wherever an archer wants to practice. It can be kicked to get it moving for in-motion shots, or whacked with an arrow at a standstill. Or how about a twelve-inch aerial bullseye target? It's black with a yellow center.

In my mind roving is the most enjoyable game of all. It's absolutely informal, although wherever two or more archers gather there's bound to be a

Roving includes good exercise if the rover decides to hike. Here, a large back quiver is used to hold plenty of arrows.

Roving has been called stump-shooting for a reason. Stumps, like this burned-out example, make good targets.

little competition involved. Roving, often called "stump-shooting" in the past, is a fine recreational activity that includes walking or bicycle riding. Walking is undeniably good exercise, and bicycling is one of the best exercises for the heart. Adding bows to bikes is very beneficial to the health. The bike provides leg action, along with arm muscle toning, and longbow or recurve shooting involves taking that deep breath and tugging back on the string. It's a great way to reduce body fat and increase endurance while having a wonderful time.

The best two-wheeler for roving is the mountain bike. Bicycling is so big the world over today that many sophisticated styles have been developed, with five major categories: road or racing bike, touring and sport touring model, track bike, cross bike, also known as city or hybrid bike, and mountain bike. The road or racing bike has drop handlebars, skinny high pressure tires, and narrow seat, usually with ten to sixteen speeds. The rider is stretched out low on this bike. It's great for fast riding, but not much good on a dirt trail. The touring or sport touring bicycle is similar to the racing model, but not as radical. It's more comfortable for on-road use and long distance travel, with better gear-carrying capability. It has wider tires and a more stable ride than the racing bike with a large gear selection, but it's still not best for off-road travel.

Our next bicycle, the track model, is also similar to a racer, but specialized for the track or velodrome. It only has one gear, and guess what? No brakes. Certainly it's not the choice for archery rovers. The cross bike, or hybrid, is a possible choice, however. This bike resembles the mountain model; most people can't tell the difference at a glance, they're that close in style. However, a closer look reveals narrower tires. Also known as a cross-fitness or cross-terrain bike, it combines features of both the road bike and mountain bike. It's at home on the road, along with trail riding where the routes are well-maintained and not terribly rough. It's generally less expensive than the better grades of true mountain bike.

The author's bicycle roving game is catching on with those who enjoy both sports. The mountain bike provides excellent cardiovascular conditioning, plus leg muscle toning, and pulling the bow is good for back and arms.

The mountain bike is the archer's best choice for roving because it's made for rugged use. This doesn't mean that a bowbender has to tear over wilderness terrain like a madman. However, the mountain bike can take it off road, where rovers may wish to go. The mountain bike has "fat" tires (for a bicycle), often with aggressive knobby tread. The seat is, or should be, more cushioned than other bikes, with shock absorbers optional. Some experts like shocks; others say they're not necessary. I like shocks; they seem to make the ride easier on my elbows, especially. A mountain bike may have fifteen to twenty-four speeds, which are changed by levers at the handlebar, or by rotating a section of the handlebar itself, called a gripshift. Its handbrakes are powerful. This bike has a good solid ride, and is stable compared with the

Bows can be shot off of bikes, like this.

Bringing friends along on a rove is the way to add enjoyment to a great sport. On this rove, the author was with his brother, who took the photo, as well as a couple of other friends.

road/racer model, as well as strong-framed, but light in weight. The archer may find himself combining two great sports—mountain biking and roving—for a good physical workout that's far more interesting than walking or running on a treadmill. When I'm biking with a bow, I don't even recognize how far I've gone. I'm having too much fun stopping here and there for shots. When this was written, my new mountain bike was not yet set up, so I was carrying my bow across the handlebars.

For true bicycle roving, several pieces of equipment are needed. The first is a helmet. Since racing on wilderness trails is not the bowshooter's interest, falls, if any, will be at slow speeds. Still, a helmet is essential because landing on a rock, even at a snail's pace, never does the pate any good. A rack on the back of the bicycle is also necessary, not only for carrying gear, but also tools, including a global positioning system (GPS). Garmin offers a special bicycle attachment for that company's excellent GPS units. A fannypack or daypack is useful for lunch and extra water. Water bottles can also be attached to the frame of the bike. There are excellent leakproof pint water containers available from army surplus stores. These olive drab plastic bottles, which are flat and shaped like a hip flask, fit neatly into corners here and there in a daypack or fannypack. Sunscreen is important, too, since the bicycle archer will be out in the sun most of the time unless it's raining, in which case, raingear is vital, and can be carried in the pack until it's needed. Gloves pay off. My hands get a little numb from vibration when I'm on the road with knobby tires, more

A safety device for roving with a mountain bicycle is a hydration pack like this Fieldline model. This model holds one and a half liters of water, fits on the archer's back, and never gets in the way of shooting a bow or riding the bicycle.

so than in the dirt. Special biking gloves are also good for the trail should a rider take a little spill. The fannypack should also contain an extra string, a bow stringer, takedown tools for bows that require them, and any other items necessary to keep an archer going instead of turning for home for minor repairs or replacements. I was roving one day when I realized that I had left my tab somewhere along the way—where I couldn't say. I reached into my fannypack, took out another tab, and kept right on hiking and shooting. Spare arrow rest or strike plate material probably won't be needed, but it takes up very little space and should be taken along. The same goes for an extra string nock and nocking pliers. The archer can easily put his own kit together by gathering up his tackle to see what he needs to keep those arrows flying, from bow to Allen wrench.

Many other goodies and gadgets can be added to the mountain bike, even cycle computers that relate time and distance as well as speed. Some have built-in altimeters, which are good for rovers who combine bicycle trips with bowshooting, going into remote areas on old mining or forest service roads, for example. Combined with topographical maps, altimeters can help pinpoint location. Of course, GPS units do this with ease. Mine is the Garmin GPS II-plus, which is efficient, yet not overly complicated to use. Currently, the United States has over a million miles of trails made specifically for bicycle riding. That's how important this sport has become. Many of those biking trails lead into fairly wild places, where the GPS becomes much more than a convenience. It's also a potential lifesaver, showing a rider the way back to vehicle or camp.

Although bicycles and bows may seem an odd combination, it's a marriage made in archery heaven. One, two, or more archers gather up their bows and arrows for the game, happily hiking or biking over hill and dale in just about any terrain, including farm or ranch. Bows shoot quietly and at short range. They don't frighten Old Betsy into giving curdled milk or Chicken Little into laying soft-boiled eggs. That's why most farmers and ranchers allow rovers access to their property, especially if the bowbenders promise to pick up debris they shoot at, such as beverage cans and other unsightly litter encountered along the way. It's a perfect partnership—bowshooters have a place to rove and farmers and ranchers get rid of junk on their property.

Targets can be whatever is safe to shoot at that won't be injured in the process, including beverage cans, pine cones, bits of wood, paper, or plastic bags, tree stumps, clumps of dirt, holes in the bank of a creek, dead bushes—you name it—but no firing on live trees or other plants. Range is inconsequential. If there's an old cardboard box a hundred yards away and it's safe to shoot at, why not give it a try? Archers of old were shooting at long-range targets in the last century and well before, informally as well as in special games with rules, such as archery golf.

In the book, *Archery*, Colonel Walrond wrote that "Henry VIII himself shot matches with his courtiers for what would now be considerable sums,

Discarded cans make excellent targets, not only for the shooting fun, but also for cleaning up an area—shoot, hit, pack out.

and archery must in his reign have served as an opportunity for a very fair gamble." Anne Boleyn also shot the bow, as proved by records of payment for "Arrowys, shafts, bracer, and shooting glove for my Lady Anne," dated 1530. Flight shooting done in days of old, as well as today, is for distance only, while long-range roving means trying to hit a far-off target. Walrond wrote: "It is an error to suppose that very strong bows are necessary for distances up to 200 yards, although after that there is no doubt that, especially in windy weather, power is essential."

One old game included shooting at "nine and ten score yards." If that meant nine yards plus ten score more, the range was 209 yards. Walrond said that "men have done well at nine and ten score with bows of 45 pounds pull." Turkish flight bows could shoot an arrow almost a thousand yards. They could be light in the hand, but heavy drawing. One of these bows weighed only twelve and one-half ounces, yet it drew 118 pounds. (Harry Drake, incidentally, is the prince of modern-day flight shooting. His wonderful bows have enjoyed great success launching arrows for distance.)

Some of my roves, especially ones that include my brother, who enjoys the game as much as I do, run all day, and others go overnight or for several days. On day outings, we carry either daypacks or fannypacks. There are dozens of commercial kits and packs available, such as Martin Archery's

A little belt kit like this one is useful on the roving trail. The army pouch is perfect for all the small accessories necessary to continued shooting, including that extra string and tab.

small or large belt packs. These, in either size, are ideal for roving, as is the leather belt pouch from Black Widow, which is one and one-half by five and one-half by seven inches. The Brookwood Eagle No. 4410 daypack with padded back and quick-release buckle, includes two water bottles, plus two side pockets, along with a main compartment with top entry (really

Long-range roving can include stay-overs. This superb Bad Lands pack is ideal for hiking into the backcountry for a longer stay. The fold-out compartments hold a lot of gear, and a fannypack is included in the package.

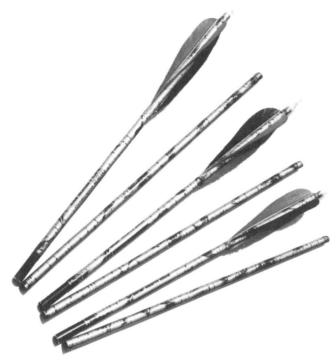

Takedown arrows from Timberline Sports were offered in the past, and will return if insert attachers come back on the market. They're ideal for carrying extra arrows in a pack.

convenient). It's just about perfect for a day on the roving trail. The same company's Navigator Case is ideal for toting the GPS units my brother and I both own and use. For longer treks, a full-sized backpack is, of course, essential. The Split Series backpack from Bad Lands has a 5000-cubic-inch capacity. Its ingenious design employs fold-out compartments that are perfect for stay-over gear, and the top lid turns into a fannypack that holds necessary items for roving all day away from camp, and it's all in one smart unit (both of these companies are listed in appendix A).

Carrying arrows for roving is no problem. On short hikes or bicycle rides, the bow or hip quiver is adequate. For long-range roving, the back quiver is best because it holds a lot of arrows, and it may have an accessory pocket. I use a Neet back quiver, for example, that includes an almost full-length zipper pouch. My pouch holds many archery accessories, along with a couple of half-pint army screw-top water containers. Handicapped bowshooters can also enjoy roving, especially along trails that one of the new motorized wheelchairs or an ATV (all-terrain vehicle) can negotiate, the latter capable of packing all sorts of equipment, from extra arrows to a big lunch.

Bows for roving include anything the archer wants to take along. Longbow, recurve, heavy draw, light draw, it makes no difference. But arrows, and especially arrowheads, are a different story. There are places where shooting good arrows—meaning tapered cedars, Sitka spruce, and other expensive darts—is perfectly acceptable. These are "soft" areas. There's a ranch I know of that includes a huge field of soft earth. I can fire arrows at dried cowpies without the least concern for breakage. Other roving places demand arrows assembled from parallel shafts bought reasonably, if not cheaply, by the hundred, because casualties can be high. Often, an archer just can't resist shooting at tantalizing targets that for the sake of the arrow should be ignored, especially in rocky terrain.

Sometimes I simply cannot talk myself out of a challenging target, especially if it means risking an arrow, which makes even more sport of the shot. A pine cone resting atop a rock is a perfect example. Hit the pine cone, or miss high, and the arrow is safe. Strike a little low and—whack! splinters fly everywhere. The point is equally risked on such shots. So instead of a point, use a spent .38 Special case to tip the shaft. These just happen to slide over an $^{11}\!/_{32}$-inch shaft with a perfect fit. Dribble a bit of hot-melt cement into a heated .38 Special case, press it into place, and the shaft is "tipped" for action. Should this roving arrow get lost . . . oh well. And if it breaks, the empty cartridge case can be carried home with the remains of the shaft for disposal or melted off for reuse. In some areas, standard target points work well for roving, such as along riverbanks or creek beds that aren't lined with rocks. Blunts are good, too, especially on flu-flu arrows. Blunts on regularly-fletched shafts can fly really far, making them hard to find.

The finest roving point I've ever tried is the JUDO, and its story is worth telling. The unlosable JUDO was born in the decades we now call traditional, and developed by archers who were bored with the big gold circle and far more interested in roving, as many of us are today, especially those who have returned to longbows and recurves. Roving archers have found that there are problems with shooting target points, especially extracting them from a rover's target, say, a stump. If the arrow really sinks in, it's next to impossible to free it without a lot of digging with a knife. Target-pointed arrows also suffer high loss. What do a snake and an arrow have in common? Both have the uncanny ability to bury themselves in a quarter inch of duff, never to be seen again.

The quest for the unlosable arrowhead began in the 1940s, when Jack Zwicky and his father, Cliff, were doing a lot of stump shooting. "Cliff and I didn't care to be restricted to shooting at plain targets," Jack said. "We wanted to be out roving all the time. So we'd go out, take a few shots, then spend the rest of our time searching for lost arrows." Jack and Cliff decided to invent a head that could not be lost for themselves as well as for their bowshooting brethren. Although they took to the task believing it might be impossible, Jack says, "With Cliff involved, I knew in my heart that someday we would succeed." It took ten years. The head had to fly at full speed with minimal drag, and snag grass, twigs, brush and other obstacles when it landed. It also had to take a beating from a stump, with limited penetration so the arrow could be withdrawn and put back into service almost immediately. Many prototypes were tried and discarded, their protruding wires bending or breaking. The inventors soon realized that wires had to be tough, and they had to have spring action.

In 1956, "Sales of our regular products went flat," Jack says. "We were practically out of business. So we went roving every day." As Jack and Cliff were pondering what to do, it hit them: they needed a new product. Why not try—one more time—to make the unlosable point? "One day Cliff got the idea of realigning the spring coils so that rather than nesting down into the body of the point, the axis of each coil would lie tangential to the hub of the head with an arm extending outward from each." Torsion springs were made with two arms, one extending outward from the point's body with a hook on the end to snag grass, the other a straight arm projecting through the adjoining coil. It was unique— and patentable. More importantly, it worked. The two Minnesota archers "took to Silver Lake Park where the terrain is rough and filled with knee-high grass. We just couldn't lose an arrow!" Jack reported.

They had to name their new brainchild, but what to call it? Soon enough, the new head all but christened itself, flipping in the air, rolling end over end, then flopping to a stop. "These antics caused us to call our new head the JUDO," Jack recalls. He and Cliff learned that four arms were just right, and their length was ideal. Shorter hooks wouldn't snag grass and longer ones snagged too hard and tended to straighten out. Thicker springs caused unwanted air drag. Thinner springs would quickly take a set. By 1958, the company was tooled up to make JUDO points in earnest. Considerable sums were spent on advertising to let the bowshooting world know that

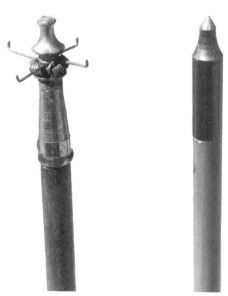

The king of roving points is the JUDO, on the left. Billed as the "unlosable point," it doesn't dive under grass or glance off the ground so readily.

something new and wonderful was available. So a few million were sold in a matter of weeks, right? Wrong. Archers were skeptical. But eventually it caught on, and the JUDO was appreciated for what I called it above—the best roving point of all.

As I roved a mountainous field near Saratoga, Wyoming, one Fourth of July, I realized how important the JUDO was to me and what fine roving it allowed without spending several minutes after each shot looking for an arrow. Not a pine cone was safe. On all my trips, a couple of arrows tipped with JUDO points go along. They provide camp fun and a challenging game to play with friends—taking shots using the instinctive shooting style that is so relaxing. The unlosable JUDO also makes roving a game of arrow shooting, not arrow searching. We're really lucky to have it.

So let's go roving.

15

Bow and Arrow Maintenance

Murphy's law says that if something can go wrong it will, and at the worst possible time. This "rule" is applicable to traditional archery. A bowstring breaks. Does it let go on the backyard range? Of course not. It fails in the middle of a 3-D competition. There are little gremlins that hang around bows and arrows that can't be seen, but they're there. They cause feathers to wilt and bows to delaminate. These nasty gremlins are afraid of only one thing—proper tackle maintenance, the subject of this chapter.

Before taking bows and arrows out of the house, give both a general check over. Consider the "whole bow" as it if were a machine, which in a way it is. Recurves and longbows are simple, with few moving parts, but things can go wrong. The arrow rest or strike plate may cause trouble. Since the arrow rest and strike plate together represent a launching pad for the shaft, if either is loose, an arrow may deflect off the shelf. This is an easy fix. If either becomes unattached, a touch of contact cement sticks them back in place. If worn, replacement is the answer. Stick-on arrow rests and strike plates are found in just about any traditional archery catalog. Caution: Use contact cement only! Other adhesives may severely damage the bow's finish, whereas contact cement holds well, but can also be cleaned off later on.

Takedown bow limbs, with certain exceptions such as Bear's Kodiak, are held in place with limb bolts. Smart maintenance requires that these bolts be tight, but not so as to crack the glass underneath the washer. "Good and snug" is the right way to tighten limb bolts, and the wise archer checks to see that they remain that way throughout shooting. After tightening limb bolts properly, string the bow and examine the limbs for warp. On the recurve bow, the string should lie in the string grooves of the limb. Sometimes a slightly cockeyed limb can be gently hand straightened. Sometimes not. The damage may be permanent. If all is well with the limbs, draw the bow. Creak! Squeak! If these sounds greet the ear, unstring the bow, remove the

Bowyer Arvid Danielson checks out one of his bows. The archer should do this as well, ensuring that his equipment is in good shape.

limbs, and apply a stingy dab of lube between limbs and riser platforms. No more creak or squeak.

Arrows demand a once-over, too, before going afield, and especially after shooting one that obviously took a hard hit, which happens often in roving. Chapter 16 describes what can happen if an arrow breaks in a bow. Test arrows by bending them, but not so far that a good one is snapped. It doesn't take much flexing to spot trouble in the form of a crack. Oftentimes, an arrow with a fracture that cannot be spotted because wood compression hides it breaks when it's bent. That's good. If it breaks from a little hand bending, imagine what could happen when the force of the bow bears down on the same arrow.

Replace frayed bow strings. There is no other solution. Do not attempt to repair them. If one strand of a string breaks, discard the string and install a new one pronto. The string serving, however, can usually be mended. This is called reserving a string, and it is a safe practice as long as the string itself is in top shape. The problem with strings is that they don't always look worn

Checking arrow integrity, including the area right behind the point, is vital to proper maintenance.

out at a casual glance. Sometimes it takes close study to detect the beginning of a frayed string that needs watching.

"You should replace strings after ten thousand shots or once a year, whichever comes first." That's good advice but you should also check for premature wear. Good strings are expensive, but cheap compared with the cost of a bow. The 10,000 shots or one-year plan is fine, but the string must be checked for premature wear, which shows up as fraying, the string looking fuzzy in places. The serving requires a look, too. If the string is in perfect shape, but the serving isn't, the string can be reserved as stated above.

String maintenance means waxing. Wax unites the strands as a unit. It also keeps a string supple, whereas a "dried out" string is prone to decay. Waxing also promotes string integrity, not only by keeping the strands unified, but also by acting as a mild lubricant between the strands to thwart friction. Wax also fights moisture invasion. Waxed strings last for years when stored in zip-lock plastic sandwich bags. Check chapter 9 for more information on strings, but for now remember to "wax and relax."

Bow quivers demand a spot check. Loose quiver bolts promote vibration, which isn't bow threatening, but it can be annoying. As part of the bow spot check, every screw and bolt should be tightened to the same torque as the limb bolts—nice and snug. It's wise to check a bow quiver for cracks, too. Again, it's unlikely that a broken quiver hood will cause damage, but good maintenance includes keeping all equipment in top working order. More important than cracks in a bow quiver are "checks" or dents in the bow itself. This is serious business. Unrepaired nicks can lead to moisture invasion, which could eventually cause limb failure. A good bow maintenance routine is to clean the bow's surface with a damp rag, then a drying cloth, followed by an occasional wax job. Hard paste wax, not spray-ons are best. Wax helps seal minute hairline cracks to prevent moisture from sneaking past the finish.

Nicks are repairable. A touch-up with a polyurethane finish can be helpful in sealing out moisture. Don't overdo it, however; too much may cause runs and unsightly finish buildup. Larger cracks or other damage to the outer "skin" of the bow should be attended to by a bowyer, who will probably sand the crack out, making a sort of valley before adding a sealer. On the same subject, storing a bow in a humid environment is asking for trouble. Likewise wood arrows. Moisture can reduce the integrity of the glues, while wood arrows stored in a high-moisture environment can warp. Store archery tackle in the right place, which always means out of the reach of children. Bows and arrows aren't toys, but children may treat them as such, injuring themselves or the equipment.

If moisture is hard on traditional bows, heat can mean death to them. "This was my father's bow," a friend of mine said sadly. Not only was the upper limb totally delaminated into its original individual pieces, it was also bent in half. The archer knew that heat wasn't good for his bow, but he underestimated how damaging the sun could be. He left his bow strung and resting upright in the passenger seat of his truck while conducting business in town. It wasn't summertime, but the sun's rays warmed the interior of the

Allowing a bow to lie directly in the hot sun is asking for a delamination.

vehicle while beating down directly on the upper limb of the bow. The moral of this story is plain—never leave a bow in direct sunlight, especially inside a vehicle. Even wintertime sun can raise temperatures in a trunk or car to blazing levels. Planning ahead is the key to keeping bows out of the heat.

This does not imply that roving on a summer day will ruin a stickbow, provided the archer doesn't leave the bow on a rock in the direct sun. On a rove, the bow goes into the shade when the archer eats his lunch or takes a rest. Today's laminated bows are less susceptible to heat damage than those of the past. New adhesives make it so. For example, Smooth-On Epoxy EA- 40 withstands temperatures at 212 degrees Fahrenheit without failing. It's not only glued joints that cause trouble. High heat can actually soften the resins in fiberglass, affect the glue holding an arrow nock in place, attack the feathers of the arrow, and damage plastic nocks. Clearly, heat is an enemy of the traditional bow.

Because traditional archers shoot off the shelf these days, feathers are king, but they do require maintenance. Stored in boxes that keep arrows separated, fletching doesn't get squashed, but in transport they can become deformed. One way to bring feathers back into shape is with steam, used sparingly, since too much steam may attack the glue joint between the feather base and the shaft. A little steam from a kettle, however, will soften the vane of the feather so that it can be pressed and coaxed back into shape. Feathers can also be waterproofed as part of a maintenance program—up to a point (see chapter 8 for a complete discussion of waterproofing). Waterproofing includes applying "duck oil" first (such as Sta-Dri Waterproofing Liquid or Dri-Tite), letting the application dry, followed by dusting with a powder that adheres to the feathers to shed water (such as Feather-PRUF Powder or R.M.C. Fletch-Dry Waterproofing Powder). Finally, for insurance a plastic bag is placed over the fletching as the arrows rest in a back or bow quiver. The Catquiver and similar arrow carriers keep fletching out of the weather altogether. Another minor, but valuable, arrow maintenance idea is occasionally touching up the forepart of the feather with a tiny dot of glue as the arrow ages. This part of the feather takes a beating as the shaft passes through brush or a roving target. A dot of glue where front of feather meets shaft helps it withstand the blow.

Arrows can also be straightened as part of the maintenance program. This applies to wood and aluminum. Carbon, graphite, fiberglass, and similar shafts don't bend. If they fail, it's due to breakage. Wood arrows can be straightened by hand. Rub a cloth briskly over the shaft to warm it up. To determine the direction of the warp, sight down the arrow, holding one end close under the eye. Then bend the shaft by hand in the opposing direction. It's amazing how straight a wooden arrow can be made with this simple method. There are also devices used to put a wooden shaft back to true, such as a hook arrow straightener, which is a solid brass tool that works as its name implies, as a hook that curves over the shaft (any size) to force it straight. To use it, the arrow is placed point downward on a hard surface. The hook is slipped over the shaft, and the archer glides the hook firmly over the bent area to straighten it.

Another tool, Straight'n Arrow, works for wood and aluminum shafts, any size. Entirely different from the hook tool, it uses a wedge system to work a bent or warped arrow back into straightness. The Hand-Held Arrow Straightener applies opposing force to take a bend out of an aluminum shaft, and the Arizona arrow straightener is a sophisticated device that includes a jeweled mechanism measuring aluminum shaft tolerances to .0005 inches. Expensive, yes, but this tool earns its keep in the long run for those who shoot a lot of aluminum arrows. The four tools cited above are all available from McMahons (see appendix A). Another fine tool, this one from Three Rivers Archery, is the Shaft Tamer. It straightens $5/16$-, $11/32$-, and $23/64$-inch wood shafts using a compression method. "You see stubborn kinks and bends simply disappear," Three Rivers promises. "This tool really works."

That speaks to bent or warped arrows, but what about broken shafts? I recommend throwing any broken shaft away immediately. My own woods are tossed into the fireplace if they show the least crack, let alone a break. Even though there are wonderful carpenter glues at hardware stores these days, some so good that a successive break in a chunk of wood may occur near the glue line, but seldom right on it, wood arrows do not mend well and should be discarded for safety reasons. However, a broken nock is a different story. Nocks can be replaced. On some carbons, the job is somewhat troublesome because the nock has a stem that runs down into the shaft. The stem can be difficult to work free, but it will come out. Aluminum arrows are a cinch. The damaged nock is broken free (gently) with pliers, or heated first with an alcohol burner and twisted off. An impaired nock on a wooden arrow can be shaved off and replaced. Heating first in hot water, can help loosen the glue. Whereas a broken nock requires a little effort in removal and replacement, a lost point is a cinch. A new one is simply attached with hot-melt cement or screwed into the threaded insert of a carbon, aluminum, or wooden shaft that has a female adapter cemented to the point taper.

Feathers can also be replaced as part of maintenance. Saunders Archery offers an excellent feather stripper. It's made of metal and it glides along the shaft, removing the fletching with a sharp, beveled cutting edge. It's ideal for aluminum arrows, and it works fine for carbons or woods—*with care*. The sharp edge can cut into these shafts. After the old feather is stripped away, the area is sanded smooth. Then the shaft can be refletched using a jig and

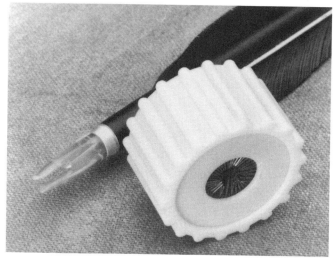

Proper arrow maintenance includes correct preparation in the first place, as in fletching a carbon arrow. This Prep Tool from Golden Key-Futura gets the carbon shaft ready for fletching or refletching by roughing up the surface. Tiny fingers within the tool create scouring edges to do the job without damage to the shaft.

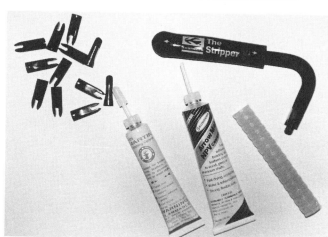

Refletching arrows is part of maintenance. Saunders Stripper works perfectly for removing old fletching from aluminum shafts, and can be used (carefully!) on woods and even carbons.

clamp, just as the arrow was fletched in the first place. It takes considerable feather damage to cause poor arrow flight. Even feathers with missing pieces of vane still fly true. But feathers that are downright ragged may not. And, of course, arrows with feathers that are stripped partly off the shaft, usually from too many pass-throughs on straw bales or other tough materials, won't speed hot and straight to the target, and must be replaced.

An often-asked question pertains to leaving a bow strung. It usually goes something like this: "My father used to have a longbow, and he told me that it had to be unstrung immediately after use, and never put away strung." The speaker's father was right—for self-bows and all older types that may take a set. Left strung, such bows "follow the string," which means the bow does not fully return to its unstrung posture, taking a set instead. A little bit of set isn't serious, but a bow can lose cast if it takes too great a set, the limb tips arched back permanently from pressure applied by the string. Modern composite bows, on the other hand, can remain strung for long periods of time without following the string and taking set. No matter what type of bow it is, however, before it is put into storage, it should be unstrung. This is partly a safety measure, but also a matter of relaxing the tension on the limbs, as well as the string. An unstrung bow left by accident in a hot area may be damaged, but a strung bow is even more in jeopardy by virtue of the pressure applied to the limbs.

What about extreme cold? Self-bows may break under freezing conditions. A friend had a yew bow crack in the cold. As an expert in woods, he was not surprised. "Yew has a reputation for freezing and breaking," he said. "It may be oil in the wood. I'm not sure." I'm not either. As for modern stickbows, however, it depends on how extreme the cold is. There is no doubt that subjecting a bow to well below zero temperatures for a long period of time can change the nature of its wood, glues, even fiberglass laminations. However, "normal" cold, even around freezing, doesn't seem to affect a modern composite bow built of high-grade space age materials. Wintertime is great for hiking logging roads and other quiet areas with bow in hand. If I'm comfortable with reasonable clothing, I have no concern for my bow under these conditions, because materials are carefully dried before a bow is built.

If corewoods or risers held a lot of moisture, the cold would certainly cause trouble, expanding that moisture and cracking the wood, like freezing a full plastic water bottle. Along the same lines, I've yet to discover a problem with rain or snow falling on a modern traditional bow. Unless the bow has breaks in its finish, rain won't bother it. I wouldn't soak a bow in water on purpose, but getting one wet is not a cause for concern. Well-finished wood arrows are moisture resistant, but I wouldn't go so far as to call them waterproof, as other shaft materials, such as aluminum, are. Feathers, as noted above, can be made somewhat water resistant, too, but moistened by snow or rain long enough, they tend to get soggy. So good maintenance calls for keeping wood arrows as dry as possible.

There are special traditional bows built for the wet and cold. Herb Meland of Pronghorn Custom Bows (see appendix B) offers a special "weather bow." It's entirely synthetic. "I don't really like to sell this bow," he says, "because I take pride in the way my regular bows shoot, without hand shock or recoil. My weather bow is smooth-drawing, but it doesn't match the best characteristics of my Pronghorn longbow or Ferret recurve." Nonetheless, this bow proved impervious to the weather, being constructed of phenolics and other modern materials designed to withstand temperature variations and moisture.

The arrow rest and strike plate of any bow should be checked for integrity.

However, it is a specialty bow and should not be ordered in place of a standard longbow or recurve unless it will be used under truly harsh conditions. Then it shines.

Now let's look at leather tackle maintenance: arm guards, tabs, quivers, and riser handles. Leather bow handles seem to last forever with absolutely minimal care. Oils from the bowhand, rather than harming the leather, act to preserve it. A touch of leather garment paste every few weeks is enough to take care of the leather grip for its lifetime. The best way to treat a leather arm guard, tab, or quiver is by cleaning first, which requires nothing more than a damp rag treatment, followed by drying and a good rub with a leather preservative. There are many different types of leather conditioner on the market. As far as I can tell, all are good. Until recently, when a friend cast a wishful eye on it and I gave it away, I owned a leather back quiver that was given to me as a boy by a man who owned it when he was a boy. He had cleaned it periodically, followed by a treatment of leather preserver. I did the same. The quiver was like new when I passed it on to another traditional archer.

Maintenance has to make sense. On the one hand, spending countless hours on tackle is unnecessary. All equipment can be kept in good repair with only minutes of effort. On the other hand, neglecting good bows, arrows, and other tackle is foolhardy. Ideally, the archer should have a place for his stuff, from bows to fletching jigs, with nocks, nock sets, extra strings, string wax, garment paste, leather preservative—everything—ready to get at. That way, maintenance becomes an

No matter the type of bow, including this primitive-backed model, maintenance is required. Bill Wiesner checks out laced-on leather handle here.

Keeping tackle up and out of the way is good maintenance in itself. Ken Wee's stands are used for that purpose, not only for his primitive bows and arrows, but also for his atlatls and darts.

easy habit. If a bowman has to look for maintenance supplies all over the house, he may settle for sticking his tackle in the closet without proper attention. Especially wise is a tackle box filled with good gear. It can be transported to range or field for on-the-spot tackle care. One last thing—insect repellent eats bows. This warning was sounded before, I know, but it bears repeating as part of maintenance. I'm not sure if all insect repellent is damaging, but I do know that in the cases I've seen, repellant had taken the finish right off the bow.

That's a look at taking care of our fine bows, arrows, and other traditional tackle. Maintenance and safety go hand in hand, with reliable performance. Well-kept tackle serves a long time. The modern composite bow, built of up-to-date materials by a professional bowyer, is long lived, especially when given a little TLC from time to time.

16

Transporting and Storing

Longbows and recurves are rugged. So are arrows, especially the latest carbons, such as Gold Tips. Neither breaks easily, but arrows of wood can crack, aluminums will bend, and even carbons may be damaged, and bow limbs, being made of wood, will not withstand a slam in the car door or trunk. Transporters aren't always careful either, be they ground carriers or airlines. So in transit or storage, stickbows and arrows must be secured against damage. Fortunately, there are carrying cases to do the job, not only for bows, but

The past provides an interesting look at how other cultures carried their tackle. This Plains Indian case holds bow, arrows, and, with attached pouch, plenty of other equipment. It was strapped on for horseback riding.

Another unique bow carrier from the past is this case influenced by Plains Indian designs. The bow is well encased, as are the arrows.

for arrows as well. There are also good ways to carry tackle in the field, including pack-in treks and bike roves.

Although the hard case is best for top protection, the bow sock has a few advantages. The sock, a heavy cloth (usually) sheath, mainly safeguards against scratches. It also offers a minor cushion between the bow and a hard place. The soft sock is lightweight, plus it makes a bow only a little bit bigger, which is important when space is a problem. Most soft bow cases are constructed of heavy cloth. Arctic fleece, thick and soft, works especially well. Tanned leather bow socks look good and provide a reasonable buffer between the stick and things that can hurt it.

One step up from the sock, in terms of protection, is the padded sheath or case. The padded case usually wears a zipper, has a handle, and, true to its name, is padded, providing a better barrier against harm than the sock. Although I haven't caught a limb in vehicle door or trunk yet, I probably will some day. Friends have. The archer grabs his bow, lays it down, gives the door or trunk a good push, and crunch! the bowtip is crushed. A padded bow case may save a limb. A bow sock probably won't.

"How do most bows break?" I asked the owner of a large custom bow-making operation.

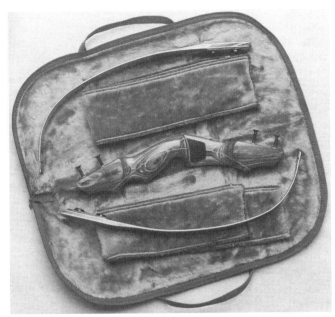

A soft case like this JD model works just fine for most applications. This one holds a takedown recurve bow's limbs and riser.

"Car and truck doors," he replied. "I don't recommend an extra set of limbs for our bows because of breakage from shooting. Doors crack more limbs than shooting. That's why I try to sell a hard case with every bow I make." Soft cases are okay, but you'd have to slam a car door or trunk lid with gorilla strength to break a bow inside a hard case. Today there are dozens of different hard case designs. One type has a cylindrical-shaped frame of PVC pipe, covered with a stout fabric, such as Cordura. Soft cloth makes a compartmentalized interior. These cases are available for both take-down and one-piece bows. They're extremely strong and quite compact. Handles make carrying easy, and some have built-in tie-downs so the bow case can be loaded on a packsaddle or backpack. Some PVC models have sufficient room to slip a few arrows in as well as a bow. Larger PVC hard cases can carry two or more bows, especially longbows.

Some hard cases are made entirely of plastic, others of wood and plastic. There are metal hard cases, too. Cases may be padded outside as well as inside. Some have foam interiors with cutouts for limbs, riser, and accessories. Or the cutout may match a specific one-piece bow. Most hard cases hinge open, forming two sections. One is for the bow and accessories; the other is for a few arrows. Hard cases for arrows make just as much sense as hard cases for bows. There are a number of different styles and sizes to choose from, some cylindrical, others rectangular. They all work great in preventing arrows from bending or breaking.

Choice hinges on personal preference and application. A larger hard case that takes the bow and a set of arrows means an archer can pick up and have everything he needs for shooting all in one hand, not only the bow and matching set of arrows, but also tabs, gloves, tools—everything right down to an extra string and other tackle. If a bow is never put in jeopardy, however, such as on a horse or in an airplane, a soft case may be ideal, remembering that it will never safeguard its contents like a hard model. One thing is certain: It makes no sense to spend a bundle for a fine recurve or longbow, only to risk the investment by leaving a bow case out of the picture. That's false economy.

Let's look first at a typical bow sock, or sleeve, as it's also called. The sock for longbows and recurves from McMahon Traditional Archery Supply is made of Arctic fleece. Noted as soft and durable, the longbow sock measures seventy-two inches by three and a half inches. The end folds over, staying put with tie straps. The recurve sock also is seventy-two inches long, but four and a half inches wide to accommodate the bent-limb bow. There's also a takedown sock available, which is forty-four inches long and seven inches wide. The same company offers a flannel longbow or recurve sock, sort of a fit-all model. McMahon's leather sleeve, at about four times the cost of the flannel sock, is more decorative, with fringe; it's seventy-six inches long and three and three-eighths inches wide. Also available is an interesting longbow case that has an attached quiver, and a strung recurve case made of Cordura that is sixty-six inches long.

Neet has a series of excellent cases. One of the more interesting models is a hard case with a cloth exterior; mine sports a handsome Navajo pattern. That case is thirty-two inches long, ten inches wide, and three and a half inches deep. A thick foam pad in the bottom half of the case has tie straps that hold the takedown bow in place, handle and limb, and the upper section has arrow inserts for over a dozen shafts. Along with bow and arrows, the case is large enough for several accessories, including bow square, nocking pliers, extra string, tabs, arm guard, and so forth. The case has a full-length zipper, and is designed to take a small lock. Web handles come together with a Velcro fastener, and an attached eight-inch-by-six-inch pocket also fastens with Velcro. My Neet case has survived several backcountry treks, including a long bicycle ride on an abandoned mine road in Arizona, where the case took a fairly good swipe against a boulder and sustained only minor abrasions.

Hoppes has been selling bow cases for some time now. They make one that holds two takedowns, plus thirty-six arrows. They also offer arrow cases. One of the models I especially like is the company's compact arrow case, which is lightweight and strong. Mine holds twenty arrows. It's thirty-six inches long, six inches wide, and two inches deep on both halves. It

Closed, this Neet bow case provides ample protection from normal hazards.

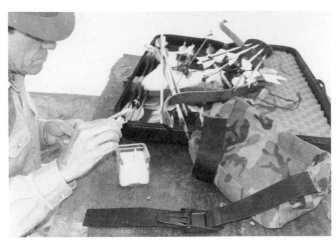

Opened, the Neet hard bow case shows how much it can contain, including a couple takedown bows, plenty of arrows, along with an array of tackle. Inside padding helps protect the contents of the case.

hinges down the center and locks, which is helpful especially for air transport. Another good arrow case is the compact model sold by McMahon, designed to protect fletching from being flattened. It holds eighteen large-diameter wood arrows, and at least twenty-four narrower carbons. Whereas the above arrow cases are for hazardous encounters, the simple arrow box will do when travel conditions aren't so harsh. Made of cardboard, they run about a buck and a half each. They're sized to hold twenty-four darts with arrow dividers to keep the fletching in good shape. They're also ideal for storing finished arrows in the house.

There are also proprietary cases. The one that comes to mind is the large hard case for my Black Widow bow.

Black Widow has a nice line of bow cases, including both soft and padded ones, and even special protective limb sleeves that can be purchased separately. I remain most impressed with the Black Widow custom hard case for my takedown recurve, which accommodates my Black Widow riser, two sets of limbs, bow quiver, extra limb bolts, strings, and more. It has a cedar accessories box built in, and the thirty-nine-by-seventeen-by-seven-inch case also holds a couple dozen arrows. The cutouts hold the parts snugly in place. I'm told that the cutouts are made with a high-speed jet of water. No matter how it's accomplished, one thing is certain: fit is excellent. Black Widow also offers a heavy-duty longbow hard case at sixty-eight inches.

There are other pack-in outfits that work well for backcountry bow-shooting. I have a Remington packframe with pack that works great. It's a narrow affair, but with a capacity large enough for several days worth of gear, if the right things are taken along. The best thing about the Remington pack for bow carrying is its two sleeves, one on each side into which fit aluminum or carbon arrows with their points removed. When I reach my destination, the arrows come out and I screw the points into place. For really long hikes, I use a Bad Lands Split Series pack with swing-out units. The pack is large enough to contain a takedown bow (taken down) plus some arrows. Takedown aluminum arrows were offered by Timberline Sports of Casper, Wyoming. They came apart in the middle and packed into small places.

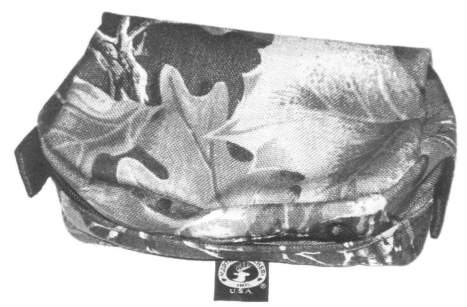

This kit from Martin Archery is designed to hold a large number of articles for the bowshooter.

The open top back quiver doesn't offer quite the same benefits, in that fletching is exposed to the elements. However, it still has the qualities of a case in that very little of the shaft is exposed. Also, like the Ice Man in chapter 5, it's possible to make a hood that fits over the top of the back quiver. So it, too, turns into a sort of protective carrying device for arrows. The bow quiver does not qualify as well as a carrying case, in that its arrows are pretty much exposed to the archer taking a tumble. While it's possible to break off the tops of arrows in a back quiver if a person falls just right, or is that just wrong, the mid-sections of arrows packed in a bow quiver are more likely to take a beating.

Utility is the byword in archery cases for bows and arrows. Even the handsome Black Widow case mentioned above is designed for hard work far more than beauty. But artistic bow cases are available. Kathy Kelly bow cases are definitely in this class with their fine craftsmanship. These cases are generally made of Cordura on the outside, with a lining of Arctic fleece, often in charcoal gray. Custom cases can be built to match certain bows. These are built of whatever the bowyer and archer decide on, including fancy tooled leather. Cases can also be made as art. Dave Carrick, who does professional woodburning on bow limbs, also builds special handmade cases of authentic Indian design. They're useful, of course, but also beautiful. I've often asked Dave to build these cases for sale, but have failed to convince him so far.

Besides storing arrows in standard cardboard boxes, which can be purchased from traditional archery supply houses, storing arrows in racks is another means of keeping them sorted and all in one place. The rack need be nothing more than a piece of wood for a base, two sides, and a top piece with holes in it. The arrows are dropped down through the holes, which are properly spaced to accommodate the size of the fletching, and their points come to rest on the base piece. Ideally, this simple rack is long, perhaps running the full length of a storage room wall, and it holds as many arrows as its length three deep (going deeper than three makes the rack stick out too far from the wall).

Another homemade rack, which normally rests on the floor, can be built with six boards. It's simply an open top box with one of the short ends missing. Imagine an apple crate with one end knocked out. The open end is upward, the bottom end serving as a base. This arrow box consists of a back, two sides, a bottom, and two arrow holders. The two arrow holders are pieces of flat wood that fit like shelves inside the box with holes in them to accept the arrows. Arrows slide through the holds in both arrow holders and come to rest on the base of the unit. Size depends on how many arrows are to be stored.

It's impossible to leave bow and arrow transportation without mentioning how to carry them on a mountain bike. This mode of travel has caught on beyond anyone's wildest imagination. Biking into the outback on one of the million miles of touring trails in the United States is faster than walking, while providing a special brand of exercise. Add the bow and the fun doubles. Toting the bow across the handlebars of the bike is okay for a short outing, but for biking any distance a rack is a good idea. It works great for carrying a takedown bow in its hard case. The case can be loaded on the rack in line with the bike. Some of it may hang out over the edge, but this shouldn't cause a problem. In open terrain, the case can go across the rack, since it won't get hung up on trees or bushes. This is the best way to carry the bow on a long ride. When the destination is reached, the bow is put together, strung, and it's ready to shoot arrows, which are packed inside of the same case, if it's so designed, or in their own hard protector.

Although not the most exciting subject in archery, cases that protect and store bows and arrows are necessary, especially when the traditional bow can cost several hundred dollars, with some arrows running several dollars each.

Bow Safety

Arguably the most important topic in our traditional archery book, safety with longbows and recurves is essential to the enjoyment of the sport. Bow-shooting is statistically safer than crossing the street, but bad things can happen to good traditionalists who are just trying to enjoy themselves. Here are a few rules that will help avoid such problems.

It's against the law to shoot bows in some areas, and for good reason, as this story illustrate. A friend of mine simply couldn't wait for the weekend to

The basic rule of archer location is met by ensuring that nonshooters remain well off to the side or in back of the person letting the arrows go, as shown here on this 3-D range.

shoot at the local archery range, and the indoor range was between owners. So one fine summer afternoon after work, he rested a target against his fence and fired away with his recurve. An arrow careened off the side of the target, speeding away at an angle that sent it right over his fence and into the neighbor's backyard. Whack! My friend heard the arrow hit. His blood ran cold.

He dashed through his gate and into the alley for a quick peek over his neighbor's fence. Oh, no—there was a barbeque going on. Facing the music, he lifted the latch on the gate, strolled through the yard past everyone, reached up just over a doorway, pulled his target-pointed arrow out of the wall, and said, "Excuse me." With that, he walked back to his own property. Nobody said a word about the arrow and he never again turned another dart loose in his backyard. The moral of the story is clear: There are safe places to shoot bows and arrows and other areas that are off limits.

The old push-pull method of stringing a bow has been replaced by the use of a bowstringer, a much safer practice.

Stringing and unstringing the bow is perhaps the most dangerous part of traditional archery. People have been seriously injured in the process. A bowyer I know had always used the push-pull method of stringing his longbows during their manufacturing. And why not? He'd done it hundreds of times without a problem. Then one day the upper limb slipped, slamming back into his face. The tempered lenses of his eyeglasses were cracked by the blow, and the bowmaker ended up with cuts on his face. He was lucky; the tip of the bow had not taken his eye out. Whereas it may not be harmful to the longbow itself to string it "by hand," recurves can be hurt by hand stringing. Another bowyer I know had an interesting experience one day when a delivery person came to his shop door. He turned to retrieve a checkbook from a desk to pay for the goods. When he turned back, he found the delivery person preparing to string a $600 recurve bow—by putting its lower tip on the cement

The bowstringer is the way to go. Both feet are on the cord here, and the head is well back from the upper limb bow tip.

floor and pushing down on the upper limb. "I hope you have a spare $600," the bowyer said just in time. The handsome limb tip was scratched, but he was able to polish it out like new. Any bow can be damaged through improper stringing, but a recurve limb is especially prone to harm by the push-pull, step-through, or any other hand-stringing method, that's because of its wide limb, which can take a permanent set if twisted.

A stringer is the only acceptable method of stringing any traditional bow. I'm sure there will be a number of primitive archery fans who won't agree with that statement, but I'm sticking by it anyway. A stringer is a length of strong, small-diameter rope with pouches on both ends. The pouches fit over the limb tips of the bow. Holding the bow face down in front of him, with pouches in place, the archer stands on the middle of the stringer, preferably with feet spread a foot or so apart to shorten the distance he has to pull. He tugs upward on the handle section, bending the bow enough so that he can slip the loop of the bowstring into the upper bow nock groove. Some stringers have a rubber or other nonscratching pad on one end that rests on top of the upper limb in place of the pouch that slips over the tip of the bow. The advantage to this type of stringer is that the pad doesn't cover the upper bow limb string groove, as a pouch may, so the area is clear for slipping the

This Selway Limb Saver bowstringer has a pad that rests on the limb to hold it in place while the bow is strung. The archer should hold his head away from the bow tip during the stringing operation.

The other end of the Selway Limb Saver bowstringer contains a pouch into which the lower bow tip is securely fit during the string operation.

upper loop of the bowstring in place. The pad-type stringer works particularly well with certain bows because of their upper bow nock and string groove configuration.

Safe use of the stringer is very important. First, the pouch on the lower bow limb tip must be absolutely secure. Since the string is already in place on that end, there is no excuse for a loose or sloppily fitting pouch. Second, the archer should position himself with his head held back and to the side, out of line with the upper bow limb tip. Should the upper stringer pouch, or the pad, slip, the limb will whiz past the bowbender's head instead of making contact with his pate. Third, it's wise to take a stance with both feet not only on the string of the stringer, but spread apart a little to reduce the distance necessary to tug upward on the handle of the bow in order to string it. Doing this will help the archer keep his head out of line with the upper bow limb tip.

The stringer is definitely much safer than step-through or push-pull methods, but it also demands care and wise use. The end pouches of the stringer should be checked carefully and often for damage. If one of these lets go, the result will be a limb tip flying upward, possibly into the archer's face. The pad-type stringer requires the same inspection, along with extra care taken to ensure that the pad does not slip during the bow-stringing process. Finally, it's vital to fit a stringer to a bow. Bow limb tips vary in design, so no single stringer can possibly fit every traditional model. End pouches have to fit well enough to stay put while the limbs are being bent during the stringing process, and at the same time leave room for the upper loop of the bowstring to pass into the upper bow tip grooves. It can be a delicate balance.

There are several basic commonsense bowshooting rules that are violated from time to time with dire consequences. One is sending an arrow in the direction of anyone. This is clearly an extremely dangerous practice. Sometimes it's not entirely obvious that an archer is shooting toward another person. That's because arrows have a way of ricocheting from hard objects. I was once invited to shoot on a beautiful backyard 3-D setup. The well-treed yard, a half-acre in size, had lots of targets arranged interestingly along a pathway. Something bothered me about one of the targets. When I drew down on it, I could see another target off obliquely to my left. Several people were shooting that day, two of them standing ready to throw arrows at the target I could see when I aimed at mine. I told my host about it. He waited until the area was clear, then he deliberately tried to glance an arrow off the side of the McKenzie. His third dart flew left, admittedly not to where the others had been standing, but close enough that the owner of the range moved the target to another position.

Bows can "blow up." This may sound like a gross exaggeration for effect, and it is—somewhat. They don't explode like a pipe bomb. They may simply shatter sending shrapnel-like pieces flying everywhere. I personally know of a blowup that caused an upper limb to break cleanly, instead of shattering. The chunk came down squarely on the archer's forehead above his right eye, cutting a nasty gash. The fellow still wears the scar.

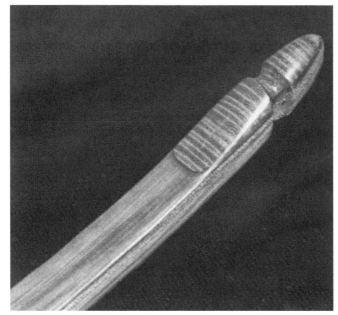

This bow tip overlay is intact and will most likely remain so for the life of the bow. However, checking overlays is never a bad safety plan. If one breaks, the string could also let go.

There are a couple of precautions that can be taken to prevent broken or shattered bows. The best thing to do is to check a bow often for cracks. This does not mean superficial lines in the finish only. Rather, we're looking for true cracks, no matter where they may be.

For my brother's twenty-first birthday some years ago, I bought him a bow. He used it for years, one day noticing a crack in the upper bow limb tip. The moment that fracture was discovered, the bow was put into dry dock, never to be fired again. He was smart. I wasn't that clever. I had a heavy-draw longbow that I much admired and shot almost every day for several years. One day I heard a crack! when I drew it. "Oh, well," I consoled myself, "I don't really know where that came from. The bow's probably all right." It was all right—for a while. A couple months later when I drew it, it broke at the handle into two parts, both of them flying back at me. Luckily, I caught a blow on the right thigh from the lower limb, instead of one on the old beam from the upper limb. I also learned my lesson. The next time I heard a bow give an insignificant creak, I let the draw down and retired the bow.

I don't want to give the impression that the archer has to worry that his bow will break every time he shoots. Today's composites, made with the finest materials the bowbuilding world has to offer, are definitely not prone to breakage. But it pays to be on the lookout all the same for any damage that could cause a problem. The same goes for the arrow. Whereas it makes nothing but good sense to hang a cracked bow on the wall or put it into the

Self-bows like this one can last a very long time; however, they are not made of laminated materials and should be carefully checked for cracks before shooting.

fireplace, this rule goes double for arrows. Serious injury can happen if an arrow breaks in its middle section during shooting. It's possible for the sharp end of the shaft to cut into the bowarm like a knife. Every so often I bend my arrows after shooting them. This doesn't mean folding them to the breaking point—just a nice flexing in the center. If there's an unseen crack, it will usually reveal itself, breaking the arrow right then, rather than during shooting. The arrow caution applies to all materials, not just wood. An aluminum dart can come up with a slight bend after glancing off a rock or other hard object, especially during a rove. This little bend may cause erratic arrow flight, which in itself may not signal danger, but it certainly says something is wrong. If the bend increases, the arrow may break at that point. Carbons may show a sliver or even a crack. At that point, there is only one place for them to go—the junk pile.

A friend of mine has a rule about bowstrings. He believes that a bowstring should not be stressed more than ten thousand times, so he keeps a crude estimate of how many shots he fires on a "normal" day at the archery range or while roving, and when a certain number of days is reached, he pulls the string off his bow and throws it away. I don't hold with this ritual myself, because I can't keep track of the number of times I fire a bow, but I definitely watch for fraying, especially at the loops. When a bowstring looks

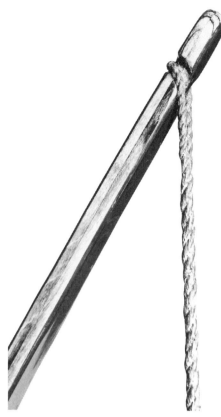

Strings must be carefully checked over for integrity. Also, discarding a string after a certain period of time is never a mistake. Bow tips are also in line for a safety check. They can be damaged from hits and bumps.

worn, or if a strand breaks, the string is immediately taken off the bow and discarded. Strings aren't cheap, but neither are they expensive enough to risk a damaged bow or bowshooter in order to strain a few more shots from a bad one. If a bow is shot routinely, it's not a bad idea to set a limit. A year is long enough to use one string. I own several bows as part of my work, so no single one gets a constant workout. Regardless, I do keep track, and my strings get changed once a year. I think it's wise.

Most of us short draw a bow, but there are some archers who over-draw. One of my best archer friends anchors between his cheekbone and his ear. His form is so pure that there is no reason for him to change anything. He shoots too well to tamper with his style. However, he definitely has to watch out for arrows that are shorter than his draw. It's possible to draw the dart back until the point falls off the shelf. Should the shooter turn loose at this time, the arrow could bury itself in the bowhand. Sound improbable? It is. Sound impossible? It's not. There are archers walking around who can show you the scars. Arrows of proper length are obviously important, but so are arrows that match the bow. Shooting a light-spine arrow in a heavy-draw bow is begging for an accident, which may include a broken shaft's sharp point in the archer's bowarm. Arrows are matched to bows not only for true flight, but also for safety.

A little thing like a broken nock can cause a serious safety problem. A chipped nock may send an arrow dangerously off course. More likely, a broken nock will cause a bow to dry fire, which can, in turn, blow a bow up, causing major damage to equipment, not to mention a chance that the archer will get beaned with a flying bow part. So even as little as it is, the nock can cause a lot of trouble and bears watching. Colorful nocks often tell the archer when they break, which will show up when the arrow is on the way to the target as a chip flying into the air like a tiny signal flare. Checking nocks is the smart thing to do, actually every time an arrow is shot. It only takes a second. Certainly a nock should be inspected every time an arrow suffers a hard landing, such as glancing off a rock.

A whole chapter of the book was devoted to gloves, tabs, and arm guards as comfort devices, but each possesses an element of safety as well. Gloves and tabs can save fingers from minor string abrasions. I suppose they could prevent serious fingertip damage, too, although I can't imagine a sensible person shooting without protection past the abrasion state. The arm guard is even more important to safety. Recall the broken arrow with it's sharp end. If the archer was lucky, it will have struck the arm guard. Most arm guards are not long enough to protect the full forearm of the bow-shooter, but at least they cover part of it. The arm guard also prevents string burn. If not medically serious, string burn is certainly uncomfortable. I've had burns that were far more painful than bee stings.

One afternoon as I attempted to drive past the local archery pro-shop, an attack of curiosity struck and I had to stop for a look. Although I needed another bow like a toothache, the shop was known for taking in some interesting old sticks from time to time. Another fellow must have been struck with the same feeling, for he was sorting through a lineup of recurves and longbows when I walked in. *Twang!* I turned fast, seeing nothing. *Twang!* I turned around again and—nothing. *Twang!* This time I was quicker. The guy was dryfiring every bow he picked up. I politely explained that dryfiring was no good for the bow and potentially dangerous to his physical well-being. He thanked me. "I've never owned a bow," he said, "but I want one and I think it's going to be a recurve." Dryfiring is dangerous. That's the point of this true story.

Many archers shoot old bows because they're interesting. But should oldies be drawn, or put on wall pegs? If the bow has been previously owned by one archer, I suppose shooting it carries only a minor chance of failure. But if a bowbender has no idea of the bow's previous history, caution is the watchword. I shoot old bows—cautiously—watching closely for delamination of limbs, cracks, and other stress problems. When an old bow looks like it's been through too many campaigns, however, safety dictates setting it aside to admire for its history, while shooting it not at all.

One of the most beautiful sights in archery is watching an arrow soar toward the heavens. It's also a dangerous game that should *never* be played. Arrows, even from low-power bows, usually sail up, up, and away until they go out of sight. Then the arrow comes, streaking toward earth with lethal power. A writer once penned something about shooting an arrow into the air,

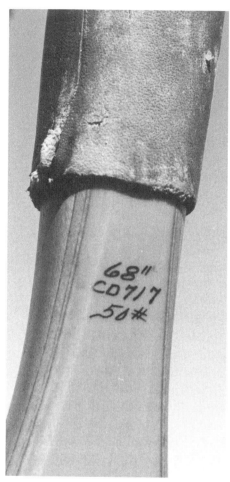

Old does not have to mean feeble; however, safety demands that well-used bows of the past be checked very carefully before shooting.

and it falling to earth he knew not where. There's more truth than poetry in that. Never shoot up into the sky.

Long-range shooting is another matter. As long as everyone knows where everyone else is, and the entire path from bow to landing site is clear of anything that can get hurt, it's perfectly all right to launch a dart for distance. A constant watch downrange, even with binoculars, is a good practice.

Stump-shooting (roving) is as harmless and enjoyable a sport as I know of. Yet it holds dangers for those who aren't careful, as the following story shows. One afternoon, two rovers were hiking the woods away from the city when one spotted an interesting target. It was a patch of debris 50 yards away, visible only through an opening in the trees. They both got ready to shoot. The first man up, however, had a funny feeling. "I don't think I want to shoot at that," he said, hardly believing his own words. It looked like a perfectly legitimate target. Going along with his friend's wishes, the second archer held off, too, and both walked up to the patch of "debris" on the ground. Twenty yards from it, they stopped and gasped. A woman was sunbathing in a clear spot between the trees, covering her sides with a silver tarp that, from a distance, looked like litter. The rule is basic: Never shoot at anything you cannot identify to absolute certainty. Using binoculars on roves is a good idea. If something looks like a plastic grocery bag, a glance through binoculars will verify, or refute, that first impression. The magnified view also helps identify the background. Every archer must know where every arrow might end up before he turns that arrow loose. Arrows are uncanny. They can fly farther than you can believe. Even after years of bowshooting, I'm still amazed at times to walk out into a field looking for a dart that ends up twice as far away as seemed possible.

Looking for arrows requires safety mindedness. Before reaching in for a hidden dart, be certain that nothing harmful resides by it—like a poisonous snake or spider.

Roving means hiking or bicycling away from city streets, where certain creatures may be present. One spring I fired an arrow into a clump of dirt lying in front of what looked like a little mine shaft on the desert floor. I could see into the mouth of the shaft; nothing was there. One of my arrows skipped across the dirt pile, flying directly into the opening of the pit. I walked over to retrieve the shaft, which was showing by its feathers. As I grabbed it, I heard a buzzzz! A rattler was poised no more than a foot from my hand. Since I already had the arrow in my grasp, I plucked it away and backed off, leaving the snake to his business as I proceeded with mine.

I wish I could say this was my only encounter with dangerous beasties, but it wouldn't be true. I've shot at pieces of cardboard, even discarded roof shingles, that had scorpions or black widow spiders under them. It pays to be careful when roving.

Stump-shooting is so much fun that it's easy to get caught up in the game, paying no attention to a sunburn coming on. Sunscreen is called for wherever sunburn is a possibility, along with a hat and sunglasses to block the rays. Some of the points for bicycle shooting, coming up later, apply to any rove. The list of precautions may seem a little long, but by adhering to certain rules, years of roving will pass without a single mishap.

Group shooting calls for strict rules that are followed 100 percent of the time. Many archers may be on the 3-D target range at once. Before firing at a McKenzie, it's imperative that no one is down by the target, or behind it looking for an arrow. Our group has a simple rule: Someone, not the same person every time, shouts, "All clear on target number four?" Then we look to ensure that no one is by or behind the 3-D target. Also, no one should ever advance toward the target until everyone is ready to go. All members of the group should have their bows in the carrying position before anyone takes a single step toward the McKenzie. Imagine what could happen if an archer figured everyone was finished and, without looking, darted out in front of someone firing an arrow.

In some areas, a strung bow in a vehicle is illegal. Bows must be unstrung until the bowman goes into the field. When he returns to his vehicle, the bow is unstrung before it's put inside for travel. An unstrung bow is a sign of good manners in many situations, such as carrying a bow unstrung into an indoor range. Around kids, especially young ones, an unstrung bow makes sense. Should a curious little person decide to see what happens if the string is worked on with a pair of scissors, the bow could spring out and hurt someone badly. As with anything potentially dangerous to children, from sharp objects to cleaning products, storing bows where they can't be tampered with shows wisdom.

There's no reason for bike roving to be less safe than sitting in the living room with a good book—provided the game is played intelligently, which means knowing the rules. There are books available that go through basic safety rules in mountain biking. A few guidelines were provided in chapter 13 on roving with the bicycle, namely, using a helmet, having some water along, carrying raingear, and so forth. How the bow and arrows are carried is important, too. Ideally, they should be secured so that they won't jab the rider should he fall.

The right clothing is important, too, but we'll leave advice on that for mountain bike manuals, except for gloves. Gloves help keep hands from getting numb on vibrating roads. Gloves also protect the hands if the rider does

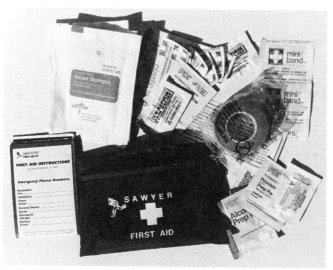

On roves that take the archer away from immediate help, a first aid kit like this Sawyer model is a good idea.

take a tumble and uses his hands to break the fall. Having a spare tube along and the means to change a tire make sense, especially for long-distance bike roving. This means carrying a repair kit and tire pump. The bicyclist should also beware of heat stroke, dehydration, hypothermia (if the rider gets wet), even altitude sickness. Energy bars make sense, too, as does a purifying pump where running water is available. Drinking from mountain streams nowadays must be considered unsafe because of giardia.

Bicycle roving is engrossing. There is always one more challenging target to send an arrow after. Time gets away, and suddenly, all bike rovers look at the horizon to find the sun "slowly sinking in the west," just like in dime cowboy novels. It's going to be a ride out in the dark. Without a good flashlight, it won't even be that. The bike rovers will simply have to stay put for the night, prepared or not. Riding a mountain bike on trails in the dark without a light is begging for disaster. That's why I wouldn't start out on any bicycle-roving trip without a good flashlight, plus extra batteries and spare bulb.

Although I'm hooked on the fascinating sport of traditional archery, there are certain high-tech devices I won't give up, such as my Garmin GPS—or my Syclone Streamlight. This versatile flashlight is only five inches long. It weighs a mere seven and one-half ounces, and that's loaded with four AA batteries. It can be handheld or attached to a bicycle helmet with a special mounting clip (provided). The upper third of the Syclone swivels into a bent position. It's waterproof, has a six thousand candlepower krypton bulb that lasts three and a half hours, or a backup amber LED that runs seventy-two hours on four AA batteries. I have the bracket mounted on my bicycle helmet, carrying the light itself in my fannypack or daypack. When needed, the Syclone slips on the mounting bracket of my helmet, and I ride through the cool of evening, headed for home with my way lighted.

The safety precautions set down here are incomplete. As the bowbender does more shooting, gaining greater experience, he will compile his own list of safety regulations. Common sense, of course, is always the number one safety rule. If a shot seems risky in any way, that's enough to shout "Don't take it!" to anyone. If a target is not perfectly identifiable, the same signal goes up. Common sense, plus a little knowledge, go a long way in keeping the great sport of archery safe.

Glossary

Archery language is colorful and interesting, as well as important to traditionalists today. This glossary includes some of the older terms that the reader may come across in older books.

ACTIONWOOD   hard rock maple in laminated form, popular as a limb core material. Although not fancy, Actionwood is strong and reliable, making it the right choice for certain hardworking longbows and recurves.

ANCHOR POINT   any specific point on the body used as a location to anchor the archer's drawn shooting hand, often a spot on the face, such as the corner of the mouth. The bow is drawn to that same location every time for consistency. Called "anchorage" in the past.

ARCHER'S PARADOX   the natural bending of the arrow as it goes around the riser of the bow, after which it straightens out and flies its normal trajectory.

ARCHERY GOLF   a game played in the past with bows and arrows replacing clubs and golf balls. Instead of holes on the range, targets were used.

ARROW REST   a piece of material on the flat portion of the shelf that the arrow glides on. Once known as the "arrowplate."

ATLATL   a spear-throwing device that may have preceded the invention of the bow, and probably did. Examples have been found in many parts of the world.

BACK OF THE BOW   the part of the bow facing away from the archer when he holds his bow in the shooting position.

BACKING   a layer of material that is attached to the back of the bow.

BANANA FLETCH   high-profile fletching (large feathers) used to straighten an arrow quickly from the archer's paradox.

BAREBOW   shooting a bow without the aid of any aiming device. In the past, a bow without an arrow rest was called a "naked bow."

BARRED FLETCHING   feathers with a striped appearance as naturally found on the wild turkey or dark domesticated bird (as opposed to white turkeys). Artificially applied to dyed white feathers.

BARRELED   the shape of a wooden shaft that tapers on both ends with a "fatter" middle section. The shaft usually tapers from $^{11}\!/_{32}$ inch to $^{23}\!/_{64}$ inch in the middle to $^{5}\!/_{16}$ inch on the ends.

BELLY OF THE BOW   the part of the bow the archer looks at when holding the bow in the shooting position. Also called the face of the bow.

BILLET   in modern usage, refers to a short piece of wood used in making a bow limb or half a bow spliced at the handle, as opposed to a stave, a long piece of wood used to make an entire bow.

BLUNT   an arrowhead with a flattened point.

BOIS D'ARC   French for "wood of the bow," meaning Osage orange, a wood admired for years in bowmaking.

BOWYER   a person who makes bows.

BRACE   an old term that means to string the bow. Still in use.

BRACE HEIGHT   the distance from the throat of the grip to the string of the bow; some bowyers prefer measuring from the string to the forward part of the bow itself. See *fistmele*.

BRACER   an old term for an arm guard.

BROADHEAD   an arrow point with a cutting edge.

BRUSH BUTTON   a rubber button-shaped device that slips onto the string of a recurve bow normally with the aid of a hairpin. It prevents brush from getting caught between the string and the limb where the two meet.

BURN   to use a hot wire device to shape a feather.

CANT   to tilt or tip the bow off the vertical during the act of shooting.

CAST   the extreme distance an arrow shoots from a bow. Also the velocity a bow imparts to an arrow.

CENTER-SHOT   a sight window that is cut away so that the nocked arrow is aligned with the longitudinal axis of the riser.

CHESTED ARROW   an arrow with a widened section near the nock that tapers in both directions.

CLICKER   a device normally attached from the belly limb of the bow to the string, making a sound when the archer reaches full draw. Useful in solving target panic.

CLOTH-YARD SHAFT   a term from medieval English archery referring to an arrow that was thirty-seven inches long, mainly the war shaft used in the medieval longbow. Brought to England by Flemish clothmakers at the time of the Plantagenets. In disuse by 1553, but a term still encountered in archery literature today.

COCK FEATHER   on a shaft with three feathers, the one that points out away from the shelf of the bow when the arrow is nocked on the string.

COMPOSITE   bow made of two or more materials, especially a traditional bow with wood and fiberglass parts laminated with adhesives.

COMPRESSED SHAFT   an arrow shaft that has been compressed for strength and straightness.

CORDOVAN   horsehide leather taken from the middle of the back and considered one of the finest materials for tabs.

CORE WOOD   the center wood in a bow limb that has laminations to either side of it.

CRESTING   colored lines that go around the arrow in narrow bands, often painted as rings. Probably for arrow identification originally, but mostly decorative today.

CROW BILLS   horn points sometimes found on English arrows of the middle ages.

CROWN DIP   the colored portion of the arrow, extending forward from the nock end usually nine or ten inches.

DACRON   a synthetic polyester fiber used in the making of bowstrings.

DEFLEXED   a bow whose limbs curve in toward the archer when it is held in the hand in he shooting position. Compare *reflexed*.

DELAMINATION   the coming apart of a laminated bow.

DRAW LENGTH   the distance the archer pulls the bow, measured in inches from the front shelf of the bow to the string of a drawn bow. A draw length of twenty-eight inches is most common.

DRAW WEIGHT   the "pull" of a bow measured in pounds at a specific draw length. See *draw length.*

DRY FIRE   to shoot a bow at full draw without an arrow on the string. Dry firing can easily break a bow.

EFFICIENCY   in archery, the relationship between a bow's draw weight and its arrow velocity. The higher the arrow speed for a given bow weight, the more efficient that bow is.

ELEVATED REST   a device attached to the bow that allows the arrow to sit higher than the shelf.

FADEOUT   in a composite bow, transition zone between the rigid handle and the flexible limb.

FISTMELE   old term for brace height, but still in use. Originally the breadth of the fist with the thumb stuck out—used to set the distance from the face of the riser to the string.

FLATBOW   a bow with wide and flat limbs, unlike the English longbow with its narrow limbs.

FLETCHER   called an arrowmaker today, the fletcher was the person whose specific job was to build arrows.

FLETCHING   the guidance portion of the arrow located on the back of the shaft; feathers for traditional archers who shoot off the shelf.

FLIGHT-SHOOT   a shoot in which the object is to see how far an arrow can fly.

FLU-FLU   also floo-floo, fletching that causes enough drag to slow an arrow down on purpose so that it will not fly as far as usual. Feathers may be completely spiraled around the shaft, or very large feathers can be used to create drag.

FOLLOWING THE STRING   a term applied to bows that take a set from being strung, the limbs not returning to their original position when the bow is unstrung.

FOOTED ARROW   an arrow with hardwood spliced into its forepart, or pile end.

GLOVE   also called a shooting glove, normally a three-fingered skeletonized glove made usually, but not always, of leather to protect the fingers of the shooting hand as the string is drawn and the arrow released.

GREY GOOSE SHAFT   Old English term referring to an arrow fletched with grey goose feathers; "whistling grey-goose wing" refers to the same arrow in flight.

GRIP   the section of the riser that the archer grasps during shooting. Sometimes referred to as the handle.

HAND SHOCK   vibration felt in the bowhand when a bow is shot.

HEELING   shooting a bow with the heel of the hand pushing against the handle.

HEN FEATHERS   on a three-feathered arrow, the two feathers that project inward toward the riser when the arrow is nocked on the string.

INSTINCTIVE SHOOTING   the method used today by most traditional archers. The arrow is shot without sights using hand-eye coordination coupled with practice to direct the arrow to the target.

ISHI   the last Yana Indian of the Yahi tribe of northern California. He lived and worked at the University of California, Berkeley, where he met Dr. Saxton Pope, who befriended him. Ishi got Pope interested in archery, which promoted the sport in the United States.

LAMINATIONS   thin layers of material bonded together to form a bow limb or riser. Creates strength in risers and high performance in limbs. Laminated bows have three or more layers while a *backed bow* has only one layer of material attached to the core, making a two-part bow.

NOCK   the notch in the arrow behind the fletching that receives the bowstring. Can be either a self-nock; which is a notch in the arrow shaft itself, or a plastic string-holding device that can be open-throated, which does not pinch the string, or snap-on, which does pinch the string. Also used to identify the tip of the bow that holds the bowstring (then called a bow nock).

NOCK POINT   the location of the nock set on the string.

NOCK SET   this is the small device attached on the serving of the string that serves to locate the nock of the arrow in the same spot for every shot. May be a shrink-on synthetic fixture, dental floss wrapped around the serving with a bit of glue, or the popular and excellent pinch-on nock set with metal body and synthetic interior ring that saves the serving from damage.

PARABOLIC   feather fletching with a rounded profile at the back.

PILE   or "pyle," an old term still used today to designate the forepart of an arrow.

PLUCKING THE STRING   release of the arrow with an outward jerking motion of the fingers.

PRIMITIVE   for this work, archery tackle older than traditional.

PUSH-PULL DRAW   drawing a bow by pushing outward with the bowarm, while pulling the string back at the same time.

PUSH-PULL STRINGING   stringing the bow by placing the lower limb against the instep of the shoe, pulling inward on the handle section (toward the archer) and then pushing the top string loop into place on the nock groove of the upper limb. Not recommended.

QUILL   the shaft of a feather, which is ground flat to fit on the arrow.

QUIVER   a case for holding or carrying arrows.

RECOIL   the tendency for a bow to move forward when shot, giving the archer the feeling that it is "trying to go downrange" under its own power. Also used to mean vibration in the handle of the bow. Not interchangeable with hand shock.

REFLEX-DEFLEX   a bow in which the unstrung limbs bend inward toward the archer, then outward at the tips.

REFLEXED   a bow that has limbs and/or riser bending away from the archer when the unstrung bow is held in the hand as if shooting it.

RELEASE   the turning loose of the arrow. A "mechanical release" is a device that locks onto the string to draw the bow and turn the arrow loose.

REVERSE HANDLE BOW   longbow and recurve on which the handle rests flush with the belly of the bow, giving the appearance on some longbows especially of the bow being strung backward. Can lower brace height in relation to limbs.

RISER   the entire middle portion of the bow that separates the limbs.

ROYAL TOXOPHILITE SOCIETY   founded in 1780 in England, this organization laid down shooting rules for the bow, as well as serving to keep archery records.

SELF-BOW   any bow made of one and only one material, such as an all-wood bow.

SERVING   the thread wrapped area in the midsection of the string that accepts the nock set. The arrow nock fits onto the serving.

SHAFT   the dowel part or body of the arrow, sometimes used loosely to mean the arrow itself.

SHELF   that part of the riser on a bow that forms a platform for the arrow rest.

SHIELD CUT   feather fletching with a concave profile at the back.

SIGHT WINDOW   that section of the riser that is cut out to bring the arrow more into line with the center of the bow (center-shot). So named because it is the section that sights would normally be attached to if the bow wore sights. Today, barebow shooting of traditional bows is more common than using sights.

SPINE   in archery, the stiffness of an arrow. More stiffness equals greater spine. Normally measured in five-pound increments for wood arrows, such as 55/60 or 60/65.

STABILIZER   usually a weighted fixture attached to the riser of the bow designed to dampen bow vibration. Seldom used on regular longbows or recurves.

STACKING   sudden build-up of draw force, especially toward the latter part of the draw.

STALLS   leather fingertip coverings that look like a shooting glove without the strap. These cover the appropriate fingertips of the shooting hand only, slipping into place.

STATIC RECURVE   a recurve bow with sharply bent limb tips that do not flex when the bow is drawn.

STAVE   a term used by makers of primitive bows to indicate a long piece of wood used to make a bow.

STRAIGHT FLETCH   arrow with feathers mounted parallel to the shaft, as opposed to offset or helical twist.

STRAIGHT GRIP   a handle, usually on a longbow, that has a very shallow throat.

STRIKE PLATE   a pad that rests on the riser of the bow above the arrow rest on the shelf, or it may be one piece making up both rest and strike plate. Makes contact with the side of the arrow.

STRINGER   a device used to string the bow, usually a strong cord with a pouch on either end that fits onto the tips or into the nocks of the bow, or one end may consist of a pad that rests on the upper limb of the bow for support.

STUMP SHOOTING   also called "roving," where the archer shoots at random inanimate objects.

TACKLE   equipment used by the archer. Originally tackl, a Welsh word that meant arrow. Also from Old German takel denoting the fittings of a ship or horse.

TAPERED ARROW   an arrow that narrows toward the fletching end, oftentimes for nine inches, and usually from $\frac{11}{32}$ or $\frac{23}{64}$ inch down to $\frac{5}{16}$ inch, thereby taking a $\frac{5}{16}$-inch nock.

TARGET PANIC   the inability to loose the arrow, but more commonly letting the arrow fly before full draw is reached. Once called "archer's catalepsy."

3-D ARCHERY   a game that has turned into a serious form of archery competition in which the targets are three-dimensional and normally shaped like some wild animal.

TILLER   bringing the limbs of a bow into balance with each other during the building stage.

TOXOPHILE   a very old word pertaining to archery; a "toxophilite" is a person who is fond of or expert at the bow and arrow.

TRADITIONAL   knowledge, custom, doctrines, and practices passed on from generation to generation. For this book, longbow and recurve types popular in the '40s, '50s, and '60s.

TUNE   to bring a bow into an ideal balance of brace height, arrow match, and nocking point for good arrow flight.

UNDERSPINED   an arrow that is too flexible for the bow it's fired in, as opposed to overspined, where the arrow is too stiff for the bow.

VANE   nowadays typically used to define plastic fletching rather than feathers. Vanes can be used on longbows and recurves with an elevated arrow rest. In the past, the term designated any type of fletching on an arrow. Originally it meant "feather." Also used to identify the softer part of the feather as opposed to the hard quill section.

WING   in archery a reference to the feather pertaining to which wing it was taken from: left-wing feather or right-wing feather.

YEW   extremely popular bow wood used over the centuries by archers in many parts of the world.

Appendix A
Traditional Archers' Buyer's Guide

Allegheny Mountain Arrow Woods
POB 582
Coudersport, PA 16915
Phone: 814-274-2282
Ash, cherry, and poplar are three wood shafts offered by Allegheny, a company that purchases its own hardwood logs locally for processing into shafts. Noted for testing many different types of woods for arrows.

Arrow Specialties
24928 S.E. 416th St.
Enumclaw, WA 98022
Phone: 360-825-5910
Makers of the Arrow Crester with adjustable nonmarring rollers and hinged motor that spins arrow from the top. Has arrow and brush holders built in, along with cresting pattern holder.

Bad Lands
1414 South 700 West
Salt Lake City, UT 84104
Phone: 801-978-2207
Fax: 801-978-2249
Makers of the excellent Split Series backpack with hydration capability (interior water container with drinking tube).

Bear Archery Company
4600 S.W. 41st Boulevard
Gainesville, FL 32601
Phone: 352-376-2327
Fax: 352-376-6115
www.beararch.com
Known throughout the world, the Bear Archery Company has about a dozen traditional bows in its catalog, along with a wealth of supplies and tackle for the archer.

Bitzenburger Machine & Tool, Inc.
13060 Lawson Road
Grand Ledge, MI 48837
Phone: 517-627-8433
Phone: 888-724-5697 (orders)
Fax: 517-627-8433
Maker of the superior Bitzenburger fletcher, a tool relied upon by arrowmakers the world over.

Blue Mountain Arrow Shafts, Ltd.
POB 2494
Venderhoof, B.C.,
Canada VOJ 3AO
Blue Mountain's method of producing strong, straight arrows from slow growth pine has resulted in a cedar alternative for traditional archers.

Bob's Archery Sales
211 South Holly
Denver, CO 80222
Phone: 303-377-4180
Phone: 800-872-2937

Bob Taylor's shop specializes only in traditional bows and arrows, as well as a long line of supplies. Deals also in both new and used custom longbows and recurves for archers who don't want to wait for a bowyer to make a bow.

Brookwood BBC Mfg. Co.
POB 3565
South El Monte, CA 91733
Phone: 626-443-5160
Phone: 888-401-2247 (orders)
Fax: 626-443-3933 or 888-301-2247

Manufactures the well-designed Eagle fannypack, with two water bottle pockets, top-entry main compartments, and two additional side pockets, ideal for daylong roving on foot or mountain bicycle.

Bull River Bowcrafters
POB 615
Troy, MT 59935
Phone: 406-295-5908

Larch and Douglas fir arrow shafts are this company's specialty. Bull River Bowcrafters is active in testing various cedar alternatives for crafting good traditional arrows. Also makes the excellent, rugged Viking tubular-style bow case.

Bushnell Sports Optics
9200 Cody Street
Overland Park, KS 66214-1734
Phone: 913-752-3400
Fax: 913-752-3550
www.bushnell.com

Excellent compact binoculars ideal for roving. Also rangefinders for setting up archery 3-D games and targets.

Butler's Traditional Archery Supply
1031 County Road 141
Durango, CO 81301
Phone: 970-247-2894
Fax: 888-495-9159

Special handmade custom arrows, with cap dip and cresting in many different wood choices. Also a full line of traditional archery supplies.

Crick-It Draw Check Co.
POB 142
East Tawas, MI 48730
Phone: 517-362-7123

Maker of the Crick-It Draw Check device that sounds every time the archer reaches full draw and anchor point.

Easton Technical Products
5040 W. Harold Gatty Drive
Salt Lake City, UT 84116-2897
Phone: 801-539-1400
Fax: 801-533-9907

Famous for fine aluminum arrows and arrow shafts for traditional as well as high-tech bows. Also offers a spine chart for aluminum arrows.

Fedora Bowmaking School
115 Wintersville Road
Richland, PA 17087
Phone: 717-933-8862

Bowmaking for fun or profit is the goal of the Fedora Bowmaking School, along with instruction in overcoming target panic, arrowmaking, string building, and more.

Gateway Feathers
POB 447
Holmen, WI 54636
Phone: 608-526-4490
Fax: 608-526-9699

Feathers in over thirty colors, barred or solids, in 5-inch down to $1\frac{7}{8}$-inch lengths, including a $5\frac{1}{2}$-inch Mag. Waterproofing available as well.

Gold Tip
140 South Main Street No. 3
Pleasant Grove, UT 84062
Phone: 800-551-0541
Fax: 801-796-8921
www.goldtip.com
Makers of the Gold Tip carbon "Graphite XT" made of 100 percent carbon epoxy with inner straight fibers, inner radial fibers, center straight fiber core, outer radial fibers, and outer straight fibers, making an arrow shaft that can be run over by a car tire and survive.

Hoppe's (Brunswick)
Airport Industrial Mall
Coatesville, PA 19320
Phone: 610-384-6000
Fax: 610-857-5980
Makers of several excellent hard cases for both bows and arrows, especially important when transporting tackle from home to field, or on long trips. Also excellent for storage of bows, arrows, and accessories.

Jack's Traditional Archery
126 Forest Road No. 20
Randle, WA 98377
Makers of high-grade side quivers, as well as a basic leather tab without finger separators, preferred by some archers. Also offers handmade leather arm guards and the Bow-Tote, an all-leather device used to attach the bow to the archer's belt with a string holder.

Jerry Hill Longbow Company
Box 231 McGowan Road
Wilsonville, AL 35186
Makers of traditional style longbows in the Old-English design.

Kustom King Arrows
1260 East 86th Place
Merrillville, IN 46410
Phone: 219-769-6640
Fax: 219-769-6641
www.kustom-king.com
Known especially for top-grade custom-crafted tapered cedar arrows such as the Commemorative and Exotic series, with numerous options in nock, feather, crown and shaft colors, and other appointments. Also offers many good books and videos, plus arrow assembly supplies and many accessories.

Kwikee Kwiver Co., Inc.
7292 Peaceful Valley
POB 130
Acme, MI 49610
Phone: 616-938-1690
Phone: 800-346-7001 (orders)
Fax: 616-938-2144
Makers of bow quivers that slip on and off in a snap. Ideal for those who want to use a bow quiver some of the time, but not all of the time.

Martin Archery, Inc.
Route 5, Box 127
Walla Walla, WA 99362-9483
Phone: 509-529-2554
Fax: 509-529-2186
E-mail: martin@bmi.net
www.martinarchery.com
Offers a complete line of archery tackle, from recurves and longbows—such as the well-known Super Diablo—to the Martin Grain Scale for weighing arrows that is adjustable to 800 grains. Also has shelf materials for rests and sideplates and silencers.

McKenzie Targets
POB 480
Granite Quarry, NC 28072
Phone: 888-279-7985
Fax: 704-279-8958
Pioneers in high-grade 3-D targets in a huge variety that are so well known in archery circles that 3-D targets are often referred to as "McKenzies."

McMahon Traditional Archery, Inc.
2 Commerce Park Boulevard
Middleboro, MA 02346
Phone: 508-261-9783
Phone: 800-627-3199 (orders)
Fax: 508-946-9500
www.mcmahonarchery.com
Traditional archery company dealing in a wide variety of supplies from books and videos to longbows and recurves in various price ranges.

Monarch Bows, LLC
POB 433
268 Corner Cut-off
Darby, MT 59829
Phone: 406-821-1948
Phone: 800-793-3224 (orders)
E-mail: monarchhb@cybernet1.com
Recurves, longbows, and flatbows are available from this custom shop. The Royal Flatbow comes in 58-, 60-, and 62-inch lengths, with a Royal Recurve offered in 58-inch length. Also offers the Raghorn Longbow, Royal Longbow, and Imperial Longbow. Risers are custom fit to the customer's hand. Tulip wood, yew, ebony, and other woods are used.

Nelsons Arrows
1181 Swede Hill Road
Greensburg, PA 15601
Phone: 412-837-6210
Fax: 412-837-9755
Bowstrings made to order, along with a line of handmade custom arrows.

Nirk Archery
A Division of Martin Archery
Route 5, Box 127
Walla Walla, WA 99362-9483
Phone: 509-527-3150
Fax: 509-529-2186
E-mail: nirkarch@wwics.com
Bows, including the X-100 recurve and Frontiersman longbow, plus side quivers, bow cases, tabs, gloves, arm guards, arrows, Nirk Nocks, and other archery supplies.

Old Cedar Tree Traditional Archery
229 Wahgouly Road
Sheboygan, WI 53081
Along with custom leather back quivers and finished cedar arrows, this company buys and sells used longbows and recurves.

Rancho Safari
POB 691
Ramona, CA 92065
Phone: 800-240-2094
Fax: 760-789-1506
Makers of the famous Catquiver, combination arrow carrier and pack, with arrows held point downward and fletching protected from the elements under a hood. Also offers tackle.

Raptor Archery
923 11th Street
Hood River, OR 97301
Phone: 541-386-4503
Fax: 541-386-2434
Staves and billets of Osage, yew, hickory, ash, and other woods, along with custom-made high-grade arrows and shafts in Alaskan yellow cedar, fir, and hard maple. Also offers custom bows, as well as used bows, videos, books, and a large assortment of traditional and primitive archery supplies.

Raven Arrows
993 Grays Creek Road
Indian Valley, ID 83632
Phone: 208-256-4341
Raven Arrows sells the "real thing." Specialties include gray, barred natural turkey feathers, gray goose feathers the company calls "naturally waterproof," and full-length or die-cut natural (ivory colored) whites. Sold in full cut for home burning or chopping or in die-cut shield or parabolic styles. Superb arrow shafts in fir, spruce, and cedar at good prices, well finished with tapers cut. Matched sets contain thirteen or fourteen arrows to ensure a dozen excellent shafts.

Rob Kennedy's Traditional
    Archery Supplies
POB 1114
Armidale, NSW 2350 Australia
Offers some of the finest custom arrows available for those who desire highly artful darts. Some archers order these for display rather than shooting.

Rocky Mountain Bowstrings
POB 504
Meeker, CO 81641
Phone: 970-878-4300
Fax: 970-878-4064
Makes strings for recurve bows
(no Flemish-style strings).

Saunders Archery
POB 476
Columbus, NE 68602-0476
Phone: 402-564-7176
Phone: 800-228-1408 (orders)
www.sausa.com
Huge line of high-grade products, including exerciser for keeping in shape to pull traditional bows, the Saco home target and many others, and a wide range of tabs and other archery tackle. Also offers the long-lasting Indian Cord Matt Target.

Selway Archery
802 South 2nd
Hamilton, MT 59840
Phone: 406-363-4770
Phone: 800-764-4770 (orders)
Fax: 406-363-0761
Makers of bow quivers in different styles using hand-stitched rawhide leather hoods.

Steve's Strings
POB 7002
Redlands, CA 92375
E-mail: stringmstr@aol.com
Flemish bowstrings custom made to order in Fast Flight, B50, Dacron, or linen. Also offers archery accessories.

Streamlight, Inc.
1030 West Germantown Pike
Norristown, PA 19403
Phone: 610-631-0600
Phone: 800-523-7488 (orders)
Fax: 610-631-0712
Manufacturers of the Syclone high-tech flashlight, as well as other high-quality lights for outdoor use, as in roving.

Three Rivers Archery Supply
POB 517
Ashley, IN 46705
Phone: 219-587-9501
Fax: 1-888-FAXX-TRA (329-9872)
www.3riversarchery.com
Billed as the world's largest traditional and primitive archery supply with 2700 items in stock, this company sells bows, finished arrows, arrowmaking materials from feathers to various glues, arrow straighteners, jigs, and much more.

True Flight Arrow Co., Inc.
POB 746
2709 South Freeman Road
Monticello, IN 47960
Phone: 219-583-5131
Phone: 800-348-2224 (orders)
Fax: 219-583-9271
E-mail: arrows@pwrtc.com
Known as the world's largest supplier of
arrows, including those made with
feather fletching for the traditional archer.

Trueflight Mfg. Co.
POB 1000
Manitowish Waters, WI 54545
Phone: 715-543-8451 (24 hr.)
Fax: 715-543-2525
Longtime makers of an extremely long
line of excellent feathers for stickbows.
Numerous patterns in ten sizes, including
dyed barred feathers in many different
colors, solids as well. Maker of the excel-
lent 5½-inch low-profile feather.

Whisperin' Pines Archery Camp
348 Holliday Drive
Poplarville, MS 39470
Phone: 601-795-8727
Unique two-day workshop designed to
enhance enjoyment and knowledge of
traditional archery. Professional one-on-
one instruction by Hall of Fame archer
Bob Wesley, on a private 3-D range.

*Be sure to check advertisements and
classified sections in traditional archery magazines for other companies dealing in stickbows and supplies.*

Used Bow Dealers

*Note: Used bow houses usually charge a
small fee for a list of bows. Be sure to send a
self-addressed, stamped envelope when writing to any of the following for information:*

Bob's Archery Sales
211 South Holly
Denver, CO 80222
Phone: 303-377-4180
Phone: 800-872-2937 (orders)

Bowzonly Inc. Archer Shop
POB 1375
Walker, MN 56484
Phone: 218-547-3890

Caribou Creek Archery
POB 2261
Palmer, AK 99645

J&M Traditions
RR2, Box 413
Sunbury, PA 17801
Phone: 717-286-7887

Ken Efaw
Box 89, RD No. 1
Waynesburg, PA 15370

Nuthin But Traditional
16904 Southwest Greentree Ave.
Lake Oswego, OR 97034
Phone: 503-880-7796

The Footed Shaft
5510 North Highway 63
Rochester, MN 55906
Phone: 507-288-7581

Vic's Archery
3957 56 S.W.
Grandville, MI 49418
Phone: 616-538-8200

*Check advertisements and classified sec-
tions in traditional archery magazines for
used bows.*

Appendix B
Traditional Bowyers

As a service to the reader, a handful of America's traditional bowyers are listed here for those who may wish to walk the trail to a custom bow. The reader is urged, however, to use two other sources in his search for a bowyer: the classified sections of magazines devoted to traditional archery, which are advertising meccas for bowmakers, and Dan Bertalan's book, Traditional Bowyers of America *(see appendix C for these sources).*

Arkansas Stick
Rt. 1, Box 77
Gurdon, AR 71743
Bowyer Terry Hughes makes simple, light recurve bows in 62- and 64-inch lengths. The 64-inch model weighs 1 pound, 9 ounces, with a 7½-inch bracing height. He uses shedua risers (other exotic hardwoods available), red cedar core material, and a low-luster polyurethane finish.

Assenheimer Bows
1005 River Road
Bucyrus, OH 44820
Bowyer Don Assenheimer makes recurves in 62-, 64-, and 66-inch lengths averaging 2 pounds, 10 ounces. All bows have a maximum 8-inch brace height and dyed, laminated hard maple risers. Takedowns have interchangeable limbs.

Autumn Archery
10151 West Asbury Avenue
Lakewood, CO 80227
Phone: 303-980-9434
Bowyer Art Hunter builds custom primitive bows in various styles. Wood staves and billets are also for sale. Hunter teaches a bowcrafting school that includes string-making, along with interesting historical notes on archery.

Bearded Horse Productions
POB 2303
Boulder, CO 80306-2303
Phone: 303-417-6279
Ken Wee, bowyer, is regarded as one of the finest primitive bowmakers in the country. He builds a variety of original-style Native American bows, as well as other types, using authentic materials. Ken also makes historic artifact copies, along with leather tackle. He also offers tools for primitive bowmaking. His atlatls are especially sought after for their workmanship and performance.

Black Swan Archery, Inc.
1895 Highway 61
Columbiana, AL 35051
Phone: 205-669-3220
Bowyer Arvid Danielson uses a computer program to aid bow design, but his longbows and recurves are individually handmade with a high regard for exotic woods

and fine workmanship. His short Bush Bow is especially noted for smooth shooting with good performance.

> Black Widow Custom Bow, Inc.
> 1201 Eaglecrest
> POB 2100
> Nixa, MO 65714
> Phone: 417-725-3113
> Fax: 417-725-3190
> www.archery.net/blackwidow

Black Widow bows have been built continuously from 1957. They have always been known for high performance, top quality, plus ruggedness in the field. There are several models to select from, including a short-window recurve, a short one-piece recurve, and a longbow.

> Bob Aragon Native American
>   Archery
> 1201 Trenton Street
> Denver, CO 80220
> Phone: 303-322-0519

Bowyer Bob Aragon specializes in authentic reproductions of historical pieces of Native American cultures, including self-bows that are true to the originals. He uses materials associated with bowmakers of yesteryear in his bows, arrows, and other tackle.

> Great Northern Bow Company
> POB 777
> Nashville, MI 49073
> Phone: 517-852-0820
> Fax: 517-852-2082
> www.mvcc.com/bu/gnbco

Rick Shephard and Jerry Brumm, both expert archers, build several different models in their Michigan shop, including the unique "Jack Knife" design, which is a folding bow, as well as the Ghost recurve, one of the lightest recurve bows available. Also makers of the Professional model bow quivers built from heavy leather.

> Howard Hill Archery
> 248 Canyon Creek Road
> Hamilton, MT 59840
> Phone: 406-363-1359

The original-style Howard Hill longbow is built and sold by this company, sometimes in limited collector editions. Materials vary. One bow, for example, uses three bamboo laminations in the limb, plus three yew laminations with clear glass on the belly and black glass on the back, along with a Gaboon ebony riser. Inlays are available on request.

> Jack Howard Archery Co.
> 21914 Highway 20
> Nevada City, CA 95959

The Jack Howard recurve bow was well known during the golden age of traditional archery, when composites ruled. The bow is back again. The company also has a line of tackle and outdoor gear, including the Western-style finger tab.

> Jerry Hill Longbow Co.
> 515 McGowan Hill Road
> Wilsonville, AL 35186
> Phone: 205-669-6134
> Fax: 205-669-0270

Nephew of the famous Howard Hill, Jerry, who is a professional exhibition shooter in his own right, sells longbows along with traditional tackle, such as the Hill-style shooting glove, arm guards, back quivers, and more.

> Old Cedar Tree Traditional Archery
> 229 Wahgouly Road
> Sheboygan, WI 53081
> Phone: 920-458-7567

Along with custom leather back quivers and finished cedar arrows, this company deals in used longbows and recurves, buying and selling.

Pronghorn Custom Bows
2491 West 42nd Street
Casper, WY 82604
Phone: 307-234-1824

Herb Meland, bowyer, builds a high-performance no-hand shock longbow in the reflex-deflex design. His longbows normally shoot over 200 feet per second with medium-weight arrows. Most popular bow in the line is the Three-Piece Takedown Pronghorn, offered with exotic hardwood risers such as cocobolo and bocote, as well as dymondwood and others. Also offers the Ferret, a lightweight, high-performance takedown recurve, normally featuring red elm limbs, but also Tonkin bamboo.

Robertson Stykbow Co.
Box 7, HCR 488
Forest Grove, MT 59441
Phone: 406-538-2818

Bowyer Dick Robertson makes self-bows as well as composite longbows and recurves, often using exotic woods for his one-piece or takedown models. His bows are noted for gifted workmanship.

Schafer Silvertip Bows
312 Helena Flats Road
Kalispell, MT 59901
Phone: 406-257-0740

Bowyer Dave Windauer builds the Schafer Silvertip custom bow in a variety of exotic woods, such as cocobolo, bocote, rosewood, and dymondwood. Risers offered in high wrist, low wrist, and medium. Also high-grade, fine checkering option for handles.

Sky Archery Co., Inc.
11510 Natural Bridge Road
Bridgetown, MO 63044
Phone: 314-731-1600
Fax: 314-731-1310

Offers custom traditional bows, including the Target Supreme T/D Model, a competition recurve designed especially for archers interested in serious target shooting, but who have a shorter draw. Left-handed as well as right-handed, the Target Supreme T/D is a tournament bow in draw weights from 20 to 44 pounds.

Smith Archery
POB 1122
Athens, TX 75751
Phone: 903-675-3118

Brad Smith, bowyer, handcrafts high-grade, top-performing primitive-style bows in his shop. His bows have been seen on TNN, not only in his hands, but also shot by one of the best longbow marksmen in the country, the talented western singer Gary Morris. Also offers a bowmaking school, as well as *How to Make Your Own Osage Longbow*, a book written by the bowyer.

Toh-Kah Bows
3010 Westwoodland Trail, N.W.
Shakopee, MN 55379
Phone: 612-445-0494

Bowyer Jim Welch specializes in custom-made Native American flat self-bows or sinew-backed bows in Woodland, Eastern, and Plains styles. Jim also offers classes in making Osage self-bows.

Wapiti Archery Company
490 South Queen Street
Lakewood, CO 80226
Phone: 303-989-1120
E-mail: 74067.1252@compuserve.com

J. K. Chastain has been building his Wapiti longbows and recurves for many years in both takedown and one-piece styles. His takedown recurves feature a tow-bolt system of limb attachment to riser, and his bows are backed by a lifetime warranty.

Zebra Longbows
POB 742
Beetown, WI 53802

Doug Duncan makes his two-piece takedown longbow with a patented handle bolt system. Also offers a one-piece recurve bow, and a one-piece longbow.

Appendix C
Magazines and Books

Traditional archers may not be interested in the history of the sport, or its romance—at first. But in time just about everyone who shoots a longbow or recurve wants to know more about the tackle and the legends. There are some good magazines dedicated to traditional (and primitive) archery, plus literally dozens of books, if not hundreds, on the subject. This brief bibliography should serve only as a jumping-off place on the road to many other good publications.

Traditional Archery Magazines

Instinctive Archer
POB 45299
Boise, ID 83711-5299
Another "slick" with excellent paper and clear photographs. Bowyer interviews are matched by how-to stories such as "Weight Lifting and Archery." Includes historical and archeological articles, as well as many tips to improve bowshooting skills. Every issue has something in it to match an archer's interest, including competitions and advertisements from many bowyers and traditional supply houses.

Primitive Archer
POB 209
Lufkin, TX 75902-0209
The title of this periodical tells it all—nothing but pretraditional bows grace its pages. "Primitive Archer Tips Exclusive" helps the reader with problems encountered in making or shooting the truly old-time bow, such as "Splitting Staves," or "Aligning String Nocks." Also included in every issue are how-to tips on making bows, arrows, strings, and other tackle in articles such as "Tillering by the Numbers" or "Follow the Grain." Interesting historical pieces include more than the story of an old bow, but also detailed instructions for building a piece on that ancient design, such as "The Mongolian Bow."

Traditional Bowhunter
More broad-based than its title suggests, this magazine, which has recently grown to well over one hundred pages, is another slick, high-color production, with articles such as "The Shelf Wood Bow—Gluing Rawhide to Self Bows," along with a column entitled "Native American," featuring archers such as Joe Thornton, a Cherokee World Champion archer. Also excellent book and video reviews every issue, plus a bowyer interview.

Books

Some of the books listed here are mainly of scholarly interest for traditional archers who want to learn more about bow history, as well as performance, and even building. Other texts are of a more general nature. The short explanation of the book's content should help the reader decide if he is interested in the title. Although some of these books are out of print, local libraries can normally find them anyway, using the inter-library loan service, whereby books can be located in libraries all over the country and mailed to the reader, usually for a small fee. Also, bookstores can often locate out-of-print books. New books, of course, can be purchased from any bookstore. Another excellent place to locate these titles is in traditional archery catalogs. Many of the best titles are currently available.

All about the Atlatl
Gary L. Fogelman
Fogleman Publishing Company
PA, 1997
The author subtitles this work *At Least as Much as You'll Ever Need to Know*. And that's right. The thirty-six-page softcover edition includes the origin of the name, how the atlatl works, throwing instructions, history (Paleolithic Europe, New Guinea, Australia, Alaska, Florida, and more locales), and much more compressed into an easy-reading reference work.

American Indian Archery
Reginald and Gladys Laubin
University of Oklahoma Press
Norman, 1980
This book begins, as it must, with a history lesson on Native American archery, followed by a comparison of bows. Bowmaking and sinewed bows are discussed, along with horn bows, strings, arrows, quivers, and shooting styles. Also included is information on the "Indian

crossbow," medicine bows, blowguns, stone bows, and harps. Illustrated with drawings, black and white photographs, and a handsome color section.

Archery
C. J. Longman and Col. H. Walrond
Longmans, Green Publishers
London, 1901
This particular edition is a reprint of the 1894 book (Longmans, Green says 1896, but all copies of the original show 1894). It's a careful study of archery from prehistoric times onward, including bows and arrows of many peoples and countries. *Archery* is complete with information on the various bows and how different cultures used them. Includes a chapter on early American target archery.

A Bibliography of Archery
Fred Lake and Hal Wright
Derrydale Press
Lyon, MS 1994
This remarkable book surfaced as a report in 1994 in a series of titles called Legends of the Longbow. An earlier copyright by authors Lake and Wright was 1974. Hundreds of titles are listed, some of which can be found through interlibrary loan, others too valuable to be checked out by the library. Periodicals and archery films as well as books are included. There is even a section on manuscripts in European languages and another on Far Eastern books and manuscripts.

Billets to Bows
Glenn St. Charles
Glenn and Margaret St. Charles
Seattle, WA
The author calls his self-published book *The Sights, Sounds & Smells of Archery*. Chapter 1 is a brief biography of the archer-writer, with photos from his early days. Chapter 2, "Harvesting the Yew," and subsequent chapters go into bowmaking. English longbows, making the

semistacked bow, making a bowstring, and other chapters are filled with tips and tricks for success. St. Charles's book also includes a few words on shooting at moving targets, and even his experience with shooting the compound bow instinctively.

The Bowyer's Craft
Jay Massey
Bear Paw Publications
Girwood, AK 1987
The late Jay Massey was a primitive archery enthusiast and expert bowcrafter. This book is mainly about types of bows, bow woods, and the manufacture of primitive tackle. The book also includes an interesting opening chapter on "The Bow in History."

The Grey Goose Wing
E. G. Heath
Osprey Publications
Berkshire, England 1971
Ernest Gerald Heath did a wonderful job in this book. The opening chapter, "Bowmen of the Stone Age," includes photographs of ancient cave wall art that show early man with his bow. Historical bows of various cultures are discussed, as well as information on the composite bow, the clothyard shaft, Native American archers and archery, the crossbow, and even symbolism in archery.

Ishi: The Last Yahi
A Documentary History
R. F. Heizer and T. Kroeber
University of California Press
Los Angeles, CA 1979
The wonderful story of Ishi, the last member of his tribe, a people who were pursued and slaughtered on their home ground in California. Ishi's influence on Dr. Saxton Pope helped to bring about a resurgence in American archery. Ishi shared not only his bowmaking and shooting knowledge, but his beliefs as well as his philosophy of life.

Longbow
A Social and Military History
Robert Hardy
Arco Publishing Co.,
New York 1977
A fine text on the early history of the longbow, beginning with prehistoric times. The author then takes the reader into Britain to famous battles of the past, including Agincourt. American archery is also included, along with a brief section on "Some Technical Considerations."

Secrets of the Omaha Bow
William Vonderhey
William Vonderhey
PA 1992
This self-published book is a gold mine of information for anyone interested in primitive archery. The author is founder of the American Indian Archery Society (1989) and a noted expert on Native American culture and archery. The book reveals the special way that the Omahas handcrafted their bows, with full instructions for the reader to do likewise, illustrated with photographs and drawings. Also includes how to make arrows and an authentic quiver/bow case.

Target Archery
Robert P. Elmer
Alfred A. Knopf
New York, NY 1946
This text, over 500 pages long, goes into the sport of target shooting with a bow, with a history of American archery as well as British. But it's much more than a history book. It includes information on bow woods, making bows, Turkish bows, wooden bows in general, arrows, bowstrings, and accessories, as well as how to shoot a bow, the dynamics of an arrow in flight, and more.

Traditional Bowyers of America
Dan Bertalan
Envisage Unlimited Press
MI, 1989

Dan Bertalan traveled to many parts of the United States to speak personally with thirty working bowyers, taking down firsthand accounts of their lives, along with their bowmaking techniques, designs, and materials. The late Jay Massey wrote the following in the foreward to Dan's book: "The bowyers written about in *Traditional Bowyers of America* also represent something else: American independence and originality, and perhaps even more important, early American Values." Massey also pointed out that "not all of America's traditional bowyers are illustrated, of course. To do so would require a book of two thousand pages."

The Traditional Bowyer's Bible
    (3 vols.)
Massey, Baker, Cosgrove, Hamm, St.
    Charles, etc.
Bois d'Arc Press
Lyons and Burford
New York, 1992-1994

This work comes in three volumes, the first published in 1992, the second in 1993, and the third in 1994. Many authors contributed to this monumental work, which includes exceptionally good information on bow woods, bow geometry, handcrafting bows, other archery tackle, including arrows, and many other subjects. For example, professional arrowmaker Gabriela Cosgrove relates her secrets to the craft in volume 3.

The Witchery of Archery
J. Maurice Thompson
Charles Scribner's Sons
New York, 1878

Maurice Thompson (he did not go by James) was injured in the Civil War. After leaving a Confederate prison, he and his brother took up longbow and can right-

fully be called the fathers of modern American archery for their efforts in organizing the National Archery Association of the United States in 1878, which brought attention to the bow and arrow. *Witchery* is a classic in archery history, a book that many dedicated traditionalists read several times over for its fine writing style and mood. It's currently offered in paperback through traditional archery supply companies.